In Pursuit of Gotham

In Pursuit
of Gotham

Culture
and Commerce
in New York

WILLIAM R. TAYLOR

New York   Oxford

OXFORD UNIVERSITY PRESS

1992

Oxford University Press

Oxford   New York   Toronto
Delhi   Bombay   Calcutta   Madras   Karachi
Kuala Lumpur   Singapore   Hong Kong   Tokyo
Nairobi   Dar es Salaam   Cape Town
Melbourne   Auckland

and associated companies in
Berlin   Ibadan

Copyright © 1992 by William R. Taylor.

Published by Oxford University Press, Inc.,
200 Madison Avenue, New York, New York 10016

Oxford is a registered trademark of Oxford University Press

Library of Congress Cataloging-in-Publication Data
Taylor, William Robert, 1922–
In pursuit of Gotham : culture and commerce
in New York / William R. Taylor.
p. cm.   Includes index.
ISBN 0-19-503904-1
1. New York (N.Y.)—Civilization.
2. New York (N.Y.) in literature.
3. American literature—New York (N.Y.)—History and criticism.
I. Title.   F128.47.T19   1992
974.7′1—dc20   91-28783

I want to thank the following publishers for permission to reprint
here material that has been published elsewhere: Little, Brown and
Company for parts of Chapter 1, Cambridge University Press for parts
of Chapter 2, the Henry Francis du Pont Winterthur Museum for an
earlier version of Chapter 3, Johns Hopkins University Press for an
earlier version of Chapter 6, and the Russell Sage Foundation for
an earlier version of Chapter 4, and for parts of chapters 6 and 10.

Frontispiece: An engineer checking the vertical alignment of columns
during the construction of the Empire State Building. Lewis Hine,
1932. From the collection of the International Museum of
Photography at George Eastman House.

9 8 7 6 5 4 3 2 1

Printed in the United States of America
on acid-free paper

To all of my children—

Charles, Geoffrey, Linda, Wendela,

William, Stephanie, and Amy—

constant reminders of cultural change

and history in the making

Contents

Acknowledgments

This book was long in the making and my obligations are correspondingly weighty. A number of institutions have provided support. The New York Institute for the Humanities at New York University has been my intellectual home away from home since 1979. It was more than chance that brought together an exceptional group of scholars interested in the history of urban cultures. The Institute seminars and conferences drew scholars from all over the Northeast. Those of us fortunate enough to work there were exposed to the best work being done on the culture of cities.

The State University of New York at Stony Brook, in addition to all the other considerations it has shown me, was generous in granting the sabbatical and research leave required to do the job, and understanding about my need to be away from the campus for much of the time. My department has supported me in every imaginable way despite the added burdens my absences sometimes incurred.

I am not sure what direction the book would have taken had I not spent a crucial year at the Institute for Historical Research at London University, but I am convinced it would have been a different, less interesting book. I appreciate the courtesy shown me as an outsider with little role in the Institute's regular business as well as the associations it provided.

Chapter 3 was originally prepared for a meeting of the Hungarian Academy of Science in Budapest in 1982. The Social Science Research Council was directly responsible for Chapter 5, which was originally written for a Council conference on New York in 1984. The Russell Sage Foundation provided important funding for the Inventing Times Square Project at N.Y.U. and published the volume of conference papers for which Chapter 6 is the introduction in revised form. I am grateful to the Foundation and its president, Eric Wanner, for the many kinds of support I received as fellow during 1990–1991, the year I completed this book. I am also grateful to the Rockefeller Foundation for a Humanities Fellowship in 1983–1984. Finally, like everyone at the New York Institute for the Humanities, I am indebted to the Daniel Rose family for its continuous support of Institute activities, most crucially for its generous support of the study of Times Square and the accompanying conferences. Chapter 10, on Damon Runyon and the origins of slang, in a slightly different form was my contribution to that study. Chapter 8 was prepared as a lecture in a series of programs on Greenwich Village organized by the Humanities Council of New York University.

I am grateful to Sheldon Meyer and to the Oxford University Press for support and patience during the long period of gestation. I believe I was among the first authors Sheldon Meyer contacted when he began work for Oxford many years ago. I have turned to him for advice many times in the succeeding years. In moments of discouragement, his friendship was a spur to get on with it. It is especially gratifying to me to have him as my editor. His sensitive reading of the manuscript, as I would have expected, exemplifies what is almost a lost art among publishers. I always learn from good line editing, as I have from that of Gail Cooper at Oxford.

As an historian inured to working alone, I am especially grateful to those with whom over the past few years I have exchanged ideas. I owe a special debt to those who participated in the Times Square Conferences in 1988–89. I took away from those intense sessions a fresh sense of the intricacies of historical change. I also want to thank Elaine Abelson, Jean-Christophe Agnew, Quentin Anderson, Barbara Balliet, Marshall Berman, Elizabeth Blackmar, Daniel Czitrom, Susan Davis, Michael Denning, Lewis Erenberg, Neil Harris, Eric Hobsbawm, Ira Katznelson, Eric Lampard, Lary May, R. Lawrence Moore, David Nassau, Anson Rabinbach, Carl Schorske, Richard Sennett, Dan Schiller, Werner Sollers, Christine Stansell, Sally Stein, Richard Swedberg, Alan Trachtenberg, Michael Wallace, Sean Wilentz, and John A. Williams.

I owe particular thanks to a number of friends and colleagues who were willing to read and comment on chapters still in draft. Whatever its faults, it is a better book as a result of their efforts and insight. I am especially grateful to my friends Peter Buckley and William Leach, who read each of the chapters as they were written, some of them several times, and provided me with detailed comments and constant encouragement. Our conversations over bag lunches at the Institute were a stimulus at points where I might have become discouraged. Others have read chapters in draft and provided me with advice that has sharpened and improved these essays in important ways: Tom Bender (who was my co-author on Chapter 4), James Gilbert, Stanley Katz, Lawrence Levine, Paul Mattick, Jr., John Mollenkopf, Richard Poirier, Anson Rabinbach, Richard Schweder, Donald Scott, Joan Scott, Fred Weinstein, and R. Jackson Wilson.

I am also indebted to an impressively talented cohort of graduate assistants, many of whom participated in my course on urban culture at Stony Brook and helped with my research. Together they enriched my sense of history and of New York's urban past: Jane Gover, Karen Kearns, Barbara Kelly, Kevin Ryan, Steven Stowe, James Terry, and Cynthia Ward. In the preparation of the manuscript for publication, Gina Grossfeld and Jennifer Parker weighed in with intelligence and skill to help pull things together this past year. Minda Novak helped me in countless ways—with research on Damon Runyon, with the illustrations and the intricacies of permissions, and with the editorial tasks.

Two good friends, Herbert Gutman and Warren Susman, died in 1985. The book would surely have been improved by their readings. The insight and support of Mark Grunes during the entire period of the study had an incalculable impact on my ability to think and to write. Fred Weinstein, the chairman of my Stony Brook department, and Richard Turner, director of the New York Institute for the Humanities, have provided the kind of support and encouragement that only good friends in power can give.

I want to note here a special kind of gratitude beyond the ritualistic to my wife, Ellen Siegel Taylor. She constantly encouraged me to get on with it and found ways to give me confidence when I seemed to lack it. She read what I wrote page by page, ever on the alert for obscurities, ambiguities, false or pretentious notes. I believe I learned from her comments something about the authenticity of my voice as a writer.

Introduction

The aspect the power wears then is indescribable; it is the power of the most extravagant of cities, rejoicing, as in the voice of the morning, in its might, its fortune, its unsurpassable conditions, and imparting to every object and element, to the motion and expression of every floating, hurrying, panting thing, to the throb of ferries and tugs, to the plash of waves and the play of winds and the glint of lights and the shrill of whistles and the quality and authority of breeze-born cries—all, practically, a diffused, wasted clamour of detonations—something of its sharp free accent and, above all, of its sovereign sense of being "backed" and able to back. . . . One has the sense that the monster grows and grows, flinging abroad its loose limbs even as some unmannered young giant at his "larks," and the blinding stitches must for ever fly further and faster and draw harder; the future complexity of the web, all under the sky and over the sea, becoming thus that of some colossal set of clockworks, some steel-souled machine-room of brandished arms and hammering fists and opening and closing jaws. The immeasurable bridges are but as the horizontal sheaths of pistons working at high pressure, day and night, and subject, one apprehends with perhaps inconsistent gloom, to certain, to fantastic, to merciless multiplication.

Henry James (on circumnavigating the Battery), *The American Scene* (1907)[1]

The quotation from Henry James sets the theme of this volume. It is not New York in its totality I have been pursuing—too big a subject—but "Gotham," a particular ironic persona of the city adopted long ago when it was only Manhattan.

It is difficult to know for sure how the name Gotham first became associated with New York, but Washington Irving's use of it in 1807, while not the first, probably made it stick.[2] Irving had a way with names. No one else has had the same success in concocting names the city would take to heart, although his success with Gotham is still something of a mystery. Irving's Gotham was a sleepy Dutch town, ill-equipped to resist any external threat. It provided him with a comic contrast, even to the bustling, provincial New York of his own time. At the root of Gotham's attractions as a name must be the impression it gave of a place that was, paradoxically, both unique *and* representative. Gotham also provided Irving with a way of objectifying and distancing himself comically from the place where he lived. Not a bad set of attributes for a nickname. The original Gotham, for example, was a town in Nottinghamshire, England, widely known in the sixteenth century as a "place of fools," one of several such places scattered across Europe, whose residents were reputed to be simpletons—or to feign foolishness out of guile (its residents, that is, were dumb and smart simultaneously). It appears to have been the role of residents of such places to epitomize the foolishness of the whole country.[3] New York has always possessed a similar attribute: it is both the epitome of America and utterly alien to it—its manners outlandish, crazy, yet somehow typical.

Irving, in adopting "Gotham" at the beginning of the nineteenth century, was apparently attracted to the name by these typifying, parodying, and distinguishing qualities. The comic contrast between the cozy village suggested by Gotham and a mushrooming commercial city must also have been appealing. The desire to find the village within the city has been a magnetic theme for writers on New York from Irving to Greenwich Villagers like John Reed, and Broadway mythologists like Damon Runyon. Irving clearly had some such idea about what made New Yorkers distinctive at the time, although his account of the conquest of Gotham by the mythical Hoppingtots—who assault the city by *dance*—does little to develop this particular quality.[4] The name, without any particular reference to its past associations, moreover, was soon used everywhere in the country as a nickname for New York, like that of its basketball team, the Knicks. Its popularity, in fact, long outlasted the nineteenth century. Why this usage has prevailed is not entirely clear. I suppose big, anonymous, unwieldy places like modern cities invite nicknames like "Gotham" or the "Big Apple." Literary representation also works best with small-scale communities. In any event, the attractions of Gotham with its associations of coziness have not entirely disappeared, even today. New York's current telephone directory still contains half a page of entries under the name, including a chicly modern and cavernous gourmet restaurant and an unusually interesting bookstore.

Because of Gotham's historical ambiguity, I have taken the liberty of assigning it a more specific meaning. Gotham, as I use it here, is a kind of ideational village embedded in New York and refers to the city as a cultural marketplace, as the site of the lively exchange between the city's commercial life and the media it developed—*pace* Diedrich Knickerbocker—for self-expression.

New York had much to express. A speed-up of the economy after the turn of the century drastically altered the form and texture of urban life. New York, an old Dutch city, had been transformed during the nineteenth century into the country's largest seaport and biggest city. This kind of growth put a great strain on Manhattan, which at the beginning of the century was a narrow island with a tangle of winding streets at its southern tip. Rapidly projected into the role of national marketplace and major *entrepôt* to Europe, Gotham, bursting at the seams, absorbed and articulated these transforming pressures in a distinctive and dramatic way. It was further set off from other large cities, here and abroad, by being unimpeded by the spatial priorities and civil-regulatory requirements of a national or state government. Its dominant business and mercantile classes, as a result, were from the outset given a relatively free hand in reshaping the city to their varying and evolving needs. Business and commerce, one might say, had the run of the city. As George Hurstwood, just in from Chicago, was to note in Dreiser's *Sister Carrie* (1900), New York had overshadowed Chicago to become in a sense the first modern business city. It soon became both a model for, and an ominous bellwether of, the city of the future; the Beleagered City of popular folklore, Superman's Metropolis and Batman's Gotham City.

From Irving's Gotham to Henry James' "terrible town" a century later with its pincushion of skyscrapers, the Gotham factor, the cultural reagent of commerce, has been the principle component of the New York subject as it has been defined by a succession of writers and artists. New York, one feels, has sometimes exercised a veritable tyranny of place over the sensibilities of these artists. Even in their moments of repugnance, they are drawn back repeatedly to attempts at defining its aesthetic uniqueness. For all of them, from Irving to Fitzgerald and Harte Crane, the city possessed, in Yeat's words, a kind of terrible beauty. From Melville's "Bartleby, the Scrivener: A Tale of Wall Street," into modern times, artist after artist has taken the cultural pulse of New York's bustling business life. For Stephen Crane the tall buildings in the financial district were "emblematic of the nation's domineering power"; they appear to have had a comparable significance in Alfred Stieglitz's turn-of-the-century New York photographs of Wall Street skyscrapers and in those of Berenice Abbott thirty years later. For Henry Adams in 1905 the city "had the air and movement of hysteria." James' "frenzied dance" of skyscrapers is refracted twenty years later in the New York watercolors of John Marin and in Edward Steichen's photograph of a dervishing Empire State Building in the 1930s. One could cite endless examples where, as in the epigraph from James, the attempt to find expression for the imprint of commerce on the forms, shape, and pacing of New York has become an artistic obsession, pushing language and graphic representation to—some might even say beyond—its limits.

The chapters that follow, written over the last fifteen years, fall within this long tradition of reflecting on the city and the ways its commerce and culture have interacted. Each of them in one way or another is an attempt, in other words, to wrestle with the Gotham factor. The chapters appear here in roughly the order in which they were written. Each of them represents an attempt to understand a particular aspect or facet of New York's evolving commercial culture. I began them with a puzzle, and I have now finished the book with fewer answers and more questions than I would have preferred. Each chapter is a true essay, in the meaning of the French word *essayer*, "to try or attempt." They are shots (to shift metaphors) at a moving target. I recently heard anthropologist Clifford Geertz explain how impossible it was to contrast the Balinese and Moroccan villages as he knew them thirty years ago with the "same" places he revisited recently. The villages had changed, he noted; the countries had changed; their situation in the world had changed; anthropology had changed; he himself had changed. There was, accordingly, no single perspective from which both encounters with these places could be compared and studied.

I feel much the same way about New York of the mid-'seventies and the city today. While my subject is historical, the perch from which I have been peering into the past has suffered some jarring shocks in the interval. There is a cyclical character to the changes that have overtaken the city. When I first began to think systematically about New York, it was experiencing a serious fiscal crisis that threatened its future. Its infrastructure—its subway system, its parks and public places—were in shambles. During the 1980s it went through an unprecedented period of prosperity that inspired, among other things, a building boom to rival any in its past. In a few short years the visual face of the city was transformed; some would argue, further disfigured. There were changes of like magnitude in the city's social and cultural life. A whole new breed of prosperous, high-consuming, young urban residents, for example, made a conspicuous appearance in a city that suddenly seemed to sprout expensive new hotels, condominiums, restaurants, nightspots, discos, and comparable "upscale" amenities every week. Then came the crash of '87, followed by a succession of economic shock waves that have placed the city once again in economic peril and threatened its museums, parks, and cultural institutions with further retrenchment. The spans of Manhattan's vital bridges, for James the throbbing pistons of its engines, are slowly being consumed by rust.

Fifteen years in the life of a discipline is also a long time. Changes of the same magnitude have overtaken the history of urban cultures, which scarcely existed as a recognizable sub-species of history when I first began to write. The serious study of popular cultures, too—a related development—was also just beginning. This *nouvelle vague* in history came as something of a shock and caught me by surprise. When an editor at Little, Brown sent me an advance copy of Neil Harris's study of P. T. Barnum and New York late in 1972, I recall wondering whether Harris was still serious about history. By the end of the decade, however, other pioneering studies in urban culture had appeared, and I had begun to piece together the early essays in this volume. The publication in 1979 of Carl Schorske's *Fin de Siècle Vienna* was an instructive addition to existing cultural studies of cities and, I believe, helped legitimize analogous studies of American cities. In any event, work on urban cultures has since proliferated.

It is only a slight exaggeration to say that I began in the 'seventies by explaining to puzzled graduate students why I was studying New York, and that, recently, I have found myself wondering, having read what is now being written, whether the field is now too much taken for granted. Scarcely a month now goes by without a new book or manuscript on some aspect of urban culture appearing. Certain overall changes are becoming clear. Work on urban cultures that appeared during the 'seventies, including my own, often derived its methods from traditional intellectual history or from American studies. This early work was also more general in scope. Recent work is much more specialized and targeted and shows the influence of new studies in social history and urban geography; other new work reflects new combinations of social history, urban geography, urban anthropology, and critical theory.[5] This volume, as it progresses, reflects some of these changes in scope and methodology.

The successive chapters in the book were written under very diverse circumstances. Rereading them now, I have discovered to my surprise that, despite discontinuities of time and circumstance, they provide a more coherent exploration of the book's theme than I would have expected.

My interest in writing about New York was awakened, ironically, in 1975, when I had left the city to spend a year in London. The first two essays in particular date from writing and lecturing I did that year. I had earlier given some thought to writing about New York but in quite a different way from the one I ultimately chose. It was the experience of London that alerted me to the visual character of modern American cities and helped me set a course through the inquiry that follows. Living in Kensington and working at London University and in the British Museum, I crossed the city daily, often on foot. Central London as seen by pedestrians from its parks and squares and principal thoroughfares is very different from modern American cities with their clustered, vertical downtowns. In its spatial organization, moreover, London expresses a tension between its existence as a capital city with all the institutional implications that role entails and its character as a vast commercial city of élite residential districts, working-class neighborhoods, factories, warehouse areas, and harbor and shipping facilities. It has also, as a royal seat of palaces and what were once palace gardens, been shaped by its monarchical heritage. London in the mid-'seventies, as I recall, had only a single skyscraper, on Oxford Street, and that stood vacant. Except for that one building, no commercial structure overtopped London's churches and government buildings. Its major thoroughfares and the cobweb of sidestreets reflect an historical tension between political and commercial pressures in the growth of the city.

Why, I wondered, had modern cities like New York developed concentrated vertical downtowns? What kind of significance had been built into the novel spatial arrangements and into the ornamentation and iconography of civic and commercial structures in such American cities? How had artists and others whose eyes had been conditioned to older cities of Europe responded to the vision of American urban modernity? These were some of the puzzles that began to tantalize me in London. There were a number of interesting photographic exhibitions that year, including a large show of photographs by Paul Strand in the early spring. This was my first exposure to his work, and I was especially interested in his New York pictures, circa 1920, with their crisp, rectilinear qualities. The first essay, "Psyching Out the City," was a direct response to this awakened interest in photography. How, I wondered, did American photographers who had lived in Europe see New York when they returned to the city from abroad? I needed a set of eyes to guide me to an answer to this question. Alfred Stieglitz, who came back to New York in 1890 after a lengthy stay in Germany, provided an interesting example of one search for an aesthetic of the modern American city. This quest to find beauty— "a terrible beauty"—in the geometry and concrete of modern New York was continued, I felt, in the work of Lewis Hine and Edward Steichen.

The second chapter, on the evolution of the skyline view of New York, is another product of my London year. Early in the year, a small shop near Bloomsbury Square placed a set of seventeenth-century prints of London on display. These prints, with their emphasis on the harbor and shipping, made me conscious of earlier conventions for visualizing the city. These and other similar, older views of cities across Europe that I located in the British Museum formed a background for my exploration of American cityscapes and of the emerging New York skyline perspective.

Much of the work that went into the next essay, on the evolution of public space, was done during the spring of 1984 in the research collections of the New York Public Library on Forty-second Street. To get to the library from where I live, I had to cross several parks whose present functions and dilapidated condition would have appalled those who planned and built them. I walked past statues of military heroes unknown today and along thoroughfares lined by buildings of monumental character whose ornamental façades and towering campaniles were generally ignored. If I traveled by subway, the historical amnesia was more evident. I spent several days in the catalogue room at the library examining every entry slip under the heading "Public." Out of this experience and the subsequent examination of many of the published items catalogued came my recognition of a relationship that was more than verbal between evolving ideas of public space and public opinion. Both concepts changed dramatically in the early twentieth century. It was only a short step from this recognition to the conclusion that "the public," as this concept was defined after 1900, referred to a physical presence, an aggregate of potential or actual consumers. I came to this recognition one day as I crossed some of the city's public spaces heading toward the library. Each day's walk was a visit to the city's dilapidated public past and a reminder of the high expectations this vision of modernity once evoked. What, I wondered, were the expectations of those who planned and built this particular New York?

For three years in the early 'eighties, a group of historians from the New York area participated in a monthly colloquium at the New York Institute for the Humanities at New York University. Its purpose was to examine different aspects of urban culture. The next chapter, "Aesthetic Tensions in the Shaping of New York," is a revision of a paper jointly written with Thomas Bender for a meeting of that group in the spring of 1982. This meeting, to which we had invited several practicing New York architects and architectural historians, was an attempt to exhume the aesthetic presuppositions underlying buildings of monumental scale in New York. We wanted to fix their place in an overall conception of the kind of modern commercial city that had evolved out of the experience of the Chicago Columbian Exposition of 1893. We had been set on this particular tack by a paper we had been shown on the conservative and progressive thrusts of Beaux-Arts classicism.[6]

This essay enabled us to examine the evolving architecture and planning of New York's commercial activities. We concluded that Louis Sullivan, Siegfried Giedion, and most modern architectural critics, in their rush to attack New York's Beaux-Arts designs, had missed the revolutionary character of the city's tall buildings. The classical repertory had provided precedents for certain "public" buildings: for municipal structures, libraries, railway terminals. Tall buildings, however, posed a problem. There was, to begin with, a psychological resistance to vertical structures. They had been technologically feasible, we discovered, long before they were actually built. One reason for the resistance to height was architectural. No one seemed to know what a tall building should look like. There were no classical or Renaissance precedents for such structures, except for church towers or campaniles. The skyscraper structures that evolved, we concluded, were an attempt to accommodate the need for height within existing horizontal conceptions of public space. The result was the rectangle surmounted by a campanile, a form that eventually evolved into such skyscrapers as the Metropolitan Life Insurance building and the Woolworth and Empire State buildings in New York.

The next chapter, "The Launching of Commercial Culture," played a critical role in the development of my ideas about cultural production in New York. The initial impetus for this chapter came from the Social Science Research Council. In 1984, the SSRC, in conjunction with the Russell Sage Foundation, held three small conferences to determine how "economic, cultural, and political perspectives might illuminate the mercantile, industrial, and postindustrial phases of New York's development." I prepared an early version of this chapter for one of these sessions. There was a disposition at the conference to see what I called commercial culture as simply an early form of mass culture that probably deflected working-class people from genuine cultural expressions. In the paper I had argued that producers of this kind of culture-for-sale could not control the ways it was consumed or the significance consumers might attach to it. Forms of commercial culture, my argument went, were often read as urban Baedekers, as guides that helped residents understand the complexities of the city. In preparing the essay, I had been especially impressed by studies of early European street cultures, and I came to see these street cultures as forerunners of the kinds of culture-for-sale that were produced in nineteenth-century industrial cities like New York.

I also concluded then that commercial culture was an interim stage in cultural production, one that followed street cultures and predated what we usually mean by "mass culture." I dated its period of ascendancy from 1880 to about 1930. In street cultures, production and consumption take place in the same locale, and producers and consumers are in close touch, as in organ-grinder street music. In mass culture there is little reciprocity beyond the marketplace between producer and consumer, as, for example, in wire-service news dispatches. In commercial culture, producer and consumer collaborate in the shaping of a cultural form, as in vaudeville. While this paradigm vastly oversimplifies a complicated argument, it helps explain why I have focused the remaining essays on the critical period of some twenty years or so on either side of 1900, when the forms of commercial culture were being reshaped into media of mass culture.

This was an hypothesis that I brought to the collaborative study of Times Square that I helped organize in 1988. Many things had to change, we then concluded, before Times Square could shift from its earlier role as a hub of New York's commercial culture to become a national cultural marketplace. Changes in production and consumption, in the promotion of goods and services; the development of wholesale tourism of cities and other historic sites; and changes in morality and religious values pertaining to leisure and entertainment had to precede such a development. If Times Square was a force in launching mass media, mass media, once they were in place, just as certainly spelled its doom.

The next chapter examines the process through which such a central entertainment district first evolves and then develops into a national center for cultural productions. It also examines the emerging commercial aesthetic that developed in and around Broadway, and, finally, it reviews the impact of Times Square on conventional morality and probes the so-called pathologies that accompanied its decline in the post–World War II period.[7]

Times Square holds still another kind of significance. It also brought about a revolution in the form of the modern city. The center of the classical city was the forum and the agora. Times Square, located at a major transportation hub, was neither. Because of its location, it became a new kind of center of amusement, recreation, and vice, the kind of area that in earlier cities was located off-center, its activities discreetly muffled. Times Square's very centrality meant that what took place was immediately in the national spotlight. When Times Square declined and became a theater of sexual entertainment, that, too, was refracted through the culture and brought about the condemnation and subsequent redevelopment of the area that is taking place today.

The chapter on Walter Lippmann is the only one in this part of the book to be written before the Times Square conferences in 1988. It is based on a paper prepared for the American Historical Association meetings the previous year. In a way, it anticipates a conclusion I was later to reach about the infectious attractions of Broadway's entertainment culture. I was already beginning to piece together the configuration of cultural practices and institutions that made up the Times Square world, and I was struck initially by the odd fact that Lippmann, a stern Progressive and an editor and founder of the *New Republic*, wrote during the 1920s a succession of articles on current events for Condé Nast's slick urban guide to fashion and entertainment, *Vanity Fair*. The midtown magazine world was located in the forties across Sixth Avenue, slightly to the east of Times Square but well within its magnetic field. I had begun to feel that this segment of New York's commercial culture, a segment that was soon enriched by the appearance of the *New Yorker*, functioned as a kind of avant-garde during the 1920s, nurturing writers and critics from Robert Benchley and Dorothy Parker to Edmund Wilson and H. L. Mencken. Once I began to read through the Lippmann correspondence at Yale, these suppositions were amply confirmed. Lippmann turned out to be an avid consumer of commercial entertainment and actively courted such entertainment figures as Charles Chaplin, George Gershwin, Irving Berlin, and Harry Houdini. The Lippmann essay was also my first attempt to place opinion-makers within New York's commercial journalism, to examine how they functioned there. While Lippmann retained, even in these associations, something of his reputed austerity, and chided Broadway, journalism, and commercial publishing now and then for lax standards, other critics within magazine journalism as different as H. L. Mencken and Edmund Wilson adopted much the same posture. This inquiry into a commercial avant-garde was one that I pursued with greater thoroughness in the long chapter on H. L. Mencken.

"The Power of the Word" was prepared as a lecture in 1989 for an extensive set of New York University programs on Greenwich Village. It presents the obverse of the coin: a safe house in the capitalist zone that turns out to have been prey to some of the publicizing mania that was simultaneously gripping midtown commerce. If one part of commercial publishing functioned to nurture an avant-garde, the avant-garde haven in the Village, its protests apart, shared an historical moment with midtown commerce and advertising. It had always struck me as curious that a lively bohemia had developed in lower Manhattan at the precise moment the culture of Times Square was beginning to peak. Who were these writers and artists, I wondered, who proved immune to the forces that were contagiously spreading through the society? Since many of them came to New York from small towns and cities across the country, were they impelled by different motives than those that drew their literary brethren to the thriving entertainment industries uptown? The answer to this last question turns out to be a mixture of yes and no, one that takes account of their mania for individualistic self-expression, but also sets them off from commercial writers and artists in important ways. The Villagers, with their collegiate, liberal values, were forerunners of generations of middle-class rebels looking for exemption from the life of business. The Village itself was the first Free City for writers and artists, a forerunner of the Expatriate City and the post–World War II University as havens for aesthetic and social refugees from an all-embracing middle class.

The portrayal of H. L. Mencken that appears here is an accidental discovery that grew out of my research into his study of the American language. I became interested in Mencken when I was working on Damon Runyon and the historical origins of slang. Mencken seemed to me one of the most acute students of the vernacular, who knew Times Square almost as well as Damon Runyon and Ring Lardner, who worked the area as journalists. I was also puzzled by Mencken's point of view, which seemed to be defined by his dual residence in Baltimore and New York. The publication in 1989 of a diary he had kept, and the publicity surrounding the secret memoirs that were to be released early this spring, were further inducements to examine the career of this part-time New Yorker.

In the beginning, I was also captive to the reputation for erudition and critical acumen that had always surrounded him. As I read through his published work, I was struck more by his clear penchant for generating quotable, often abusive opinions than by anything else about him. It is this factor, the creation and marketing of opinion, that I have emphasized here. I have attempted to fill in the historical contours of what I describe as the "New York opinion factory," and I have tried to suggest how Mencken's career as a journalist fits into the vector of the emerging magazine industry directed toward prosperous, middle-class, urban readers. Magazines such as *Vanity Fair*, *Vogue*, the *Smart Set*, and the *New Yorker* introduced readers to a complex of ideas about the city and city life, what I call "the new urbanity." New York in the pages of these magazines became the center of what was fashionable, what was clever, and what was new. The stress on fashion, sophistication, and "upscale" living made an attractive base for new kinds of advertising beamed at prosperous urban residents who wanted the last word on everything from clothing and food to theater and entertainment. They were avid consumers of opinion, always alert to the dangers of deception, and appreciative of sharp, colorful criticism, which became by the 'twenties another form of lively entertainment.

There were many things about Mencken himself that made him an enigmatic figure in this journalistic world. His attachment to Baltimore, his middle-class German-American background, his deeply conservative social and political views, his absence of collegiate or patrician polish, and his pronouncedly masculine persona all clash with the character of the liberated urban sophisticate he portrayed himself as being. He appears here as a figure deeply divided, quick to anger, with a ready pen. He was the verbal cartoonist of the cultural rebellion that followed World War I.

Finally, in the concluding chapter on Damon Runyon, I try to show the linguistic fallout from the Broadway world in the form of a rapidly spreading national slang. Damon Runyon in 1911 arrived in New York as a seasoned journalist from the West, and, after his Broadway years writing for Hearst's *American*, he left for a new career writing and producing films in Hollywood. Runyon's years as a reporter working the area brought him in touch with the volatile linguistic world surrounding Times Square, a "language funnel" for the special argots that had developed in the area. The sporting world (especially horse-racing and boxing), bootlegging, the underworld more generally, and the worlds of vaudeville, carnival, and show business had all developed rich and expressive argots by the 'twenties.[8]

Journalists like Runyon, Ring Lardner, and Jack Conway of *Variety*, I try to show in Chapter 9, were quick to exploit the vitality of these languages in forging new journalistic styles for themselves. In doing so, they were in the vanguard of the creation of an American slang that rapidly spread through the local, then national, press, magazines like the *Saturday Evening Post*, which published Runyon's Broadway stories, and, finally, during the 'thirties, through national network radio and through Hollywood films to the rest of the country. Walter Winchell, writing for *Vanity Fair* in 1927, included a list of slang expressions from the area and called New York "the slang capitol of the world." Ten years later, the list of slang expressions he included had, thanks to the work of Runyon and others, become part of a national slang that was quite generally employed. A whole cast of Broadway characters out of *Guys and Dolls* with their colorful monikers and vivid speech had found a place in some national dramatis personae. The authority challenged by Runyon's softhearted gangsters and gamblers was less the law than the formalities of written English and Emily Post, the same authorities challenged in Irving Berlin's lyrics. One revolution that Times Square had helped bring off was a revolution in vernacular speech, a revolution against the conventions of classical civility that a sometime habitué of the area, H. L. Mencken, had labored to track in the various editions of *The American Language*.

Readers will soon discover that the first five chapters in their general tenor are, in effect, essays in search of a subject. The last of these, written in 1984, on the "launching" of a commercial culture in New York, also had the effect of launching me on the five more-focused studies that follow.

All of these last five grow out of the collaborative study of Times Square, and they reflect my growing interest in the history of publishing, in newspapers and magazines as important expressions of New York's commercial culture. They demonstrate, I believe, that language is one of the most sensitive barometers of cultural change. The chapters on Walter Lippmann, H. L. Mencken, and Damon Runyon also reflect my reinvestment in biography as a way of focusing cultural studies. Biography, I found, is one way of pinpointing the relation between culture and commerce by considering the ways writers gain a living through the circulation of information and the sale of entertainment.

There is no real stopping point in such an inquiry. It is not possible, like Irving's Diedrich Knickerbocker, to put this manuscript history in a drawer and walk off into the sunset. There are not only conclusions to be weighed but judgments that might be made; if not here, then privately and introspectively. It is hard not to ask whether, for example, these vast modern cities like New York show an increment of progress over the nineteenth-century industrial cities with their Dickensian squalor that they have replaced; or whether, perhaps, they may be speeding us even more rapidly to the brink of disaster, into uncontrollable costs and unimaginable human suffering. Answers to such questions, when they can be formulated, lie heavy in the air. The urban mythology of the comics is only one indication of what such answers might be. Superman's Metropolis and Batman's Gotham City are modern cities salvageable only by supernatural intervention.

This volume ends with Runyon and the moment in the city's past that fed his imagination and gave us much of our slang. But there are countless other inquiries fairly waiting to be taken up. It is the mode of questioning that seems to matter, the search for revealing details, surprising relationships, contrapuntal occurrences. If these chapters stimulate fresh encounters of this kind with the city's past, they will have more than served their purpose.

Clearly, new cultural configurations are replacing, have replaced, those that are described here. Gotham no longer visually registers the dramatic impressions in the way it once did from the shifting economic life of the city. These changes are now registered invisibly. No wonder the modern city of the comics must resort to the supernatural for explanations of change. Much of what was once fully visible and above ground, on the streets and in the air surrounding its tall buildings, now takes place out of sight, fiber-optically, electronically. What at one time required a tight neighborhood of related activities, physically adjacent, can now be accomplished severally and apart by signals beamed in from great distances. In the arts, too, physical interaction plays a much smaller role. The shouts of appreciation or the hail of rotten fruit that once registered theatrical success or failure have given way to telemetered ratings. The hum of computers has largely replaced the jingle of coins and the shuffle of bills. Catalogues and video displays are replacing the street, even the great department stores, as markets where we prefer to buy. And so on.

It is a familiar refrain, but one must take care not to sentimentalize the past. Each moment in the city's past possesses a kind of integrity of its own, with its own shifting equation of good and evil. The city, moreover, is constantly changing. There are fresh and daunting problems, and they are present on a scale no one could have anticipated fifty years ago. The population of 1905 has been replaced by another, even more multi-ethnic and multi-racial, with grim potentialities that are yet to be explored. There are as many different accents, as many different languages and cultures in the city today as at any time in the past. The problems already posed by these changes are as daunting as those imagined a century ago by people like James.

Some things, on the other hand, do not change; at least not out of all recognition. One of them is the steady pressure on the city, for good or ill, from its economic life. New York is still a place where commerce has a free run. More than anything else, it has retained its role as Business City. Today's commerce is more one of financial markets and services than tangible goods, but the pace is still brisk, although not the driving, throbbingly energetic movement described by James in 1907. From the terrace of my apartment on the edge of Greenwich Village, I can hear the hum of taxis each weekday morning soon after daylight as they head down Broadway, a block away, toward Wall Street, the city's other downtown. It is the same stream of south-flowing traffic that Stephen Crane, Theodore Dreiser, and John Reed had noted ominously from their differing perspectives more than half a century earlier, although its significance, along with that of the city it now personifies, has been further complicated by the triumph of the capitalist marketplace almost everywhere in the world.

In Pursuit of Gotham

ONE

Psyching Out the City

"All is changed, changed utterly,
A terrible beauty is born."
   W. B. Yeats, "Easter 1916"

The modern skyscraper city ringed by successive industrial and residential districts appeared with startling suddenness at the end of the nineteenth century. Before that time cities had expanded without assuming any particular or characteristic shape. The process through which these sprawling, low-rise cities of the nineteenth century gave way to modern cities consumed the first three decades of the new century. It was a process, moreover, fully as disruptive in its consequences as the more frequently discussed transition from country to city that was taking place at much the same time. The disruption was of every kind: economic, social, and aesthetic. The very conception of the city was radically transformed as a wide range of new activities and values accrued, in popular thinking, to the idea of city life. The economic and social costs of such a process have been extensively discussed by historians and others. Less attention—indeed, little at all—has been given to examining how such a radical process of change was perceived by those who experienced it, or how they learned to live with it and to enhance its disruptive character with a new aesthetic that found positive qualities in its forms and modalities.

   Chicago was the first American city to develop a typical "downtown" of tall buildings clustered about activities that ranged from commercial to service: office buildings, banks, wholesale and retail stores, hotels, theaters, and restaurants, all fed by railroads and other arteries of public transportation.[1] For a long time it was the most modern of such cities, widely acclaimed as the home of the skyscraper. But the same developments that created Chicago soon transformed other American cities. New

York, in particular, early became known for its modernity, and it soon surpassed Chicago as the embodiment of a new style of urban life. Its importance as a port of entry, its constricted location that made at once for high population density and vertical construction, and its vigorous ethnic theatrical, and literary life helped it establish a reputation for modern urbanity.

The stamp of modernity was early put on New York, in part by a succession of photographers and other graphic artists who were sensitive to the visual character that the city was assuming and who saw in these new shapes and forms a vision of the future. For the French avant-garde painter Francis Picabia, for example, New York had become by 1914 "the Cubist city."[2] For a whole generation of photographers, its buildings, its streets, and its people came close to being an obsession. New York was as important to photography, moreover, as photography was to New York. The creative potential of photography, an art already half a century old by the turn of the century, was strikingly unfolded in the work of those who first tried to grasp the meaning of these changes.

One common problem faced by all significant urban photographers in this period was that of how to relate the people of the city visually to their surroundings. There was, first of all, an aesthetic problem to be confronted. The modern city violated virtually every artistic convention developed over the centuries for linking man to his environment, even those that were suited to the visual character of older European cities, such as Venice, Paris, and London. During the nineteenth century, landscape painting, in the hands of John Constable, Joseph Turner, Jean François Millet, and the Impressionists, developed into a major artistic genre, and photographers were quick to adopt many of its conventions. Photographs of people in a setting of fields, hills, woods, rivers, lakes, or shores were commonplace by the end of the century. In particular, photographers, like painters, were excited by the magic of light reflected from water. In the face of such conventions the visual properties of modern cities like New York must have seemed a kind of antipastoral version of the beautiful. It was one thing to portray people scattered across fields, at work and at play; it was quite another to depict them against a background of concrete, glass, and asphalt. There was something, too, about man in relation to machine that seemed initially incongruous, even grotesque. Tall buildings, furthermore, blocked the horizon; created dark, sunless canyons; overshadowed waterways; and dwarfed those bits of vegetation their construction had not eradicated. Clouds of smoke replaced trees against the sky; a network of rails, the familiar stream of waterways. It proved difficult to portray people in such settings without dwarfing or dehumanizing them.

In view of such problems, it is scarcely surprising that few photographers before 1915 sought to capture broad panoramic sweeps of the modern city. These perspectives on the city that have become the familiar conventions of today's photography and cinema—the skyline view and the bird's-eye view—had to await a more minute exploration of the city's new visual character, and represent a later visual accommodation to it. Indeed, it is very likely that during the transitional years before the modern city became a recognized visual entity, it was difficult for anyone, photographer or not, to conceive of these sprawling, amorphous communities as a whole. Such an impossibility, moreover, places the present discussion in a context of the history of perception and helps give it a significance beyond the history of art and architecture.

If the photograph can be shown to record in some fashion how the modern city was perceived and how such perceptions changed over time, then historians have at their disposal a valuable and largely unexploited source. There are two aspects of photography that tend to support such a claim. First, the photographer is both a man of his time, sharing its interests and anxieties, and also a kind of antenna for the public, probing, clarifying, and channeling the visual signals of a new environment. The photographer's relationship to a public is a complicated one, like that of any graphic artist, since he must both anticipate public taste and, if he is to be understood and appreciated, finally satisfy it. Any art form, to stay alive, must speak meaningfully to some public, however small. During the opening decades of the century, the public for photography enlarged immeasurably. Public interest and taste, moreover, dogged that of photographers. At the Empire State Building, where the photographer Lewis Hine perched his camera one day, the public swarmed the next. The second aspect of photography sets it apart from the other graphic arts. The photograph not only reflects the perceptions of the photographer, it often records and documents some of the perceptions of his subjects, when the subjects are human. Being photographed in this period was an event, something that happened to you and your surroundings, something novel and memorable. The photograph itself thus became a bit of "reality" snatched from a moment of someone's existence. Sometimes, for example, the very artlessness of the way people grouped themselves before the camera tells us something about how they conceived of themselves and how they wished to be seen. Indeed, as we look at these photographs today, part of their interest and humanity lies in the different meanings that were ascribed to the experience of having one's picture taken.

A new kind of urban photograph began to appear in the 'nineties that, even in the beginning, was easily set off from most earlier photographic work about the city. Among the first photographs were quite a number by

Alfred Stieglitz, taken in the years immediately after his return from Europe in 1890. These images speak directly of the time and place—New York in transition to the modern city. They provide evidence about the beginning phase of the process through which photographers were to size up modern urban life.

The occasion of Stieglitz's photographic scrutiny of the modern city is a little unclear. By 1890 he had completed some study in Germany, had exhibited photographs abroad and mastered existing photographic technology. He was soon to abandon any pretense of following a vocation other than photography. Bolstered by independent means, which freed him from some of the economic pressures that preoccupied his contemporaries, he first launched himself into the New York photographic and artistic world in a series of bold and imaginative steps. These included the founding of his influential quarterly, *Camera Work*, in 1903, and the opening a few years later of the Photo-Secession Gallery at 291 Fifth Avenue, a succession of moves that kept him a focus of modernism in the arts for almost half a century.[3] Unlike Jacob Riis, he was not a reformer bent on changing people's minds. He did not, like Riis or Lewis Hine, take up the camera in the course of other work. Taking pictures, at least for a time, was his work.

In his approach to the city, Stieglitz was neither carping nor idealizing. He struck, overall, some sort of balance between communicating a sense of loss and a sense of aesthetic excitement, except for the fact that he seemed possessed by the city to a singular degree—annoyed by it, antagonized, exhausted to the point where he had to get away, yet continually fascinated and drawn back, at least in these years, for still another look. Indeed, he himself traced the inauguration of his photographic career to an experience of the city that seems curiously like a religious conversion. When he returned to America in 1890, Stieglitz had found New York, by contrast with European cities, dirty, empty of excitement, and without culture or artistic interests of any traceable kind. For a time he went through a period of deep depression, which included weeping at night. In reminiscing to his biographer, he associated his early work and the end of his feelings of depression with a succession of aesthetic experiences in and of the city. One of these was his discovery of theater in the winter of 1893, when he almost accidentally witnessed the Italian actress Eleanora Duse in a notable production of *Camille* and, at about the same time, the comic team of Weber and Fields in a performance that came as almost a revelation to him. He closely associated these two experiences with his first photographs in his new, probingly realistic manner. "This is the beginning of a new era," he later recalled exclaiming to a fellow photographer as he finished the first of these new prints. "Call it a new vision if you wish."[4]

The photograph that evoked these remarks was made during a Washington's birthday blizzard in 1893 and is entitled "Winter, Fifth Avenue." The exposure was made as Stieglitz, equipped with a recently purchased hand camera, stood at the corner of Fifth Avenue and Thirty-fourth Street facing south (*Figure 1, photo section*). It portrayed coaches lumbering north along a deeply snow-rutted avenue against a background and foreground of laterally driving snow. The buildings lining the streets are reduced to shadowy abstractions and the human figures to tiny silhouettes. It was considered a work of great technical brilliance, one that pushed photographic technology beyond its recognized limits. At the time it was taken, for example, Stieglitz reported that the light was so dim that he himself had doubts about what he could capture on his plates. Those who first saw the plates were doubtful about whether recognizable forms would emerge in prints made from them.[5] Yet the result, in accord with Stieglitz's hunch, was a photograph of considerable interest. In it a carriage in the near foreground (which Stieglitz actually described as a "stagecoach") appears to be arriving out of some mythical past into the midst of a busy, modern city, with the almost magical blizzard providing the illusion necessary for such a transforming vision. The photograph is also well composed and interestingly ambiguous. The long, straight line of ruts running laterally across the picture parallels the lines of driving snow and therefore seems to suggest either a country road penetrating the city or an added bit of geometric design to score off against the vertical lines of the modern buildings.

It is easy to see why such a photograph would have seemed to Stieglitz "a new vision" and to promise a new kind of potential for photography. It was all done, moreover, without the artificial procedures that often characterized pictorial photography of the day. No pigmented paper had been used in printing from the plate to simulate brush strokes, nor had the negative been scratched or scored for the same effect—both techniques that even the best of his contemporaries commonly used. Nor had it been necessary to "import" a Whistlerian fog by artificially softening the focus. Instead, the photograph was as sharp and the focal distance as great as lens and available light would permit. The picture was thus the direct result of the unfiltered play of New York winter light on a slow photographic plate, a triumph of what would become known as "straight" photography, in order to distinguish it from its more heavily cosmetic stylistic rival.

Not long afterward, Stieglitz made another photograph of a somewhat similar kind, a picture of a horsecar and team standing at the terminal, the horses steaming as the driver, back to the camera, tends to them (*Figure 2*). Once again, the steaming horses have an almost primeval quality, as though they had just sprung fresh from creation. In the background is the old Post Office with its Doric columns and rectilinear windows capped with snow. This photograph, too, has a visual immediacy and the arresting quality of expressing temporal displacement and skewed chronology. For Stieglitz, the making of these two photographs was powerfully associated with his theatrical initiation of a few days before: "The steaming horses being watered on a cold winter day, the snow covered streets and the Stagecoach in 'Winter—5th Avenue,' my sense of loneliness in my own country, all seemed closely related to my experience when seeing Duse."[6] Just as clearly, from Stieglitz's obtaining of these visual effects, a new kind of street theater had been born.

During the next fifteen years or so Stieglitz continued to develop and broaden his conception of urban photography. Between "The Asphalt-Paver" of 1892, the earliest picture that roughly fits this form (and a photograph of considerable interest), and his "Excavating, New York," a picture that still retains in 1911 some of the qualities of his early work, Stieglitz made at least a score of other photographs of great variety and range. "The Asphalt-Paver" is a good example of how this process began. In this particular photograph the subject and the center of attention is a paving machine in the foreground of the picture, virtually enveloped in smoke from a nearby asphalt-melting fire. A single human figure whose outline is scarcely discernible against the machine is bent over it. The smoke rises in a great cloud to partly obscure the bare branches of a row of trees behind and, farther off, the geometric line of a viaduct. This viaduct crosses the picture at a slight angle. There is no horizon, no clear division of earth and sky. The whole photograph, in fact, is a study in shades of gray. The darkest forms are those of the viaduct and the vertical stack of the paving machine, which cross at right angles in the center of the picture. Even lighter than the sky is the cloud of manmade smoke.

The meaning of such photographs, at least out of context, is somewhat enigmatic. The objects portrayed, the paving machinery and the viaduct behind, seem very much from the present, in contrast to those in "Winter, Fifth Avenue." Their lines are contrasted with the lacework of bare branches, the soft outline of the smoke, and what little one can detect of the single, hunched human figure. Stieglitz seems characteristically to have employed smoke to soften and qualify the starkly linear quality of his urban scenes.

Sometimes in his cityscapes, mushrooms of smoke billowing from stacks almost seem to take the place of trees in the conventional landscape, as in his picture of railyards, "The Hand of Man" (*Figure 3*). Even more telling, in this case, is the bleak, wintry tonal range. There is no beauty here, at least not in any easily recognizable form, though the picture has the quality of offering a perception of where things are, measured against the more or less constant values of earth and sky. All in all, one would have to say, the photograph presents a not-very-optimistic reading on the building of roads. Some kind of hostile invasion of the natural world is clearly under way in this portrayal of man-in-the-machine as an enemy encampment.

The direction in which Stieglitz was moving in his portrayal of New York becomes clearer if one contrasts two photographs: one of a Paris street scene made in 1894 during a wedding trip to France and the other a New York street scene made eight years later. The Paris photograph, "Wet Day on the Boulevard," is of a tree-lined street. Despite the rain and grayness of tone, this is an aesthetically agreeable picture, in perspective and subject very much in the manner of contemporary Pissaros. The wet, puddled street reflects what light there is, and there is an interesting bustle of people freely moving about in carriages or under umbrellas: all in all, a scene out of the European urban past. Paris and other European cities were always to strike Stieglitz this way, as they did most contemporary photographers. Another photograph of Paris made by Stieglitz seventeen years later, for example, is roughly similar in character.

There is no analogous portrayal of a New York street scene by Stieglitz, nor, so far as I can determine, by any other "art" photographer of the time. New York streets were usually photographed by Stieglitz, as by others, at night or when mostly deserted, the parks virtually empty. More and more, the vertical lines of buildings rising on either side of the street, or the geometric patterns of streets and buildings viewed from above, tended to dominate or dwarf any human figures in sight. A good example of this is "Spring Showers, New York," made in 1902. In the foreground of this photograph is a sapling surrounded by a fence, a small remnant of nature caught in a cage. Near the small tree is a street cleaner in a white coat, back to the camera and broom in hand, working alone. Way off in the distance and barely discernible are some carriages and what appear to be the forms of pedestrians, but the scene is overshadowed by the obscure forms of tall buildings rising on either side of the street. As though to emphasize the strikingly vertical character of the picture, the print itself is tall and thin, in contrast to the horizontal and rectilinear squatness of the two Paris prints.

The significance of such a shift in emphasis does, I think, prove something of a problem, though certain things can be said that do clarify the situation somewhat. For one thing, this shift was not unique to Stieglitz. A growing and analogous photographic interest in abstraction began to mark the work of a number of photographers at just about this time. Such a change can be seen in the work of Edward Steichen, Paul Strand, and Alvin Coburn, to name but three art photographers, as well as that of a documentary photographer like Lewis Hine. While the subjects and objectives they worked with differed, a comparable development took place in each of them. The explanation of this change, therefore, does not seem to lie in the work of any one artist. A careful examination of Stieglitz might tell us something about the idiosyncratic style he worked in, might help explain his total commitment to his art and, indeed, much else, but it could scarcely supply an answer to the central riddle: why does this particular kind of geometric and abstract vision of the city appear in just these years?

This was not, as we know, a phenomenon of photography alone, since such painters as John Marin and Joseph Stella seem to have perceived something comparable only just a little later. Nor was it the product of any particular avant-garde influence. While many of those involved were associated with the Photo-Secession movement and with Stieglitz's "291" gallery, Hine and Stella worked alone.

Stieglitz's *Camera Work*, while an invaluable source of what became known as "pictorial" photography during the whole of its existence from 1903 until its discontinuation in 1917, is scarcely dominated by this kind of photography, since most Photo-Secession work does not conform to this pattern. The examples cited here have had to be culled from masses of photographs of a widely differing character. *Camera Work*, furthermore, contains little editorial comment on the city as a subject of photography, and apart from a few references in letters, there is little recognition in Stieglitz's writings that such a development was taking place. Since Stieglitz himself was editor and retained a controlling voice concerning what was printed throughout this period, one would have expected him, had he been fully conscious of the importance of this shift in his own perception, to have given some indication of it, at least in the selection and grouping of his own photographs included in the volumes for 1905, 1911, and 1913. The only hint of this came in 1910 when he grouped a number of cityscapes made during the previous year.

Nor does the appearance of modernism in European painting and sculpture seem to hold the answer. The notorious Armory Show in 1913 and the arrival in the Stieglitz circle of European modernists such as Picabia and Marcel Duchamp came too late to provide a satisfactory explanation. Stieglitz's own style of abstract representation was well developed by 1910, the year before the first Futuristic Manifesto and the year of his first, faltering exposure, during a trip to France, to the art of Pablo Picasso and Henri Matisse.[7] Instead, the change in Stieglitz, as in the others, seems to be the product of the aesthetic promptings of New York itself, an almost communal experience of the city by those who lived there and whose perception was in some way specially attuned to what they saw.

One of the most interesting careers in American photography began some nine years earlier, in 1901, when Frank Manny, superintendent of New York's Ethical Culture School, placed a camera in the hands of a young botany teacher from Wisconsin named Lewis Hine—in order for him to improve his teaching.[8]

Hine's career as a photographer was closer to that of Jacob Riis than to those of more consciously artistic photographers like Stieglitz and those associated with the Photo-Secession movement, which he originated and led. During the next thirty years or so, Hine, with seeming artlessness, photographed America's new laboring classes from the time of their arrival at Ellis Island. He found them, child and adult, in their homes, on the streets, sometimes at rest or at play, but most often at work.

While his photography was not confined to New York, the city was the focus of his most interesting studies—and all but a few of his pictures concerned subjects that were in some sense urban. Indeed, his photography was informed almost from the start by an interest in urban sociology acquired first at the University of Chicago and then at Columbia, where he completed a Pd.M. in 1905. Out of this latter association, in fact, came his lifelong involvement in Progressive social reform and in the beginnings of investigative journalism. He served first as staff photographer for Paul Kellog's *Survey*, an influential national magazine focusing on all aspects of social service and reform. Subsequently, he was photographer for the National Child Labor Committee, for the Russell Sage Foundation, which then had a pronounced sociological orientation, and finally for such prominent "muckraking" national magazines as *McClure's* and *Everybody's*.

The most striking feature of Hine's photographs is the way they question the relation of his human figures to their setting. It is the faces we remember in these pictures: the face of a child standing beside a power loom, the white faces of boy miners, the look of concentration on the face of a construction worker dangling from a beam of the Empire State Building, the slightly puzzled look on the face of a boiler worker lying in the end of a boiler. For Stieglitz the setting always seems to dominate, and his human figures, when they appear at all, seem part of the setting. Indeed, the feeling we often get from Stieglitz's pictures of the city as a soulless place partly derives from the way human figures are submerged in his urban photography. The titles he sometimes gave his photographs support such a reading: "The Asphalt-Paver," "The City of Ambition," and, for a railroad yard, the ironic title "The Hand of Man."

With Hine, human figure and setting are kept in balance, and one's attention is absorbed in examining the character of the juxtaposition. His documentary style is inclined less to judge than to question the seeming disparity of (for example) child and machine. The precise way this relationship between subject and setting is presented varies from picture to picture, but from the outset Hine was unusually successful in capturing the formal character of his settings and in isolating the details that give them visual meaning. In particular, he dwelt upon the pervasively abstract and geometric character of both city and machine.

Hine's "Madonna of Ellis Island" (*Figure 4*), for example, is an extraordinary early photograph taken of an immigrant woman with her two children, which is part of a sequence of such portrayals made about 1905. This is a very modern "madonna," compassionate and ironic, as the title would suggest. She is seated on a bench against the background of one of the high windows of the immigration hall. The window, with its parabolic curve and its somewhat blurred geometric tracery, faintly suggests a church window. The group of figures is arranged to parallel the lines of the window, one child seated on each side of the mother. The woman, to judge from other photographs of the same time and location, is probably Jewish; if so, still a further ironic turn on the title.

But here, as in almost all Hine's work, it is through the portrayal of the faces that he achieves his most powerful effect. In this case, the faces are illuminated by bright sunlight shining through the hall, and all three are smiling, somewhat enigmatically, again with the slight suggestion that there is more to it than simple joy and relief after a safe arrival. The mother, in fact, appears quite unconsciously to have assumed a Mona Lisa smile. Is this, one is made to wonder, simply a happy family group? Perhaps. For example, the family is grouped together in a way that suggests closeness and, through the clustering of hands, tenderness, too. Yet there are puzzling features in the way these three faces are caught by the camera. In traditional Madonnas the mother's face is generally bowed over or attentive to the infant's. This mother's is not. She looks at neither child. Instead, her eyes are slightly averted, her smile faint and enigmatic, with perhaps a touch of complacency. There is a suggestion that her thoughts may concern something a long way removed from the present moment. Neither child, moreover, is looking at her, nor are they looking at each other. The older has what appears to be a "faraway" look, across her mother's lap and over her baby sister. Even the infant, whose eyes reflect the bright light originating behind the camera, gives the impression that she, too is wrapped in some private reflections.

These faces drawn from the crowds of immigrants moving through Ellis Island are highly individualized and photographed to suggest that, conceivably, figures so portrayed have separate destinies in the New World. This ability to individualize his subjects, even in pictures of large groups like his "Breaker Boys" (*Figure 5*), is achieved by such devices as highlighting the eyes or patterns of wrinkles around the eyes. This preoccupation is characteristic of Hine's photographic work until the 'twenties and un-doubtedly explains some of the force his work carried as evidence with legislators and reformers bent on social justice. It is this very ambiguity in the expression of his subjects that gives his work such power and di-rectness. His photograph "Forty-Year-Old Woman," made at Hull House in Chicago in 1905, portrays a lidded, wrinkled face that is virtually sphinxlike in the ambiguity of its expression (*Figure 6*). The title, too, is characteristically ironic, since to the "comfortable classes" this woman must have appeared closer to sixty than to forty. What kind of experience, the viewer must have wondered, has etched those premature wrinkles and lowered those lids? Such faces radiate the historical mystery of the abrasive transition from peasant to urban slum dweller.

Hine, in selecting his subjects, seems to have had an extraordinary sensitivity to the effect of his camera on those he photographed. His subjects in their responses span the whole range from extreme self-consciousness before the camera to utter indifference. Hine seems to have sensed, too, that these responses to the camera's presence were an impor-tant part of what he could reveal as a photographer. In puzzling through his gallery of urban figures and trying to define what we see, it is important to remember that the camera itself was an unseen participant. Uncertainty about how to respond to it figures as significantly in his work as uncertain-ty about the machine and the new shapes and forms of an urban setting. Much of the value of his photographs as historical documents derives from these flickerings of uncertainty and what we can infer from them about what people perceived was happening to them. Some adult subjects appear to have ignored the camera, or pretended to, like those performing in *cinema verité*, partly to avoid a feeling of self-consciousness and partly because they *were* busy and only tolerated the distraction. And then, too, remaining at work must have been important as well because for many of these subjects their working selves must have been their most comfortable identities. Staring at the camera lens or looking vaguely off into the distance would have struck them as awkward and artificial. Children, who are more "open" anyway and who identify less with their work, appear to have expressed this experience of being photographed much more directly and overtly—and with the widest range of gestures and stances.

Photographers seldom photographed themselves in this period, at least with full paraphernalia, and there are accordingly few pictures of what people confronted when their photographs were taken. One interesting exception is a 1910 portrait by Hine of a family in a New York tenement (*Figure 7*). Part of what makes this such a striking photograph is the presence of a wall mirror in the upper right-hand corner of the picture, which seems to be reflecting a black-hooded camera with clouds of smoke rising in the background. The rest of the photograph shows what Hine found in the way both of setting and of human response. For example, here the camera seems to have had a still further effect of causing crowding and congestion in the room. The family group seems almost herded into a corner. Other effects are evident. A small child seated at the lower right seems in the midst of a cry or gasp; it is hard to know which. The baby in the mother's arms is slightly blurred, probably from having started at the flash or having stirred during the exposure. Another child standing by the window is starry-eyed. The other children give evidence of varying degrees of interest and surprise. Only the mother can maintain something approaching normal composure in the face of it all.

In other ways, too, the photograph portrays what is essentially an adult's world. A fancy nineteenth-century clock, conceivably a family heirloom, stands on the mantelpiece on top of a lace cloth, well away from the reach of children. Beside it are a small porcelain figurine, a vase, a bottle of medicine. What appears to be a cut-glass pitcher and one or two other items, along with a coal-oil lamp, stand on the dresser behind the group. On top of the lamp is a man's hat, or so it appears, perched almost jauntily. On the walls are several "pictures"—it is hard to tell whether they are prints, photographs, or aquatints, and whom or what some of them represent. One such picture is cut off by the camera, another is obscured by what seems to be an item of clothing hanging on the wall. A frame containing what looks like several photographs is partly obscured by the hat. Only the milk, Karo syrup, and baby bottle on the table by the mirror and the small child's stool give evidence of the seven children in residence.

It takes some careful looking to find what may be the most important object in the room, a sewing machine off in the left-hand corner piled high with clothing. Is it the family's clothing that is being made, or is it "putting-out" work? Only one leg, the wheel, and what looks like a spool beneath are caught by the flash. Thus we see this family, and we see, furthermore, what they see, in this case even the camera in their midst. We perceive the texture, the perspectives, the feeling of congestion—or is it closeness?—which these individuals must have been alive to. Yet much that we think we see or sense is conjecture, and our overall impression fully confirms the importance of ambiguity in photographic representation.

What we see is very much a visual event constructed or (better) puzzled out by the viewer. The clock, for example, says one-thirty. Is no one in school, or is it summer or Saturday? If this is a "family" photograph, why is there no man present? No particular hardship is depicted in this case (although the number of other rooms is also unknown), and one is left to wonder what the photograph "means," or was intended to mean. Most forcefully, perhaps, one is left with the impression that this small domestic "invasion" has trapped its subjects in a singular moment of history, frozen a frame from lives in which viewers may see undefined destinies. In particular, it has caught something about the physical scale of life, the human density and the Old World aesthetic values of those portrayed; something too, perhaps, about the spatial limitations of those undertaking an uncertain social existence in one of the most densely populated urban areas of the world. The belongings of several generations of family life, such as the picture of some ancestor on the wall, are crammed, like the people themselves, into a corner of a single room, as if to dramatize the discomfort of a transition from a more spacious to a severely constricted social scene. Indeed, the very absence of melodramatic evidence of poverty and the presence of some bourgeois comfort make this aspect of the picture even more dramatic.

This kind of universal significance tends, I believe, to supersede intended meanings of the time, even in those photographs of a more overtly documentary kind, such as those of children whom Hine caught in factories, mills, mines, or on city streets. One sees them today looking into his camera, some of them insolently, some almost introspectively, close enough, some of them, to be able to see their own faces reflected in the lens. Still, it would be difficult to determine what being photographed meant to his subjects. It must have meant many different things. To the black man dying of tuberculosis whom Hine photographed in 1908 in a Washington slum, it appears to have been yet another indignity to be suffered stoically by someone too sick and too weak to do more than cast his outer garments over the head of his bed and let rubbish collect at his feet (*Figure 8*). To the "newsies" taken at close range in 1910, the occasion seems to have called for a macho show of adulthood with much mugging and puffing of smoke (*Figure 9*). To the Negro orphan, aged about two, the experience was both frightening and significant, to judge from her erect pose, her wide eyes, and the tight grip of her hands on the arms of her baby rocker (*Figure 10*). To his "Breaker Boys" from the mines or to his mill workers, picture-taking seems to have brought a few moments of respite from hard, draining work. Few give the impression of according the experience the significance that viewers must have given it, nor do Hine's subjects appear to have expected anything like redress from the appearance of an alien photographer in their midst. The camera must have seemed to them still another machine, leveled at them to uncertain effect. Yet, ironically, to Florence Kelly, Jane Addams, and other social reformers the camera had become the one incorruptible measure of social conditions—another kind of mechanistic instrument of scientific measure. None of the ambiguity of Hine's work, for example, was apparent to Florence Kelly, who saw the photograph as providing a kind of metric scale of reality. "The camera," she wrote, "is convincing. Where records fail and where parents forswear themselves, the measuring rod and the camera carry conviction."[9]

For Hine himself, the machine he carried about was necessitated by a breakdown or failure of language to portray social circumstances. The ability of language to get at the character of human pathos, he felt, had been steadily eroded by three-quarters of a century of sentimentalizing and sermonizing. Such a development had left the actualities of human existence covered over with a soft yet impenetrable shell. For him it was narrative art that had suffered most as a gauge of reality. "If I could tell a story in words," he wrote to Paul Kellogg in 1922, "I wouldn't need to lug a camera"—an odd formulation which suggests that Hine may have underestimated the unique force of his own work.[10] One of the great virtues of his photographs lay precisely in their not telling a story in the traditional mode but, instead, in their inviting plural, even conflicting, interpretations.

Photographers like Hine were never wholly innocent about the importance of illusion in photographic work, although they rarely discussed this aspect of their art. At the same time, even the best and most artistically self-conscious photographers of the time, like other artists, seem never to have been fully conscious of the range of meaning that could be assigned to their work. Their obsession was the operational aspect of camera work. They almost prided themselves on their accidental artifice, the way they acted from hunches, the happy effects obtained from minor mishaps such as double exposure or kicking the leg of the tripod while the shutter was open. Once they had broken their dependence on painterly modes and perspectives, they quickly began to explore the potentialities of their machinery in an openly experimental fashion. They seemed, in fact, to have been fully as preoccupied with learning from their machinery as with "instructing" or guiding it. This search gave a somewhat restless character to the best photography of the period. No photographic mode or style, except perhaps the studio portrait, settled down or remained in any sense constant. To be a photographer of standing between 1890 and 1930—to set an arbitrary outer limit—meant to experiment and hence to change, to feel one's way in a medium that played tricks with light, flattened distances, blanched color, and distorted human features at close range. For photographers with such aspirations to art, it was a complicated business of learning to see the world afresh through the narrow squint of a single glass eye, almost like a Cyclops.

Hine is in this sense quite representative. He had changed his own style of social documentary photography out of all recognition by the end of his life. From the outset his pictures had betrayed an interest in abstract design, as a photograph like "Madonna of Ellis Island" suggests. He had always shown an interest in the machinery surrounding his human figures, especially in the pictures of children at work in the prewar years. Over the years, however, his machines were increasingly moved from margin or background to visual center, and they soon began to assume an importance as great as or greater than that of his human figures. His "Steamfitter" of 1921 could almost be a still from Chaplin's *Modern Times* fifteen years later (*Figure 11*). Finally, his figures were almost literally swallowed up by machines—as in "Man at Dynamo" of 1921 (*Figure 12*)—dwarfed by them into Lilliputian figures dancing about on abstract forms, or hidden within them. There is some evidence of this growing preoccupation with machinery in a photograph taken as early as 1910 that portrays a group of children in the process of clambering up the corner of a railroad boxcar, a photograph somewhat uncharacteristic of Hine in this period, since the camera has caught the spectacle from the rear and no child's face can be seen. A later, more striking example is "Boilermaker" (1929), which shows a worker flat on his stomach and perched in the opening of a huge, cylindrical boiler, boiler cap in hand, still for a moment and looking at the camera with interest (*Figure 13*). Other geometric shapes fill the picture: the regular lines of wartlike welts recede down the boiler, and there is an abstract arrangement of what appear to be crates or boxes at the upper left. If photographs such as this make a statement, it is not precise. Yet any viewer is left to ponder the oddity of such a normal-looking man, his hair carefully combed, lying with apparent comfort in such a space-age habitat. The ironic play, if one was even intended, seems to be directed neither at the man nor at the machinery. The man's steady eye, indeed, seems to send some kind of question back to the viewer for consideration: what do you think of what you see? It is, in fact, a long way from the crowded tenement of 1908, both formally and in substance.

This preoccupation with abstraction in genre photography is apparent even in Hine's early work. One of his newsboys, Danny Mercurio, is shown against a foreground of starkly geometric blocks of cement sidewalk that recede like merging parallel lines into the background. The background is further dominated by a fretwork of rectilinear window casements in a distant building. Another newsboy, photographed at about the same time, is shown standing against a perfectly plain brick wall. In what seems at first the straightest of documentary photographs, Hine in 1910 photographed a Bowery derelict, hands in pockets, who appears virtually cornered by camera and flash. In this case the soft lines of the huddled, dazed figure are set off against the ornate, geometric masonry of the dark wall behind him and against the equally fancy tile work underfoot (*Figure 14*). In another, similar contrast, a woman beggar partly obscures an advertisement for safety razors and stands surrounded by abstract Art Deco ironwork railings. It is hard to find photographs at any period of his work that do not embody this preoccupying contrast of humanity and geometric form.

Hine was, of course, not alone among photographers, to say nothing of artists more generally, in taking such an interest in abstract machine forms. Paul Strand at the time had shifted his interest to machines; for example, to photographs of motion-picture cameras he was then using, their mechanism open to view, as in "Double Akely" of 1922 or his earlier "Automobile Wheel" (1917). And this was the moment at which American "Precisionists," such as Charles Sheeler, appeared on the art scene with representational abstractions of a geometric character. This almost simultaneous discovery of the "beauty" of abstract form by photographers, sculptors, painters, and architects warrants more careful examination. The gradual emergence of this mechanistic vision among photographers seems to be a preoccupation of an autobiographical sort, a kind of running portrait of the artist as or in machine, through which for a few years these photographers allowed their "machinist" selves to play a more and more prominent part in what they see.

This sudden appearance of the mechanical Narcissus is evident even in the prewar years. With the 'twenties came an even more apparent and widespread recognition by all kinds of artists that they were in part welders, chemists, machinists, aviators, motorists, students of optics—a whole range of technological specializations. They possessed, in other words, a fractured consciousness of being part artist and part scientist-engineer that was embedded in perspective as well as in form and subject. These were years, of course, in which art generally carried on a love affair with science and technology, and the effects of this romance had a dramatic impact on the shape and imaginative image of cities as well as on the way people saw themselves. The motorcar exerted horizontal pressures on the vertical, aggregate character of cities in much the same way that the welder's torch modified the human figure in the work of such sculptors as Giacometti. The flat perspectives of the camera appear to have played some role in inspiring the flat, almost photographic human faces that appear in the painting of Viennese Expressionists like Gustav Klimt and Egon Schiele, just as the aerial photograph flattened the profile of cities and further heightened their perceived geometric character. The human face, like the modern city, was caught by the camera at crazy angles and flattened by the lens. It was never to look the same again. A revolutionary new chemistry of paints did the rest, making brilliant, posterlike colors that were almost irresistible.

What was true of the graphic arts was even more pronouncedly true of architecture. For all his Whitmanesque rhetoric, Frank Lloyd Wright had the soul of an engineer, and only his brilliantly intuitive sense of the potential of reinforced concrete made his abstract and geometric cantilevering possible. Finally, what began in the studio and laboratory reached the public through equally revolutionary changes in printing, graphics, and photoreproduction that brought the modern art of book design and illustration into existence and created a whole new industry of advertising.

Among the best photographers, the new modern consciousness arrived very early, partly because photographers were almost by necessity machinists and emulsion chemists whose darkroom laboratories interpreted what their cameras saw. In 1934, Paul Strand, who had studied with Hine, lamented the slowness with which photographers relinquished the idea that a camera was a brush or a pencil and recognized it for "what it is, a machine."[11] Even Stieglitz, perhaps the least modish and most restless artist among the "pictorialists," got the fever and seemed for a time imaginatively caught up by the new interest in the machinery of the sky—in airplanes and dirigibles. This symbiosis of camera, city, machine, and abstract form was never more interestingly expressed than in the striking portfolio of photographs Hine took in 1931 and 1932 to document the erection of the world's highest skyscraper, the Empire State Building. As in "Empire State Building" (1931), his human figures crawl about doing their work on an immense framework of steel against a background of other urban geometry that is rendered even more abstract by a gauze of smoky haze (*Figure 15*).

Indeed, the groping of photographers in pictures like these now seems uncertainly and cautiously heuristic rather than ironic. Their aim appears to have been to attempt to recover or re-create human scale, to find some way of reimposing it in a new and disruptive visual setting, for very much the same reasons one suspects landscape painters like Millet and Constable place human figures engaged in everyday activities in the foreground of even their farthest-ranging landscape perspectives. For the photographers the object seems to have been one of weighing and testing the human impact of these new urban sites. Photographers, like others living through this period of transition, were educating their eyes, attuning their perceptions in a way that often made their conscious artistic objectives and expressed verbal attitudes seem almost irrelevant. The overall effect, however, was to further enhance the aesthetic excitement of the modern city and thus to join hands with others whose work tended toward the same end.

The full significance of the work by urban photographers during these crucial decades cannot be appreciated unless their explorations in spatiality and perspective are seen in the context of parallel and still larger efforts to enhance the aesthetic character of urban life. Photography, as we have seen, arrived in the twentieth century with an accredited capacity to document the everyday life of city people. It soon demonstrated an equally dramatic capacity to portray the modern city from striking new perspectives that became part of an emerging urban identity. This identity was composed in part of those coded perceptions, now largely taken for granted, which at the time registered the dramatic accommodation that city dwellers were forced to make with a new technological and aesthetic environment that had drastically altered the shape and scale of communal life.

It is this emerging sense of urban identity, if one may so describe it, that seems such an historic development. It was the product of a process in which art came to the aid of sensibility, a process that began with the adumbration of visual images to represent how it felt to live in such utterly new surroundings—surroundings that the city dweller found a kind of house of mirrors, in which perceptions and self-perceptions were crazily confounded, in which one could both see and see oneself from strange new angles. But it seen became clear that more than visualization was involved in these new perceptions. The objects portrayed in the new photography—like the skyline view of the city—soon began to take on aesthetic values of their own. What began as orientation to a new setting ended as romance, although the line between documentary representation and flattering portrayal remained thin and elusive. In a matter of decades the city underwent a process of aesthetic transformation—from aesthetic terra incognita to the "stylish" city of urban mythology—the New York of Frank Crowninshield's *Vanity Fair* and Busby Berkeley musicals.

In retrospect it seems evident that such a process of visualizing—or, if you will, spatializing—urban experience was central to the two decades after 1910, both in America and in Europe. Not only was it preeminently an age of architecture—keyed to such names as Frank Lloyd Wright, Le Corbusier, and those of the Bauhaus group in Germany—but it was an age of the architectonic, too. The aesthetic interest in geometric abstraction already noted in photography and the close association of this interest with urban life was suddenly evident everywhere by the 'twenties. New York continued to remain central to these developments, as the inspiration and subject of portrayal and as a source of artistry. The dazzling futuristic drawings of cities by the architectural renderer Hugh Ferris, the stark vertical stage sets by Joseph Urban, and the bold and colorful geometrics that permeated the design work of the Bauhaus, the Vorticists, and Art Deco found their counterparts in painting in the New York–inspired work of the French painter Francis Picabia, in the New York Precisionist work of Charles Sheeler and Charles Demuth, and in the representational urban abstractions of the city by Joseph Stella. Much of this fretted against the static limits of existing art forms. In particular, painters and designers, like photographers, were fascinated, almost obsessed, with the problem of representing movement—through multiple perspectives, through the shattering of geometric image, through almost any means that gave expression to the kinetic reality of urban life, the feeling of haste, pressure, and near-frenzy that came to be associated with New York. This new preoccupation was accompanied by a developing aesthetic of kinetics and of the film, which began to get an airing in Stieglitz's *Camera Work* and other intellectual journals.

This heightened preoccupation of graphic art with the spatial and kinetic, while it had implications for every art form, seemed most immediately threatening to literature, since, more than any other, it seemed bounded by linear temporal limits. Despite the fact that this was a great age of literary experiment and creativity it is possible to detect a strong undertow from these new forces undercutting the sufficiency of verbal discourse. This development was most apparent in dance and cinema, in the work of Isadora Duncan and Chaplin where the silent poetry of movement tended altogether to supplant verbal expression, but it seemed an undeniable feature of the sudden upsurge in dramatic art of all kinds. The series of historic collaborations between dramatists and musicians from Richard Strauss and Hugo von Hoffmannsthal to Bertolt Brecht and Kurt Weill, further reflected this new departure in expression. A feeling that words were insufficient, timebound, somehow lacking in imaginative reality, while it spurred some literary artists to bolder and bolder experimentation, also dictated changes in the traditional setting in which readers encountered literary art—the magazine. A new kind of collaboration developed, not only between writer and illustrator, but between editor and layout artist, which gave increasing prominence to the visual experience of the magazine reader. "Graphics," as they came to be called, were sheared from their dependence on literary expression and began to assume a certain autonomy. In advertising, for example, verbal expression as set off from photography and graphics more and more assumed the subordinate role of the subtitle in the silent film.

We have grown so accustomed to finding good fiction and "liberal" reporting surrounded by slick, sophisticated advertising—the short story or "Talk of the Town" and the ad for French perfume—that we forget how novel it must once have seemed. Nor can we reckon how much these glossy pages, either now or then, figure in one's perception of the accompanying fiction. It seems clear enough, however, that this juxtaposition of style and stylishness is historically significant, and it seems likely that the fiction that appeared in this new pictorial setting must have seemed at once, by a process of infectious proximity, better "furnished" socially and more visually class-conscious.

One process, therefore, that can be traced through this whole period from the 'nineties to the end of the 'twenties is one through which groups within the urban middle-classes gradually took visual possession of the whole city, as we have seen with these photographers. It is a process of aesthetic appropriation through which an older and narrower parochial consciousness succumbed to a more expansive and inclusive point of view about the city. The older point of view lived on, of course, in ethnic neighborhoods in which possessive pride in one's neighborhood gave way much more slowly to possessive pride in the city. For a time the problems inherent in such an enlarged point of view—the political implications, for example, of aesthetically underwriting modern skyscraper architecture— remained submerged in the joyousness of aesthetic discovery of the modern city.

The history of our own time is in part the story of how this bright, possessive vision was gradually challenged and has given way to the more somber and introverted attitudes about the city and the culture of cities we now hold. By the end of the 'twenties this shift was well under way. After the 'thirties the metropolis, however much it might be "used" as a setting, would never again hold the bright place in American imagination that it had obtained during the previous thirty years. These were years of orientation, accommodation, and aesthetic compromise, as we have seen, but they were also years of intense, exploratory, aesthetic excitement where even the "compromised" artistic works seemed enhanced by the very innocence of the period in which they had been produced. Like the English landscape after Turner and Constable and the still life after Paul Cezanne, the artistic journey of the city thereafter plunged inward, even downward into those "interborough fissures of the mind" first evoked in Hart Crane's vivid portrayal of the New York subway in *The Bridge* (1929). These and later evocations of New York were to form part of a new repertoire of urban expressionism that has since dominated American literary and artistic culture. An already somewhat threadbare consensus about how the city was to be perceived—and how its forms, shapes, and tempo were to be valued—shattered into idiosyncratic symbolism of the kind already discernible earlier in the evocations of T. S. Eliot and Ezra Pound. Later versions of this use of the city for lyrical symbolism can be found in the phantasmagorical Manhattan of Ralph Ellison's *Invisible Man*, and, more recently, in the nightmarish mockery of New York as a center of fashion and sophistication in works such as Sylvia Plath's *The Bell Jar*, or in the ghoulish evocations of city life in the photography of Diane Arbus.

The city led still another kind of subterranean existence as part of the consciousness of writers and artists who carried it with them wherever they went, internalized, half-dissociated from place—a metaphor for the artificially complex, the socially pluralistic, the pressured and frantic pace of modern life they were yearning to shake off—as in Chaplin's great film of the 'thirties, *Modern Times*. This is the city that will not release its hold on the fugitive in Hemingway's "Killers" or on Robert Penn Warren's Nick Burden as he drives through the Western desert, or on a host of fictional heroes hiding out in far-flung places, any more than earlier it had fully relinquished its grasp on Fitzgerald's narrator Nick Carraway after he had left New York and returned to the Midwest.

In either case, the tones were soon to be autumnal. It seemed evident that a certain conception of New York—the city as the very embodiment of modern times—and the idea of modern man as capable of mastering, even anticipating the demands of such an environment, had passed into history. No art form ever promised such mastery more unreservedly than architecture or portrayed it more appealingly than the tap-dancing sequences of *Singin' in the Rain* (1952), as when Gene Kelly floated almost effortlessly through city streets. But by the 'fifties, when Kelly choreographed these scenes, musical comedy was itself becoming nostalgic for the previous era, and the mastery he evoked was already a fading memory of a hope.

TWO

New York and the Origin of the Skyline · The Commercial City as Visual Text

We are getting to be more accustomed to the lofty structures, and so conventional ideas born of what we are accustomed to look at, are being gradually modified.
  Harper's Weekly, 1894

How do we visualize our large cities? What kinds of shapes, overall, do we imagine them to have? These questions would have brought different answers in each major period of urban change in the country's development. Each period seemed to develop a favored perspective. Eighteenth- and early–nineteenth-century New Yorkers thought of the city as it looked when one approached it by sea from the harbor. Mid–nineteenth-century viewers imagined a city seen from a bird's-eye view like that provided by the Latting Observatory on Forty-second Street, looking to the north. By the end of the century, the approach to New York by rail and road began to encourage a new perspective on the city, silhouetted against the sky— what we have come to know as the "skyline view." Each of these perspectives reflects something about the urban culture of the period that created and favored that view. The skyline view is no exception.

The skyline perspective first became associated with rapid change, registering successively the appearance of new skyscraper towers and clusters as New York became a vertical city. It was not long before it began to evoke other, related values, most notably modernity and sophistication. The process through which these values became associated with a skyline view is a long one, taking over half a century.

The skyline perspective—the profile of a city's tall buildings seen from a distance in relief—has become the identifying signature of modern cities (*Figure 16*). The skyline is, of course, only one of a set of related perspectives on the city designed to take account of its novel vertical and geometric character. The bird's-eye view and the night-light pattern are closely related perspectives (*Figures 17 and 18*). These ways of visualizing the city, of characterizing and identifying particular urban locales, have become part of our culture and are therefore largely taken for granted. They confront us daily in our newspapers, in the opening frames of television programs, and in advertisements. While such conventions were a response to the swift transformation in the appearance of cities like New York, they have just as clearly evolved from older ways of visualizing the city, which date from the close of the Renaissance.

The process of change that ended in the skyline view began during the seventeenth century with popular urban panoramas of London and other European cities. It is possible to trace a developing modern perspective through the nineteenth century, when the first skyline drawings and photographs appeared, and the word was first applied to urban views. There are significant developments during the 1920s, when the most dramatic changes in cityscape photography took place, and in the early 1930s, when Hollywood began to exploit these new conventions in musicals and in the films about sophisticated city life. After the 1930s there was, until recently, comparatively little change.

From its beginning, the portrayal of cities was governed in some measure by the emerging conventions of landscape. By the seventeenth century a number of artists on the Continent were producing urban panoramas that incorporated foreshortening and geometric perspective. Characteristic of these is an engraving of London after the Great Fire of 1666 by a Dutch artist, Frederick de Wit (*Figure 19*). The extent of anticipated interest in such views is suggested in this case by the caption in four languages—Dutch, French, German, and English—at the bottom of the engraving. It reads, in part, "London, formerly called Londonia, a City of Great Traffic . . . being by the late great fire almost consumed . . . but now through the great wealth of the citizens built again." One authority estimates the date of this particular panorama as circa 1690. London, the first great city of modern times, was itself a subject of considerable interest, but the fire of 1666 had clearly enhanced this interest, to judge from the volumes of similar work in the British Museum that purport to show its devastation. This picture is carefully indexed to show the exact location of such notable structures as Whitehall (which had escaped the fire), the Tower, London Bridge, and the Globe Theatre.

There are a number of details worth noting here. First, the entire city is framed within a landscape. Fully half the engraving is devoted to a portrayal of sky and cloud patterns. Only a handful of ecclesiastical and public buildings, most notably the new St. Paul's, still without its dome, rise above the horizon. In the foreground on the south side of London Bridge are two groups of human figures and a few dogs, placed there to establish human scale. These figures, also spectators of the scene before them, are looking toward the city. The fact that London was a "city of great traffic" is clearly indicated by the volume of Thames River traffic in the middle distance. This convention for portraying the commercial wealth of seaports survives well into the nineteenth century.[1] Most important, the way the perspective of the picture places the city within the countryside of river and hills surrounding it brings out the extensiveness of London, clearly the measure against which its size is gauged.

How little such conventions for portraying cities changed during the next century and a half can be seen from this engraving of New York done in 1823 (*Figure 20*). The engraving is by John Hill from a watercolor by William Wall entitled *New York from Heights near Brooklyn*.[2] Once again there is the low horizon characteristic of Dutch landscapes, and half of the engraving is devoted to cloud patterns. In other ways, too, the pictures are similar. In both cases the city is viewed from a rural setting, across water, and both contain foreground figures to set the scale. Shipping in the middle distance and along South Street is clearly designed to suggest a busy port. The horizon is broken only by an occasional church spire, most notably by that of Trinity Church at the head of Wall Street (just to the right of the largest sailing ship).

The nineteenth century developed its own conventions for portraying the emerging shape of big cities and placing them in the context of their geographical surroundings.[3] The century, for example, produced a succession of striking bird's-eye views of New York from imaginary aerial perspectives (*Figure 21*). Moreover, each time a taller structure was constructed, someone clambered to the top of it to sketch the city as it actually looked from the new perspective—from church towers, armory towers, the observatory tower near the Crystal Palace, the towers of the Brooklyn Bridge, and each new skyscraper. The engraving of the view from the spire of Trinity Church, made in 1849, is an early example of this genre (*Figure 22*). This engraving is interesting for a number of reasons: First, except for the glimpse of the river and Brooklyn Heights in the distant background, the scene is one of a wholly manmade environment. There is no horizon, no sky or cloud pattern, and few of the curvilinear lines that characterize landscapes. Instead, both artist and engraver have chosen to stress the geometric pattern of windows, roof tiles, paving stones, and the buildings themselves, as in the case of the Merchant's Exchange (in the distance on the right, toward the foot of the street). People are portrayed as minuscule from this great height, dwarfed by the massive scale of such buildings as the Exchange. The arrangement of people and carriages in the street itself seems designed to suggest crowding and congestion, a different kind of "traffic" from the array of sailing ships in the earlier views of New York and

London. In other panoramas of the same period, the city is portrayed as extending grid by grid in an almost monotonous geometric design.

Those nineteenth-century cityscapes that do not fall within the conventions of the emerging genre of landscape have a somewhat utilitarian character. The 1834 engraving of Wall Street from Trinity Church is interesting, partly for its guidebook quality (*Figure 23*).[4] The artist has opened up Wall Street so that the façade of buildings on both sides of the street can be seen, as they could not in fact have been. The margins on either side of the engraving contain the profiles of buildings along each side of the street, each margin a kind of mini-skyline. Each building is labeled by name, as in later pictorial city directories. While there is little pretense of placing such city views within the frame of a landscape, there is one notable concession in this direction. The top margin contains a view of what could be seen from the opposite end of Wall Street: the shipping along South Street, the river, Brooklyn, and the horizon beyond. The awkwardness of such a device suggests how firmly the conventions of landscape had been imposed on urban perspectives.

In the next decade photography began to shape the visual consciousness of the city. Beginning with the photographs of French photographer Victor Prevost in the 1850s, New York was to be photographed by scores of skilled picture-takers, many of them professionals by the 1870s. It is in this period, for example, that the "canyon shot" down a street between a row of buildings establishes itself as a major genre of urban photography. While most of these early pictures portray street life or building façades, a certain number of photographs show the city and adjacent buildings from the perspective of some newly created height. The skyline as we know it appears to have evolved from this kind of perspective. It also seems to have been an almost accidental discovery of the camera. By the close of the 1870s, the only thing still needed was a structure of sufficient height and mass to dramatize the possibility.

Such an opportunity came along with the construction of the Brooklyn Bridge towers on either side of the East River during the 1870s. Not only did the towers provide an unrivaled perch to photograph the city from, they became themselves photographic subjects of considerable interest, as the panel from a five-part panorama made in 1876 suggests (*Figure 24*). The other four panels portray the city—from the Battery to above Fulton Street—so as to show its extent. Indeed, the present panel, were it not for the tower, shows only a uniform density of construction from river to river. Note how the vertical thrust of the bridge tower, rising as it does above city structures, dominates the older extensive perspective on the city behind it. Once the bridge was finished, it afforded a new perspective on, and proximity to, the tall buildings that were beginning to cluster at the

Manhattan end of the bridge. A photograph from 1888 is the earliest to show the profile of buildings uniformly dominating the horizon (*Figure 25*). The thrust of the Mutual Life Building, still under construction (on the extreme right) above the horizon, seems to be measured against the spire of Trinity Church (left of center) at the end of Wall Street, the city's traditional promontory until the 1890s.

The taking of pictures that were precursors of the skyline shot during the 1880s was accidental. By the 1890s, the stage was set for the appearance of the skyline in a more self-conscious way. A key development was the interjection of the term into this urban context. The first use of the word "skyline," according to John Kouwenhoven, was in an article in Hearst's *New York Journal* on May 3, 1896.[5] The first attempt to capture the New York skyline through photography had appeared in *Harper's Weekly* two years before, on August 11, 1894. Many elements of the older, extensive perspective on the city are still present. The picture surveys the city from an elevated point in Brooklyn. Fully two-thirds of the panels are devoted to the Brooklyn piers, shipping on the river, and the busy South Street docks. Only in the background can one see the faint outline of the tall buildings along the horizon, with the profile of the newly completed Manhattan Life Building rising above the spire of Trinity Church (to its right).

Yet the idea of a skyline view, once it was conceived, was not permitted to fade, despite technical difficulties. Another drawing, made for the same issue of *Harper's* (*Figure 26*), represents a much closer approximation to what we now mean by "skyline." The perspective is from ground or sea level, so that the profile of buildings is projected into the middle of the picture. The artist has also emphasized the silhouette of the buildings by making them darker than the surrounding river and sky. The editors of *Harper's* were clearly conscious of the novelty of this array of new architecture, since, out of deference to their readers' curiosity, they included captions in the upper margin identifying each tall building from the Battery north. This new perspective, once its details were worked out, was reintroduced at regular intervals to clock vertical changes in the city's profile, as another drawing from 1897 suggests (*Figure 27*). The cameras then in use were not equipped with the lenses or filters required to focus on the sweep of tall buildings along the horizon, as drawings could more easily do. In this second drawing, the perspective has moved closer to the Manhattan shore, as though seen from shipboard. The dramatic change from three years before is apparent in the number of tall buildings that now seem to eclipse the spire of Trinity Church (in the center). The "sugar-lump" effect of such buildings side-by-side that F. Scott Fitzgerald was to note twenty-eight years later[6] is already evident, and the artist has chosen to include more geometric and architectural detail. It is interesting to note that one convention from the older perspective has been re-introduced—with a vengeance, one might almost say. The frantic marine activity in the foreground, far from eclipsing the tall buildings, seems to have been included to indicate the kind of commerce these buildings are all about.

In an article accompanying this 1897 drawing, Montgomery Schuyler, an early and interesting architectural critic, ruminated about this kind of visual development. The article, entitled "The Sky-line of New York, 1881–1897," has the character of a survey of recent building.[7] The point that Schuyler seems most anxious to stress is the utter novelty and eccentricity of New York's visual presence as compared to that of any major city in Europe. In Europe it is always a cathedral, a castle, or some other public or government structure that looms over the city, not a newspaper office or insurance building. To any European arriving by ship, the dramatic view from the Hudson River symbolizes the society that is about to be visited. "As his steamer picks her way through the traffic which crowds the river, past huge utilitarian structures that dwarf into obscurity the spires of churches and the low domes of public monuments, it seems to him that he has never before seen a waterfront that so impressively and exclusively 'looked like business.'"[8]

Schuyler made a number of interesting points about the skyline view. He noted, first of all, the chaotic quality of New York buildings that resulted from each structure's being conceived in isolation from those surrounding it. He also took account of the constant competition to go higher, the lapses in taste and in architectural design in some of the new buildings, and their lack of monumental proportions when viewed from a distance. Yet, despite his attention to the qualities of individual buildings, Schuyler was forced to admit that the skyline view was not essentially architectural in character. The emerging silhouette of the city, he concluded, was more symbolic than architectonic. "While the architectural excellence of the skyline must be sought in the parts, and not in the unattainable whole, it is in the aggregation that the immense impressiveness lies."[9]

It is clear from the context that this "immense impressiveness" of the New York skyline is still not perceived as aesthetic. Despite the attention paid to individual buildings, there is little concern elsewhere in the article with the aesthetic character of the whole. The only exception is the rather tentative use of the term "picturesque" at one point to refer to the potential qualities of a skyline view. Schuyler's use of this term, with its immediate reference to painting and its close association with landscape, is nonetheless significant since it suggests that the process of aesthetic accommodation to skyscraper architecture in the mass has begun, as, indeed, an article in *Harper's* had stated two years before. "We are getting used to the lofty structures, and so conventional ideas, born of what we are accustomed to look at, are being gradually modified."[10]

Nonetheless, the strength of "conventional ideas" was such that the process of adaptation was bound to be slow and uneven. It was not simply the size and shapes of the new architecture that presented problems. It was the absence in New York of almost every familiar feature of the older cities that made the inevitable comparisons so invidious initially. The usurpation of the horizon, the almost treeless, natureless character of the downtown, along with the commercial values the tall buildings were coefficients for, continued to bother observers. As late as 1904, Henry James could refer to the skyline seen from the Hudson River as "a pin-cushion in relief" and go on to conclude, "The great city is projected into its future as, practically a huge, continuous, fifty-floored conspiracy against the very idea of the ancient graces."[11]

This process of accommodation appears to have taken place in large part between the turn of the century and the First World War. One finds numerous skyline views of New York and other large cities after about 1910 and, increasingly, in contexts that indicate that the perspective was itself perceived as striking and interesting. One example in this period comes from an unlikely and sober-sided treatise on Pittsburgh sponsored by the Russell Sage Foundation in the prewar years. Here, amidst specimens of the new social science and sociological photographs of workers and factories by Lewis Hine and others, is a striking night skyline of the city[12] (*Figure 28*).

The camera clearly played an important role in awakening this kind of visual interest in the city. William Ivins, former curator of prints at the Metropolitan Museum of Art and historian of perspective, has described what he calls a "photographic revolution" that took place during the last half of the nineteenth century. As a revolution, it appears by his description to have been characterized more by stealth than by violence. "The change," according to Ivins, "had come about so slowly and gradually that after the first explosion of interest and excitement which accompanied the announcements of Talbot and Daguerre in 1839, very few people were aware of what was taking place under, and especially *in*, their eyes." The first photographs were seen as distortions of reality, but the process of accommodation thereafter was rapid and radical, even if unacknowledged. "It was not long," he concludes, "before men began to see for themselves what it had taken photography to reveal to their astonished and protesting eyes. Just as nature had once imitated art, so now it began to imitate the picture made by the camera."[13] The camera, by seizing upon every conceivable kind of "reality" and thrusting it with newly acquired authority before the eyes of viewers, thus contributed to the process of breaking down older, monolithic ideas about what was considered beautiful or aesthetically interesting. The camera did this by the sheer variety of the representations it was able to introduce from the visual clutter of urban life. As Susan Sontag has put it, "So successful has been the camera's role in beautifying the world that photographs, rather than the world, have become standards of the beautiful."[14]

Despite an early tendency of photographers to mimic the pastoral conventions of painting, there was from the outset a peculiar affinity between the camera and the city. The organizing during the 1880s of amateur photographers into camera clubs in most large cities provided a further stimulus for the practice and discussion of photography, as well as for the photographing of the city. By 1900, the camera, with the introduction of halftone prints in most magazines and newspapers, had probably become the single most important agent in extending the sensory experience of people beyond their immediate surroundings.[15] Moreover, the same groups who organized the camera clubs also organized bicycle clubs, as in New York, where the two clubs were closely affiliated. Both bicycle and camera thus became mechanical means for expanding the visual range of a certain kind of middle-class city dweller from a preoccupation with his neighborhood to a consideration of, and a reflection on, the city as a whole.

An even closer affinity developed between the camera and the city for the first generation of photographers who were preoccupied with establishing photography as an art in its own right, independent of painting. Between 1900 and the First World War, one group of such photographers loosely affiliated with Alfred Stieglitz and, after 1903, with his journal *Camera Work*, succeeded in making the cityscape an important genre of the new photography.[16] The photographers most actively engaged in photographing the city were Stieglitz himself and occasionally Edward Steichen, Alvin Coburn, and Paul Strand. While their work was diverse and by no means confined to the city, to say nothing of buildings, they soon began to interest themselves in the city as a physical presence, as form. Tall buildings jutting into the sky that were fragments of skyline by night and by day, and even skeletal construction sites and unfinished skyscrapers, piqued their interest.

Daniel Burnham's Flatiron Building, from the moment of its completion in 1903, appears to have had a fascination for photographers, partly because of its height and partly because of its triangular shape. Both Stieglitz and Steichen photographed it soon after its completion, with differing results (*Figure 29, 30*). Alongside the Steichen photograph, that by Stieglitz seems austere and stark, like so many of the urban photographs he took. Yet the important point was not whether the shapes and forms of the new visual world of the city were perceived as "beautiful" in some formal sense. Clearly, Stieglitz was himself critical of the city and ironic in most of this work. The novel feature of this photography was that the city was being explored with obvious aesthetic interest. It was photography, moreover, more than anything else that seemed to excite this kind of exploration.

This process of visual, photographic exploration of the city, of aestheticizing the emerging contours and outlines of the modern city as they appeared one by one, is central to an understanding of what the skyline perspective came to mean. Stieglitz, in his recollections, attributes extraordinary self-consciousness to himself as he remembers taking certain pictures during these years. The Flatiron Building, for example, appears to have interested him only after its completion. Once it was encased in its wintry surroundings, however, it began to assume a pointedly symbolic meaning that he tried to capture in a succession of photographs.

It became clear, I think, from comments such as these, that a novel feature had been introduced into urban aesthetics with this concept of "Parthenons for a day." Beautification was conceived as a process. A structure acquired beauty and gradually lost it as it slipped from history. It was somehow the photograph itself that legitimized the structure or prospect in its moment of beauty. It is evident that the photograph did for buildings and views what they could not do for themselves: it encouraged an appreciation of them as forms rather than as concrete physical presences and, hence, facilitated acceptance by those who found them initially abhorrent, like Stieglitz's own father. The elder Stieglitz, his son reported, had found the building "hideous." A photograph forced him to reconsider. "I do not understand," he reportedly told his son, "how you could have produced such a beautiful picture of anything so ugly."[17] In making such a concession, he had stumbled on a contradiction at the center of urban aesthetics: that in the eye of the beholder, the representation of structure differs essentially from its "reality." The value placed on the representation, furthermore, was itself transient. By the 1920s, New York was a city with many former Parthenons. Amassed side by side, they formed the city's skyline, as changing and transient a prospect as the buildings that composed it.

Skyscraper and skyline—tall buildings singly and en masse—thus became historically significant because they helped structure the experience of new urban residents. As the urbanites watched skyscraper surpass skyscraper, as they observed the canyons along their principal streets deepening and the outer contours of the city changing form, they were virtually forced to perceive themselves as part of an environment of restless and progressive change. One function of camera and photograph was to stop the clock at successive moments in this process and give the viewer occasion to reflect upon it. The photograph helped give legitimacy to this urban kinesthesia by evoking it as an aesthetic value. The photograph became, in effect, the entering wedge of perceptual reality, the arbiter of what was now real and, ultimately, of what was deemed attractive or beautiful. The acceptance of the city as image preceded its acceptance as fact, just as it had for the elder Stieglitz with the Flatiron. One explanation for the sheer volume of cityscape photography after 1900 was this appetite, whetted by the introduction of halftone technology, to metabolize urban novelties of scale, materials, or design through visual representations of them.

The new ways devised by the camera for perceiving the city, as they were progressively elaborated, soon began to influence the way other urban phenomena were represented and perceived. By the beginning of the 1920s, geometric and architectonic perceptions had become both pervasive and stylish. Few photographers contributed as much as Edward Steichen to this new sense of urban style, already evident in his photography as early as his "Flatiron Building" (*Figure 30*). This photograph is set off from the similar picture by Stieglitz most obviously by its being a night scene in color, one of the first autochrome pictures to appear in *Camera Work*.[18] The glow of lights in the distance and the silhouette of coach and coachman along the park in the foreground cast the city in a romantic light. The building itself is softened by the darkness, the setting, and by the lacework veil of branches, in contrast to the deserted, wintry scene in the Stieglitz photograph.

During the 1920s, Steichen went on to do a succession of cityscapes from the window of his studio on Fortieth Street (*Figures 31 and 32*). The night-light pattern, the effect of photographing a street canyon through rain on the window, or the Gothic forms of an adjacent building illuminated by the city's own light, characterized Steichen's work during this period. By the 1920s he had fully engaged in commercial work as chief photographer to the Condé Nast publications, *Vanity Fair* and *Vogue*, and as chief photographic consultant to the advertising firm of J. Walter Thompson. His cityscapes parallel his portraiture of the same period in interesting ways. The use of dramatic lighting, the architectonic background he provided for those he photographed, and his persistent preoccupation with geometric, vertical form helped set a new, sophisticated style for photographing stage and screen stars and other celebrities, as in his dramatic photograph of Isadora Duncan at the Parthenon in 1921 and his study of Chaplin in 1925.

Finally, while the particular character of urban sophistication and "style" that developed during the 1920s lies outside the scope of this essay, it is important to see that these photographic representations of the shape and visual character of the city quickly became charged and contradictory. The complexity and contradictions of such symbols were to be commented on endlessly by literary artists during the decade, sometimes in almost photographic terms. In 1925, for example, F. Scott Fitzgerald struck just this note in *The Great Gatsby*, in a description of the skyline of the city as seen from the Queensboro Bridge as Nick Carraway and Jay Gatsby sped toward Manhattan.

> Over the bridge, with the sunlight through the girders making constant flicker upon the moving cars, with the city rising up across the river in white heaps and sugar lumps all built with a wish out of non-olfactory money. The city seen from the Queensboro Bridge is always the city seen for the first time, in its first wild promise of all the mystery and the beauty in the world. [19]

The virginal quality that Fitzgerald detected in the New York skyline in 1925 suggests how rapidly this perspective on the modern city had been emptied of its social meanings and its human implications. It is a vision similar to that invoked at the end of his novel, when Long Island, before its settlement, is perceived "as a fresh, green breast of the new world." The irony of this description, in the context of *The Great Gatsby*, lies in the gap between this portrait of the city and the characterization of Manhattan in the novel. The city here has a sugar-lump skyline produced by "non-olfactory money"; but the Manhattan we come to know through events in the novel is a very olfactory place, which most of the characters have in fact fled to, lured by their involvement in moneymaking, sexual intrigue, and crime. The skyline, on the other hand, is the city seen from the outside looking in, the city as artifact, a creation of the commuter's fleeting glance.

By the end of the 1920s, the skyline view had receded from a middle-distance architectural codification of corporate aspirations, which formed an important part of its signification in the earlier period, to become something wholly "picturesque" (to reinvoke the term introduced by Schuyler in the 1890s). In effect, corporate aspiration and the symbolization of power had in popular perception been mythologized by an invocation of the city as silhouette, the city as theatrical façade, the city viewed from across the river. Thus cosmeticized, it was this perception of urban society, ironically, that was invoked to sell every imaginable product, not the least of which was urban life itself.

THREE

The Evolution of Public Space ·
The Commercial City
as Showcase

The opening decades of the twentieth century witnessed the creation of public spaces that projected a new sense of urban order and, at the same time, celebrated an emerging commercial culture. What evolved during these years was a novel kind of city, a city designed as a showcase, at once a stimulus and a gratification to the mass of consumers, whose identity was being redefined by a new concept: "the public." A new kind of space for New York—public space—and its architecture and iconography are the focus of this essay. The center of new urban order was a conception of what was public that was woven into the city's commercial culture.

It is scarcely surprising that, before 1920, planners and architects in New York devoted much of their attention to the commercial arteries that ran through the city's center to the axes where these thoroughfares converged to form small open spaces—"squares" or "circles"—and to the creation of parks and playgrounds. After about 1890, vast new structures were designed to monumentalize these central vantage points in the commercial life of the city. The city's principal commercial institutions—department stores, newspapers, hotels, office buildings, and theaters—were clustered around these axes, and architectural treatments worthy of public or ecclesiastical edifices in other societies were devised to give them visual character and prominence.

An older order was rapidly superseded by these developments. Before about 1870, New York had grown without developing the kind of concentrated business and recreational center that began to appear thirty years later, as the commercial life of the city and its related services became compressed into the area between Thirty-fourth and Forty-second streets and continued to creep northward. Only along the central spine created by Broadway and parts of Sixth Avenue (the retail stretch known as the "Ladies' Mile") was there early evidence of the kind of commercial activities that later defined the central functions of modern New York. An increasingly intricate system of transportation filled the center of New York daily with the volume of employees and patrons necessary to assure continued commercial growth. New kinds of hotels, restaurants, and theatrical entertainment made the center increasingly enticing as a place to stay. The city was converted into a vast and efficient emporium for the handling of goods, a gigantic superstore and superwarehouse that could provide services and offer amenities to those who took part in the many transactions of such an *entrepôt*. Efficiency and visual seduction were the watchwords of the new order, which required the creation of countless service vocations—sales clerks, floorwalkers, buyers, elevator operators, drummers, copywriters, window display artists, doormen, busboys, bellhops, typewriters (as the first typists were called), and countless others.

New York soon assumed the leadership in public spatial planning. New York parks created by Frederick Law Olmsted inspired a national movement for the creation of planned open spaces within major cities, but the city's innovative role did not end with its parks. A pioneering spirit initiated a succession of services and amenities designed to enhance the public life of the city, encourage its commerce, and provide a comfortable, scrubbed-up aesthetic world for its citizens. Thanks to the energy and vision of architects and planners, New York's innovations were widely imitated in other American cities. In 1892, Daniel Burnham called upon New York architects and planners, including Olmsted, to design Chicago's immense Columbian Exposition. By the 1890s, the city had achieved a reputation for the distinction and singularity of the design of its spaces.

Only recently has this reputation been exhumed from the disgrace it fell into at the hands of historians of modern architecture. A revival of interest in Beaux-Arts design has awakened appreciation for these public buildings and spaces.[1] A critique of modernism as aesthetically barren, especially in the clichéd form it assumed after World War II, has stimulated an appreciation of the architecture in New York that modernists had rejected as derivative and nonfunctional. An architectural aesthetic has now developed that, among other things, celebrates this decorative and ornamental elegance of turn-of-the-century public buildings and early skyscrapers.

Major rethinking of the historical rationale behind New York's elaboration of public space clearly seems in order. The building boom of the 1980s has altered the character of almost every focal point in the older city's design, as in the case of Times Square, which evolved rapidly following a succession of business and municipal decisions in 1904. A sense of the city's spatial past, rather than informing the debate, is rapidly being buried in the rubble created by new construction. One reason for neglecting this past may lie in the mistaken assumption that the modern city of 1920 was an immense ornamental luxury at the time. Nothing could be further from the truth.[2] Those who designed New York's buildings and elaborated its squares and broad avenues conceived of those spaces as parts of a vast commercial city with particular needs that had to be satisfied. Among these needs were the flow of traffic—both people and vehicles—the provision of dignified recreational space for a burgeoning middle class, the enhancing and monumentalizing of commercial enterprise, and the communication of commercial values to the society at large. In a sense, the streets and squares of the city foreshadowed the airwaves that carry radio and television signals: public spaces became the vehicles used by civic and business leaders to transmit information about the city to their constituencies.

These spatial changes were made in the names of the public. Banks, insurance companies, newspapers, auditoriums, department stores, and hotels deemed it in the public interest to facilitate communications within the city, to speed the growth of commercial life, and to call visual attention to the locations and institutions where these activities were taking place on a rapidly expanding scale. They expanded the perception of what was public to include their own arenas, which were, strictly speaking, privately owned and administered businesses, but served and addressed the public in dramatic ways. Those who promoted the building of such monumental new institutions and services were referred to as "public-spirited," and they modestly believed themselves to be responsive to public opinion.[3]

The concept of "public opinion" was scarcely a novelty in 1880, when the most intensive examination of it began, but the growth of large cities quite suddenly placed the discussion in a strikingly different context. During most of the nineteenth century, "public opinion" had been employed in an almost exclusively political context. It seems most often to have meant the opinion expressed about public issues—*res publica*— rather than the thinking of any particular group.[4] Successive developments conspired after the 1880s (and even earlier) to modify this usage. The cumulative effect of these developments was a slow devaluation of the independence, assertiveness, and wisdom that earlier had been attributed to the "omnicompetent citizen," which gradually gave way to the "bewildered herd" as described in Walter Lippmann's *Phantom Public* in 1925, and to the machine-made opinions of the man-in-the-mass described in John Dewey's *Public and Its Problems* two years later. This conception of a mass culture emerged in discernible stages out of the interplay between changing perceptions of public space and opinion during the critical period before 1920.

The first discernible stage was the increasing tendency after the mid–

nineteenth century to perceive the public as a physical presence—a human aggregate—rather than simply as opinion dispersed within the population. Cities as large population centers had existed previously, but never before had such numbers of people poured in and out of cities on a daily basis. Each morning, ferry boats and commuter trains unloaded their human cargoes, only to retrieve them the same evening. This further encouraged a second change: the perception of urban populations as fluid, circulating crowds of people. Beginning with Central Park, the facilities planned for such populations were designed to accommodate them, not as static crowds, but as a mobile, circulatory flow of human beings. This appears to have been true even earlier with P. T. Barnum's American Museum of the 1840s, which was designed to keep its clientele moving through the exhibition halls. Barnum boasted in his autobiography that he had made the sign "To the Egress" so alluring that his crowds, ignorant of the meaning of "egress," poured out of the museum as readily as they poured in.[5] A language of fluids became attached to all references to urban components, as in the "wave" of immigrants and masses of people "streaming" in and out.

The plan for Central Park conceived by Olmstead and Calvert Vaux in 1858 reflected even better the changing conception of how to accommodate the city's population, although the concept of a public as a body of people also made its appearance there. The thinking behind this plan invented earlier ideas concerning optimum public space. For the static arrangement of crowds in early nineteenth-century theaters, Olmstead and Vaux substituted circulation, decentralization, and distribution. A circular road was designed to carry park crowds to a wide variety of activities distributed over its 700 acres; the park could be entered and exited at several points.[6]

A development in the changing perception of the public was manifest in the need to segregate various streams of people, a form of spatial rationalism that grew in importance toward the end of the century. First, Olmstead and Vaux segregated each form of park traffic—carriage traffic from pedestrian paths, and bridle paths from both—with bridges and underpasses provided at points where these streams intersected. Perhaps even more significant was the planners' decision to sink the four east–west roads required by their commission below grade and out of sight to eliminate any contact or conflict between park crowds and the commercial traffic of the city.

Later in the century, because the population at large in the city had become more ethnically mixed and more mobile by the 1880s, it was no longer possible to make the same kind of clear distinction between the coarse, vulgar stream of the city's commercial life and the public, as

Olmstead and Vaux had done in their plans for Central Park. The advent of large-scale immigration from southern and eastern Europe brought into the city large groups that were perceived by indigenous Americans as wholly alien to American life and, consequently, as untutored in civilized ways. Public spaces and facilities were subjected to novel mixtures of people and overwhelmed by unprecedented numbers. The spaces that were constructed reflected in their massive scale and impersonality their anticipated usage. Accordingly, new services were soon perceived as urgently needed. Finally, the vision of these massive and commercially inexperienced crowds moving through the streets and ports stirred visions of unprecedented economic and political opportunities. Down the same road lay both the mass-marketing and the mass political movements of the twentieth century. The following examples suggest some of the ways these developments reflected a changing perception of "the public."

Grand Central Terminal opened to the public February 3, 1913. With its surrounding hotels, shops, restaurants, and offices, Grand Central was a city within a city—it was originally called Terminal City—the hub of an extensive real estate development and the capital of a railway empire that stretched from coast to coast. The terminal had been in the works since 1900, and the need for it had been felt even longer. The growing volume of passenger, freight, and commuter traffic arriving in the city had made its predecessor, Grand Central Depot—even enlarged—wholly inadequate. The increasing recognition that the Grand Central yards were occupying real estate of incalculable value in the center of the city and the advent of underground electrification of trains entering the city combined to encourage the terminal's designers to build an almost self-contained mini-city.[7] It was purpose-built, as the English say, in the center of Manhattan, and it rapidly changed the character of the entire midsection of the city. Park Avenue, built over the rail bed and stretching north to Ninety-sixth Street, was one consequence; Forty-second Street as the principal east–west link between the commercial and the entertainment foci of the city was another. In its interior, Grand Central Terminal's decorative space became a harbinger of the vast hotel lobbies and atria of contemporary cities (*Figures 33, 34*).

The language used by the press to characterize the completed terminal suggested a changed perception of "the travelling public," as the intended clientele was described throughout the long period of design and execution. In 1904, a reporter for the *Railroad Gazette* commented:

In preparing the plans for the new station everything has been sacrificed to the comfort and convenience of the travelling public. The distinguishing features of the arrangement of the yards, platforms, and headhouse may be summarized as follows: Ample facilities for getting to and away from the station. Cab stand situated in most convenient place for arriving passengers. Outgoing baggage room convenient to ticket offices and incoming baggage room convenient to the exits. Separation of incoming and outgoing passengers, thus avoiding confusion. Ample waiting rooms and accessories and a grand concourse large enough to accommodate the largest holiday and excursion crowds. Separation of suburban and through passengers but with arrangements for easily getting from one part of the station to the other. Comfortable waiting rooms for those desiring to meet incoming passengers. Ample baggage facilities.[8]

In the *Gazette's* language, the public was a monarch dictating what should be done. There is an obvious preoccupation with reducing the confusion of travelers by easing their transfer from one transportation system to another, providing comfortable and relaxing spaces to wait in, and even reducing their physical exertion as they moved down an interconnecting system of sloping ramps, rather than steps, that were designed to carry pedestrian traffic down from street level by "gravity flow."

Although the design of Grand Central Terminal was interpreted as a model of utility and accommodation that catered to every need of the public, its spatial design introduced conflicting perceptions of the same public. One perception involved the fascination with quantification that became evident in every description of the terminal: square and cubic footage of the terminal itself; train arrivals and departures per day; annual, weekly, and daily tons of freight and mail; and rapidly growing track mileage in the New York Central system. These statistics were cited regularly, along with the growing numbers of each kind of passenger— through, commuter, and subway—expected to use the terminal. Tables in descriptive literature also introduced the concept of the "passenger mile," which reduced travelers to a mobile unit of rail-traffic measurement. In such discussions, a different sense of the public emerges—that of traveler-as-commodity. This delight in human quantification was an anticipation of the movement to study public opinion through sampling and polling that appeared at the end of the 1920s.[9] Such fascination with translating every feature of the project into numbers and justifying every expense through numerical projections clearly played to the company's pride in its expansion and growth.

Further illustration of the change in interpreting public space is seen in the cross-sectional drawings of the terminal and its surroundings that were produced during the ten years of planning and construction (*Figure 35*). In these drawings, human figures serve as minuscule units of measure in depicting the scale of the structure. This kind of graphic interpretation seems closely related to the verbal discourse that grandiloquently described these spaces and crept into common usage after Grand Central Terminal's opening.[10]

Descriptions focused on the immense concourse—at the time the largest interior space ever designed for a conventional building—with its vast, vaulted ceiling decorated with a zodiacal and equatorial belt to simulate the solar system. The concourse was described as "lofty," "majestic," "awesome," even "sublime."[11] This language echoes the aesthetic vocabulary commonly employed in nineteenth-century descriptions of the most dramatic aspects of nature: Niagara Falls, the Western mountains, and the wildest, most rugged features of the American landscape. In its American usage, this vocabulary still retained some of the religious overtones that Edmund Burke ascribed to it in the eighteenth century, but in its application to the urban setting it quickly came to take on proprietary values for those who had constructed record-setting spaces and towers, just as it had earlier been employed to bolster American national pride. To nineteenth-century contemporaries, Grand Central's iconographic ceiling had a more specific reference. The representation of the world in the universe also spoke the language of modern global commerce with its hub in midtown Manhattan and its trade routes that circled the earth. It was the same impulse that peopled the world with American missionaries and that brought "savage" peoples to be put on display at "world" fairs and other commercial expositions.

These novel expressions all had a revolutionary effect on the perceptions of the people using these spaces. Faced with public space conceived in these grandiose terms, nineteenth-century travelers must have been awed by the grandeur of the terminal and the company that had created it, Grand Central Company, as they moved through the great barrel-vaulted concourse with its replica of the heavens arching overhead. As much as the facilities were designed to accommodate the public, the structure was also meant to impress—and overarch—its visitors with its power. The company, and more specifically, the Vanderbilt family, were clearly enhanced by space that was ecclesiastical in scale.

Although its active management passed to a consortium in 1903, Grand Central Company had been the creation of three generations of Vanderbilts, who had put together their railway empire out of many local companies across the Northeast. Beginning with founder Cornelius V. ("Commodore") Vanderbilt, whose original fortune had begun with steamship lines, a succession of sons had added to the network that became Grand Central Company. Despite their great wealth and Dutch lineage, the Vanderbilts were slow to win acceptance in New York society. Spurned by society's legendary Astor family and by social arbiter Ward McAllister, they did not "arrive" until well into the 1880s. The huge terminal sitting athwart Park Avenue, with its many reminders of the Vanderbilt family, was therefore a symbol of social as well as economic triumph in the city. Further homage was paid at the surrounding hotels—

the Commodore and the Biltmore—which commemorated the pro-
prietors' families, as did such streets as adjacent Vanderbilt Avenue. But
the terminal's grandeur was also—and equally—designed to dignify the
public. Nothing functional dictated such scale or height; no holiday or
excursion crowds would ever require a ceiling 300 feet high that replicated
the heavens.

The terminal's iconography further expressed this ambivalence toward
the railway's clientele. The statue of Commodore Vanderbilt facing north
along Park Avenue was clearly proprietary. Facing south over the parapet
clock stood winged Mercury, symbolizing both commerce and speed. The
public that worshipped technology probably saw nothing ambivalent
about this kind of divine sponsorship. Theodore Dreiser's *Sister Carrie* had
caught something of this overwhelming feeling about New York public
spaces when one of the characters, Hurstwood, arrived in the city from
Montreal and remarked, "The entire metropolitan center possessed a high
and mighty air calculated to overawe the common applicant, to make the
gulf between poverty and success seem both wide and deep."[12]

Grand Central Terminal served daily travelers with novel commercial
services: "dressing rooms," "kissing galleries," "hair dressing parlors," "arcades," "restaurants" "post offices," and "bathtubs." It would be more
accurate to say that it was designed to serve simultaneously and efficiently
different groups of travelers: through-coach and Pullman passengers laying
over between trains, long-run passengers terminating in New York, and
daily commuters—all in all, some 250,000 people daily, not including
subway riders using Grand Central as a destination or point of departure."

For the most part, the various streams of travelers were separated on
different levels of the terminal complex, demonstrating how a diverse
public group created new spatial needs. At the same time, Grand Central
Company was not alone in its efforts to reckon with these needs, nor was it
alone in devising ways of both gratifying and appropriating them. Novel
strategies similar to those used by Grand Central Company for manipulat-
ing and orchestrating the public were employed by the other new institutions catering to the public.

There is probably no more revealing instance of this process of manipulation at work than the campaign launched in the 1890s to create public
"comfort stations" throughout the city (*Figure 36*). The extent and inten-
sity of this agitation perhaps for a time exceeded that of any other municipal reform. The volume of pamphlet literature produced over a thirty-year
period supports this claim. The historic importance of this particular
campaign lay in its active intervention in what had previously been considered a private, domestic realm. The revolutionary aspect was the assumption that a man's personal hygiene and cleanliness, how he provided

for his intimate needs, was a matter of public import. The pamphleteers exercised this reasoning to recruit him for the burgeoning middle-classes, as an early publication made clear: "To make an habitually dirty man clean is to create in his inmost soul, even if but temporarily, a desire to rise out of the squalor and filth with which he may be ordinarily encompassed." The massive campaign to create these facilities and to promote and encourage their use thus opened the way for a whole range of orchestrated intrusions into the lives of urban populations, under the banner of public health or welfare. This one cause finally became the focus of a whole range of related worries about urban populations, their health, their political vulnerability, their welfare, and their accommodation.[14]

It appears to have been the surge of interest during the 1890s in public health that first drew attention to the deficiency of toilets available to people moving about the city far from home.[15] Early epidemiologists pointed to the dangers of the public defecation and urination then prevalent, but a more general preoccupation with "regularity" and "the prompt elimination of poisonous residues" is clearly evident in the pamphlets. During the 1890s, the agitation for comfort stations tended to form part of the larger agenda of municipal reform in New York. At the Conference on Municipal Progress held on April 26, 1894, for example, the combined issue of lavoratories and mortuaries was only one of four topics discussed, the others being free baths and washhouses, neighborhood guilds, and rapid transit. The yoking together of rapid transit and issues pertaining to personal hygiene emphasizes the dual aspect of the new meaning of "the public": its *embodiment* and its mobility.

A year later, a subcommittee of the powerful Committee of Seventy recommended "the establishment of adequate public baths and lavoratories for the promotion of cleanliness and increased public comfort in appropriate places throughout the city."[16] The Committee epitomized the values of the emerging commercial culture. It was a citizens' collective made up of almost every private association or organization concerned with municipal reform. The Committee included men prominent in business, finance, and philanthropy and enlisted the support of those active in sponsoring new monumental spaces such as Grand Central Terminal.

The subcommittee had discovered that American cities lagged far behind their English and other European counterparts in providing comfort stations, although interest in this issue rapidly spread from New York to other American cities during the next twenty years. Philadelphia had five public toilet facilities in 1895, for example, whereas there were more than 200 in Liverpool. In London, the subcommittee reported such stations had been placed underground at the congested junctions of major thoroughfares. More than five million people had used the facility in Piccadilly Circus during the first three years of its existence. Usage of the Charing Cross Station facility had been almost equally heavy. The subcommittee pointed out that in England and on the Continent, where these facilities had grown up in connection with the development of the underground railway systems, they were often combined with other services to travelers: bootblacking stations, barbershops, telephones, and newsstands. The subcommittee recommended that such complexes be places at key locations in New York where they might be combined with millinery and notion shops to help defray the cost of attendants and maintenance. Suggested locations for such complexes were Fifty-eighth Street at Eighth Avenue (Central Park West), Fifty-ninth Street at Fifth Avenue, Madison Square Park, Cooper Union Park, and Chatham Square. A later report suggested that information stations also might be located at such points to aid those seeking their way in New York. [17]

Serving travelers, however, was only one concern of the reform groups advocating comfort stations. In this sense the European example was only part of the argument. The decision not to adopt the English practice of charging a penny for the service is one indication of differing objectives. The major aim in almost every American city was to reach the "vast mass of humanity," as the Committee of Seventy report called it, that was currently at the mercy of saloonkeepers. In America, saloons provided the only available toilets outside large hotels and department stores. Those lured into saloons by "nature's demand," the argument went, ended up buying a drink out of common courtesy for the service provided. A survey taken in St. Louis in 1908 found that saloon keepers acknowledged receiving over thirty percent of their clientele in this fashion, making their toilets, in their estimation, a bigger attraction than the free lunch. The literature also emphasized another consideration that fueled the popularity of the campaign. Patrons who bought "the fatal glass of beer" were apt to end up in the meshes of machine politics because of the close association between the saloons and the political boss systems. Public toilets would, therefore, emancipate this portion of the saloon clientele from Tammany's clutches. [18] In this respect, those who would use comfort stations were the same group bathhouses were being built for during this period. It is not surprising, therefore, that the locations for many other comfort stations were in tenement districts of the Lower East Side and similar areas of the city: Tompkins Square, Washington Market, and Essex Market.

By 1907, New York had constructed eight comfort stations at a cost of $20,000 to $25,000 each. Annual maintenance, including attendants, was estimated at $5,000. In the eleven months between November 1907 and October 1908, almost ten million people—8,004,309 men and 1,267,827 women—had used the facilities. Perhaps the most striking feature of this statistic is the gender ratio of roughly six to one, suggesting that far more men used these public facilities than the figures revealed by the early 1920s, when the gender ratio dropped to roughly three to one.[19] By then, additional comfort stations in many different locations, some far from the city's axial thoroughfares, made comparisons a little hazardous. Moreover, women in the early 1900s were much more likely to be in the city to shop and attend the theater than for any other reason, and the large department stores and theaters prided themselves on their elaborate toilet and resting facilities for female patrons. Nonetheless, the discrepancy is too great to be accounted for by these considerations. It seems clear that the gender composition of the street population was another characteristic that was masked by the homogenizing concept of "public."

Only through such masking could the collectivity that became known as "public" be expanded to include a significant proportion of the population. As rhetoric, the term became like a beacon to summon all and sundry citizens into a burgeoning middle-class and to direct them, through advertising, to higher and higher levels of consumption. If the lure of being included as part of the public was spelled out in comfort, convenience, speed, hygiene, and civic instruction, as it was for patrons of Central Park, Grand Central Terminal, or comfort stations, such a collective designation held quite a different lure for those who did their business at street level.

A careful student of the expanding public was Frank W. Woolworth. He based his "dime store" empire on the modest resources of people moving through the streets of American towns and cities. He also based his success on his close observation of the consumer habits of ordinary people. From the time Woolworth opened his first store in upstate New York in 1879 until the completion of his skyscraper headquarters in New York City in 1913, he had been obsessed with studying the sidewalk behavior of the public.

When interviewed in 1913, Woolworth said he had based his entire career on cash payment and people-watching. He had selected store sites under the motto "Take the Store to the People," choosing areas where sidewalk traffic was densest. He soon learned that stores not sited in this fashion quickly failed. A key shift in Woolworth's thinking seems to have occurred after the financial panic of the 1890s, when he opened a store in the conservative Pennsylvania Dutch community of Lancaster. Unable to secure one of his preferred sites, he decided to build a large, highly visible store in a location that local community leaders warned him was unpromising. His reason for taking this unwonted risk is almost as interesting as what happened. [20]

"Modern America was growing up all around Lancaster," Woolworth observed, "and it just *had* to move forward." By "modern America," he left no doubt that he meant New York, where he had opened a purchasing agency on Chambers Street some ten years before. From his New York office, where he spent an increasing amount of time, Woolworth had observed the changes taking place in the city, the advent of skyscrapers and the crowds that swarmed through the streets. He therefore elected to build a large store in Lancaster that would be clearly visible some distance away. What occurred confirmed what he had shrewdly guessed: "The thing that pleased me most was that business immediately swung over to the wrong side of the street. The wrong side of the street was now the right side—it was the fashionable side and it was the prosperous side. Things grew so rapidly over there that I had to add to my new building before it was completed. I did that to accommodate a restaurant the public demanded." [21]

The next step in the evolution of Woolworth's thinking about the public was his decision to build a skyscraper office building, not a store, in New York. He had already surmised that an important connection existed between a merchandising operation like his own, with stores spread across the country, and a highly visible, highly publicized central headquarters in the city. As with other such corporate skyscrapers, rent from office space, which included most of the building, would also fatten the company purses. His precedent was the success of the Singer Sewing Machine Company with its New York headquarters. He told an interviewer in 1913: "When in Europe a few years ago, wherever I went the men with whom I came in contact asked me about the Singer Building and its famous tower. That gave me an idea. I decided to erect a building that would advertise the Woolworth 5 cent and 10 cent stores all over the world." [22] What could be better? In one package, a solid investment in Manhattan real estate *and* unrivalled advertising.

If his intention was to provide a beacon of worldwide publicity, however, his method of choosing a site continued to be localized and old-fashioned. With his rental space in mind, he acted as though he were choosing the site for a store rather than an office building. Again he took to the streets: "He looked at the crowds, watched them as they turned into side streets . . . and saw where the traffic was the most dense." Ultimately, he chose the corner of Reade and Broadway, considerably downtown from the other tall buildings and the recently completed world-record 700-foot tower of the Metropolitan Life Insurance Company, which he had already decided to "overtop."[23]

The most striking feature of Woolworth's career is his progression over thirty years from stalking the public, to orchestrating it, and finally with his tower, to luring, even overwhelming it. But he never fully abandoned his earliest idea of the public as a mobile physical presence and a collective will that was discernible upon close observation, even when he chose the much more abstract course of creating an aura around his business by constructing both a Gothic cathedral of commerce and the world's tallest building. The tower of the Woolworth Building, Montgomery Schuyler observed in 1913, had been added to lighten its appearance and give it grace "at the cost of pure utility." The tower, he concluded, "commemorates [Woolworth's] sense of *civic* obligation."[24]

Schuyler's use of the word "civic" is certainly consistent with the use this term had acquired in characterizing a new form of public space: private business headquarters as architectural spectacle. Schuyler accordingly compared the Woolworth Building to both the Metropolitan Tower and the Municipal Building, designed by the firm of McKim, Mead, and White, across City Hall Park. Woolworth's bent toward practicality and caution about excess—he paid out $13.5 million in cash for his skyscraper—were by then legendary. What was it he intended to memorialize with such a building? Woolworth appears to have been preoccupied with communicating in physical terms the grandeur of his own commercial triumph—hence, his choice of the Gothic style, reminiscent of the Houses of Parliament, with its echo of civic and ecclesiastical power. An early photograph illustrates the degree to which the building is a Gothic version of New York's typical campaniles on rectilinear bases (*Figure 37*). (Later construction concealed the base, and the tower now appears to rise straight up.) His first concern beyond setting a world record in height, was what the public would perceive at street level. He wanted the building to be at once imposing, instructive, and self-aggrandizing. He wanted his building to serve as a model to the public through its depiction of his career and as a monument to himself.

Woolworth opened his first New York office in 1886 when he was thirty-four years old. He was in the midst of making his fortune with street-level merchandising across the Northeast. He belonged to what might be called the "sidewalk generation" that flourished from the 1890s to the 1910s—one of pedestrians, strollers, shoppers, and cyclists, keenly attuned to the panorama of goods and people provided by New York's streets. It was a generation that was both spectatorial and aggressive. This was precisely the time when the term "window shopping" entered the language, along with the word "show" for any theatrical presentation. By the 1890s the display of merchandise in department store windows was becoming a highly developed art form. The delight created by sensuous display was still fresh and unencumbered.[25] The generation of this time was the first to feel the full allure of New York at night, and the phrase "The Great White Way" was used to describe the bank of illuminated theater marquees arrayed one beside the other along Broadway from Fourteenth to Thirty-fourth streets.

By 1913, the perception of the public had clearly changed. There is probably no better symbol of this change than the moment in early February when Woodrow Wilson pressed a button in Washington, D.C., that illuminated 80,000 bulbs in the completed Woolworth Building. Some reports said that the flash could be seen 100 miles away. The telegraphic signal from Washington and the spectacle of an illuminated tower sixty stories high may have brought the sidewalk generation to an end. In the following days and weeks, one source estimated that some two million words of free publicity about Woolworth, the building, and the event filled American newspapers and magazines, as Woolworth must have confidently expected.[26] In that moment he had succeeded in shifting the focus of attention away from the Metropolitan Life Insurance Company, from the sidewalk to the building's buttresses and pinnacles 792 feet above, and from goods seen close at hand in his many stores, to the more abstract image of a "brand" name. In planning his stores across the Northeast, Woolworth had emphasized the sidewalk perspective of his customers and sought to attract them by luring them into the horizontal, streetlike aisles of his stores. By creating a vertical monument rather than a horizontal access route, he was dramatically adopting a new, modern strategy.

Choosing a moment for marking such a change in perception is clearly arbitrary, since the process of change had been a long one. Even before the 1890s there had been a succession of events that issued in other vertical expressions of the evolution of the city's public spaces. These events were often compounded with related changes in communication and orchestration of public opinion, as in the welcoming celebration in 1899 for Admiral George Dewey, commemorating his victory over the Spanish fleet in Manila Bay. On that occasion a barrage of newspaper publicity had produced a spectacular parade marching through the city, but it also featured a huge, electrically illuminated sign atop the Brooklyn Bridge and the vertical spectacle of searchlights probing the sky over the harbor as the naval parade moved through the night. Then, in 1910 (if not earlier at the parade for Dewey) came the first ticker-tape parade—that perfect dual symbol of commerce and verticality—as New York celebrated the return of Theodore Roosevelt with a march uptown from the Battery. Ticker tape dropping from the upper windows of the new Wall Street skyscrapers emphasized the vertical reach of financial power.[27]

The nature of the changes signaled by these and other related events was to become more obvious by the 1920s, but already by the turn of the century there were those who sensed the connection between communications and the use of vertical space. Tall buildings, because they could be seen from afar and because their construction and design advertised the company building them, anticipated the importance of towers and other vertical structures in the transmission of telegraphic radio signals. It was no accident, for example, that New York communications industries were among the first companies to build towers, beginning with the Tribune Building in 1876, followed by Western Unions' own office tower three years later in 1879, and the campaniled Times Building in 1905.

The skyscraper towers, viewed in the aggregate, made up the Manhattan skyline. If the classic New York skyline was always a cosmetic fiction, it has now become largely a superseded one, evoked only in moments of nostalgia when we hanker, as in Woody Allen's New York films, for the city of the 1930s before modern transformations swept it from view. It probably matters that most new arrivals in the city are now by air rather than by rail or road. The city, visually and functionally, is less clustered, and it has spread along the Atlantic seaboard and become part of an aerial landscape. Other changes, too, have altered the ways we perceive the city and the significance we attach to its tall buildings and the visual patterns they form. The fact that the skyline silhouette has gone the way of older conventions for imagining the city, such as the harbor view, tells us something about the state of our urban culture.

New York today, after one of its largest building booms, continues its vertical course unabated, but the function of tall buildings has shifted dramatically. While here and there distinctive corporate towers such as the Citicorp Building or the new AT&T building continue to beam out of the skyline, the most characteristic tall structure is the anonymous glass commercial office building, virtually identical to its neighbor, and built on speculation. The most spectacular explosion of such structures, scarcely surprising in a city now identified with financial services, has been in the Wall Street area, where a high-rise glass subcity has crowded from view the pinnacled silhouette that characterized lower Manhattan in the 1930s.

Across the city one can discern scores of a second genre of tall building, the so-called luxury apartment tower, equally indistinguishable one from another and meant to house New York's new managerial and professional upper-service tier. Even the few distinctive corporate towers function differently in the city from their counterparts of fifty years earlier. The "broadcasting" function of the original campanile towers that had led companies to their erection has been successively superseded by radio, television, and electronic communications. A new communications culture has succeeded the old commercial culture that produced the city of the 1920s and 1930s. It matters little that the art deco tower of the Chrysler Building can scarcely be glimpsed behind the new developer towers. The crowds that surge through the city's streets rarely see past the new buildings.

Here and there, to be sure, historical preservationists have succeeded in staking out older landmark buildings, as in the cast-iron district of SoHo. Something resembling an older consumer culture still thrives in the interstices of new construction, but scarcely like it once did. New public space is largely confined to the atria of tall buildings like Citicorp or Trump Tower, created by builders in exchange for a relaxation of the limits on height in area building codes. Fifth Avenue continues to provide the city with luxury stores of unparalleled opulence, but pockets of an earlier Manhattan do not evoke the pattern or ensemble they were once a part of. A different urban configuration has replaced that older design, and a series of revolutions has transformed the meaning of location and distance in the city. The Federal Reserve's vast bank clearinghouse that processes over a billion dollars daily is, in one sense, the hub of the city's commerce and the successor to Grand Central Terminal and the old Penn Station as a grand landmark, but few New Yorkers know, or even need to know, its location, any more than buyers need to know the geographical location of the catalogue companies from whom they order goods. An older, more visible city, whose arrangements could be "read" taxonomically like display counters of the "superstore" that it once was, has disappeared. Circuitry has replaced district and neighborhood. New York itself, its older functions diffused by change, has become an integral part of a vast megalopolitan entity that sprawls along the East Coast from Maine to Maryland.

FOUR

Culture and Architecture · Some Aesthetic Tensions in the Shaping of New York   *with* THOMAS BENDER

It's possible a little dose of history
May help us in unravelling this mystery.
W. H. Auden

In May of 1981, the New York State Urban Development Corporation invited proposals for the Forty-second Street Development Project. This request was accompanied by an impressive two-volume compendium of detailed design guidelines, prepared by the architecture and planning firm of Cooper, Eckstut Associates. The publication of guidelines for Forty-second Street, moreover, followed by only a few months the selection of Cesar Pelli's proposal for the development of Battery Park City, a plan based on another, equally ambitious, set of design guidelines by the same firm.[1]

What was most striking about these guidelines, at least to an historian, was their recognition and evocation of the city's past. They presuppose an older New York belonging to common memory, like panels in some imaginary mural. Even more striking were the tacit assumptions about how the city "worked" at particular moments in its past and the evident desire to recapture the operational magic of its shapes and vistas—some of the dramaturgy of its principal thoroughfares and public places.

The past evoked in these guidelines might be styled "Early Modern" New York, a city caught up in the throes of dramatic changes—a vast influx of immigrants and an invasion of corporate headquarters—and a booming center of American intellectual and cultural life. Perhaps most important, it was the city of progressive urban reform, which involved as one of its principal aims the definition, in politics and architecture, of modern public life and civic culture. Between the 1890s and 1930, New York acquired its famous skyline, as well as the monumental classical structures that continue to define its public spaces. It was also a period when an indigenous New York urban aesthetic became evident.

The authors of the guidelines, clearly aware of this past, seemed unable to articulate it. This is probably because they were operating on fundamental cultural premises that are, by definition, assumed and not stated. But one of the tasks of history—of intellectual history in particular, as Arthur O. Lovejoy pointed out long ago—is to extricate unstated premises so that reflection on them is possible.[2]

The task assumed by Cooper, Eckstut Associates in the case of Forty-second Street was to give architectural expression to the street's importance, to monumentalize a street as a public space. Almost instinctively they seem to have drawn on a suppressed history of New York when they stated their assumptions: that a horizontal monumentalism in buildings implies civic or public purposes, and that vertical structures such as towers represent the power of corporate capitalism. In their guidelines they proposed emphasizing the civic or public character of Forty-second Street by keeping the "5-story building wall" uniform in order to produce a "low-rise corridor." Towers were to be kept well back from the street wall. The plan, in other words, made a strong statement for public values, and it appealed to the city's history as its authority. This essay, an early attempt at articulating such a tacit history, seeks to locate the cultural origin of this aesthetic distinction between horizontal and vertical.

Probably no modern city—and certainly none with its acknowledged importance—has been dealt with as harshly and as arbitrarily by architectural historians as New York. Ironically, New York, the first modern city in the world, has, until recently, received only scant and damning mention in the historical works that have canonized modern architecture and planning. New York's parks and parkways receive ritual praise. Otherwise it has been depicted as a city dominated by a monotonous, mindless grid, Neoclassical or French Renaissance façades, and devotion to mercantile values and derivative Beaux-Arts aesthetics. Nowhere does one find discussion of the interesting tug-of-war that took place between private and civic values: between vertical and horizontal structure, and, in planning, between laissez-faire attitudes and deliberate efforts to give shape and unity to the city's heterogeneous and often conflicting functions.

With an important exception—Le Corbusier—the giants among the moderns have been uniformly abusive of New York's architecture and planning achievements. Louis Sullivan, for example, characterized lower Manhattan as "a plague spot of American architecture."[3] In no one modernist work is the combined condemnation and neglect of New York's place in the history of urban design more clearly registered than in Siegfried Giedion's now classic *Space, Time and Architecture: The Growth of a New Tradition* (1941 et seq.). Giedion unfolded what has now become the authoritative cultural history of modern architecture and planning in its relation to the realities of its time and to modernism in the other arts.

In Giedion's story, late–nineteenth-century Chicago fared very well, since it was there that architectural expression most closely matched structural changes. That city, accordingly, produced more than its share of modernist forerunners. New York, for Giedion, represented neoclassical architectural and planning schemes, sometimes referred to broadly as "Beaux-Arts" or "eclectic," which he scorned as being in the "troubadour spirit, pitting song against the din of modern industry." New York developments were perceived as detours, even perversions, of the logic of modernist architectural progress. He made the dual charge that the Beaux-Arts eclectic neoclassicism was not responsive either to technology or to function. In a similar way he dismissed those who engaged in city planning from a neoclassical perspective: "the urbanist like the popular painter, lost himself in the composition of idylls."[4]

These charges must now be examined skeptically and critically. More than that, it seems appropriate to make a counterclaim. Such a claim would go something like this: buried within the Beaux-Arts education and locked into the work of Americans trained in Paris was a preoccupation with "ensemble," with the pattern of construction perceived collectively. This particular concern with ensemble in turn resonated with certain civic attitudes toward the city that have now all but disappeared. New York in the 1890s had the largest concentration of Beaux-Arts–trained architects in America. There they developed an evident self-consciousness and seemingly lay in wait for the opportunities provided by the ebullient turn-of-the-century building spirit.[5]

A certain preoccupation with planning was implicit in the way Beaux-Arts architectural students were trained. The full implications of this aspect of French training have never been adequately appreciated. Beaux-Arts training may not have insisted on specific sites for buildings, but it emphasized the importance of the site and it focused on street-level perspectives. Not surprisingly, the best students at the École des Beaux-Arts soon went on to develop an urban perspective: they began to conceive of individual buildings as parts of a larger ensemble of structures and spaces. These Beaux-Arts "radicals" included Henri Proust, Ernst Hebrard, and (the only one acknowledged by Giedion) Tony Garnier.[6] This radical side of the Beaux-Arts tradition was also available to "provincials" who traveled to Paris from other countries. Some Americans trained in Paris were very receptive to it. The American version of Beaux-Arts appears to have had its most pronounced expression in the architecture and urban design of New York, although Daniel H. Burnham may well have given it its most concise expression.[7]

The Chicago Columbian Exposition of 1893, identified so often with

Burnham and the New York architects, is the crucial event in the historiography of modernism in America. How one interprets that event, located in the American Midwest, largely determines, ironically, one's capacity for understanding the urban heritage of New York. The modernist interpretation (much simplified, to be sure) goes something like this: in Chicago in the decades after the 1871 fire, the orthodox story goes, a commercial ethic and new technology had produced a steel-frame architecture of tall commercial buildings exemplifying the later dictum of modernism—form follows function. When Daniel H. Burnham, whose firm had pioneered this new architecture, invited a group of New York architects to help design the Exposition, the logic of architectural history was perverted. The Neoclassical White City they built in Jackson Park was in stark contrast to the modern architecture being born downtown in Chicago. Louis Sullivan's lament echoes through the history books: The Fair unleashed a "virus" that produced "an outbreak of the Classic and Renaissance in the East. . . . The damage wrought to this country by the World's Fair will last a half century. . . ."[8] According to Giedion:

> At the very moment when the Chicago school gained a mastery of the new means which it had created, its further development and influence was abruptly choked off. The event which directly effected this change was the Chicago World's Fair of 1893 (the World's Columbian Exposition), but influences working in this direction had set in long before in another section of the country. American architecture came under many different influences during the nineteenth century, but none was so strong or came at such a critical moment as the rise of power of the mercantile classicism developed in the East.

Giedion also provided a truncated historical motivation for this anomalous turn of events.

> Public, artists, and literary people believed themselves to be witnessing a splendid rebirth of the great traditions of past ages. The immense appeal of this recreated past in "the White City" can only be laid to a quite unnecessary national inferiority complex. . . . Only Louis Sullivan had sufficient inner strength to hold fast in the midst of a general surrender.

New York, as the home of "mercantile classicism," had a sinister role to play.

> Mercantile classicism had been developing and gaining strength in New York since the 'eighties, but it won its country-wide ascendancy at the World's Columbian Exhibition of 1893. The spirit behind it had now come to possess authority for American architecture as a whole. The Fair should, indeed, have stood in New York; it so thoroughly represented the influence of that city.[9]

Giedion, in a way, was right. There is a sense in which the Fair belonged to New York. But first it is important to understand what Burnham and his New York associates were up to and how their achievement was received and interpreted. New York's Beaux-Arts architects brought to Chicago their preoccupations with a unified neoclassical city: at the Fair, under Daniel Burnham's supervision, they nursed into reality something that was broadly urban, rather than narrowly architectural. Writing at the time, Montgomery Schuyler, the best architectural critic in America, observed that "the success is first of all a success of unity, a triumph of ensemble. The whole is better than all its parts." This claim could not be made of any American city at the time. Schuyler went on to point out that this unity derived from two decisions: first, the choice of a neoclassical architecture, and second, the regulation of cornice heights, which produced a "visually continuous skyline all around the Court of Honor." It was this horizontal visual unity that gave the Fair its public impact, not the character or architectural expression of individual buildings. Among classicists, at least, this lesson was remembered. In a major article published in *Architectural Record* (1916) under the title "Twenty-five Years of American Architecture," A. D. F. Hamlin acknowledged the "revolutionary" impact of steel framing developed in central Chicago, but he also insisted on the importance of the Exposition. It represented, he argued, the first example of American design since Thomas Jefferson's plan for the University of Virginia in which a "monumental group of buildings [was] planned as an ensemble." It was, he continued, "an object lesson in the possibilities of group-planning, of monumental scale, of public decorative splendor and harmony. . . ."[10]

In retrospect, it seems clear that the modernist preoccupation with individual buildings, with overturning the architectural style of surrounding structures, and with historically singling out the new and experimental architectural expression of any age, overlooked the aesthetic lesson that can be learned from the progressive side of the Beaux-Arts tradition. This side of Beaux-Arts classicism found its fullest realization, not in Paris, but in America, in projects deeply influenced by New York architects. The most important of these projects were the Chicago fair and the plans for Washington (1901) and Chicago (1909). It is probably accurate, moreover, to say that it was Charles McKim, whom Burnham most relied on at Chicago, who deserves the greatest credit. McKim took the lead in the collaboration with Olmsted and Burnham on the "Plan for Washington" (1901) and brought this Beaux-Arts ideal, via New York, to Burnham and Chicago. In Chicago the classical ideal was clarified and purified before returning to New York.[11]

This New York neoclassicism sought to monumentalize and unify the late–nineteenth-century city. It moved from the architecture of individual buildings to the urbanism of comprehensive planning. It stressed the street perspective, the uniform cornice, the nineteenth-century tradition of the five-story street wall. It provided, moreover, for a functional expression of new technologies of urban transportation. Giedion and other historians of modernism were able to dismiss the whole enterprise because—despite their ideology of organicism and functionalism—they focused their attention, ironically, on stylistic detail and on surface. The neoclassicists "decorated" buildings; form did not express function, nor did it reveal the building technology. That was enough, apparently, to justify dismissing Burnham and the New York architects. Giedion, preoccupied with style, did not see the important urban achievement of the Fair's neoclassicism. Such an oversight is hard to comprehend in a critic of Giedeon's intelligence, since the crisis of the industrial city was clearly one of ensemble, not one of style. Most surprising of all, differences in style made Giedion overlook the remarkable similarities between New York neoclassicism at the Exposition and ensemble designs he admired, between the *Cité industrielle* plan of Beaux-Arts rebel Tony Garnier, a hero in Giedion's story, and Burnham's *Chicago Plan*.

Garnier's plan for an "industrial" city, first developed between 1901 and 1904, though published a decade or so later, is architecturally modern in a way that Burnham's contemporaneous Chicago Plan is not. (Garnier, for example, used reinforced concrete and emphasized functional expression and the cleanness of materials.) Yet as understandings of urban form—and reform—the two are remarkably similar, even though one is the work of a European "socialist" and the other, one of corporate capitalism's most favored architects.

The impulse behind all these plans was a desire to rationalize the perceived chaos in existing cities and to link these sprawling, amorphous conglomerations of population to the countryside and surrounding communities. It is difficult for us to realize how high a priority such an object could have had, or the price those making such plans were willing to pay for their fulfillment—or even something approaching fulfillment. For such planners, transportation and movement were the fundamental reality of the city. They sought to have lines of movement converge on a city "center" that was at once functional and symbolic, a central axis in a wheel-and-spoke arrangement.

In no city were the issues faced by architects and planners as vexing, the aesthetic tensions as visible, as in New York, where in the compass of half a century, record population growth, explosive commercial and industrial expansion, and a shift to metropolitan status were heaped upon a restricted island and an old premodern city. The conflict of competing demands that resulted from these changes, and the unique character of the aesthetic treaties that resulted from it, gave New York much of its architectural interest. New York has the reputation of being a vertical city, and indeed the tall buildings crowding the Battery have long been a spectacular symbol of its modernism. Yet, if we grant modernist legitimacy to certain horizontal structures that were designed to meet its planning needs and try to see New York's vertical tendencies in building in a dialectical relationship with its horizontal development, New York turns out to have a far richer heritage of architectural invention than a simple preoccupation with unrestrained thrust for height would have given it.

When Henry James returned to the United States in 1904, he was displeased by the sight of the skyscrapers that had risen over the five-story city he had left twenty-five years before. James suggested that the thinness of American culture had rendered it incapable of resisting such expressions of unrestrained commerce. New York grew skyscrapers, he seemed to say, because it lacked the density of culture required to guide growth away from purely economic and technical considerations, because it lacked, in his words, "the ancient graces." There was no higher aspiration capable of keeping the buildings down, so they "overtopped" his beloved Trinity Church.

James' interpretation is in some ways compelling, but it is possible to read New York's development quite differently. One can see technology, economics, and a particular cultural disposition in favor of horizontal urban order interacting to form a distinctive configuration in New York City. The evidence of a sustained resistance to vertical architecture is striking. Even the look of verticality appears to have been resisted when it first appeared.

A case in point is the Haughwout Building, a cast-iron building put up in 1857 and still standing on the corner of Broome Street and Broadway, one of New York's most remarkable buildings. It is the first building to have an Otis elevator, and although it is only five stories high, Ada Louis Huxtable has credited it with anticipating all the essential elements of the skyscraper. Illustrations of this building tell us how the perception of structures shifted from horizontal to vertical during the century after its completion. This evidence of a shift is important because it points toward the essentially horizontal perception of urban form during the nineteenth century.

Two illustrations of the Haughwout Building, one a wood engraving made when the building was new, the other a photograph taken when the building was nearly a century old, provide some fascinating evidence (*Figures* 38, 39). Today, we, who have accepted the aesthetic of a vertical city, apparently view the building differently from the New Yorkers who first confronted it. The engraving makes the building look flatter, less high, and wider than the photograph does. Note also that the engraver faces the building head-on at street level, while the photographer, used to vertical perspectives, chooses a location well above street level to snap his photo. Since New Yorkers were unused to tall buildings in the 1850s, one would have thought that contemporaries would have been struck by the height of a building like the Haughwout and that an engraving might have exaggerated its height rather than diminished it. A modern photograph of such a five-story building, on the other hand, might be expected to reduce its vertical qualities. Apparently, the engraver was prepared to perceive the city in terms of horizontal rather than vertical lines.

Such a perception of the city is suggested by a contemporaneous series of drawings of New York architecture (by many hands) run in *Putnam's Magazine* in 1853. The anonymous author of this series, probably Clarence Cook, expressed the mid–nineteenth-century urban bias toward horizontalism when discussing A. T. Stewart's famous department store (1846), the Italianate structure still standing at Broadway and Chambers Street. While he admired the building, he worried that it was too tall, or that it gave the impression of being too tall. "This might have been remedied," he reflected, "by making the horizontal lines of the building more prominent than the perpendicular."[12]

This perceptual, or, if you will, cultural, resistance to verticality or height provides a crucial context for some comments of Montgomery Schuyler's concerning the slow development of the skyscraper. Writing in 1909, on the evolution of the skyscraper, Schuyler insisted that the technology and economic incentive for them were available before tall buildings were actually constructed. His discussion reveals how the technology Huxtable finds in the Haughwout Building fitted into a frame of cultural or architectural perception of the traditional five-story city. The elevator, Schuyler remarked, did not suggest an unlimited number of floors. Rather, its "humble office" was simply "to equalize the desirableness of rooms on the fifth floor with that of rooms on the second." Such was the case for nearly a decade. "Such a creature of habit is man . . . that, throughout that decade, it did not occur to anybody that the new appliance might enable the construction of taller buildings." The first building to go beyond five stories with the assistance of the elevator was the Equitable Building (1870). It went to seven. "The addition of two stories now seems timid enough; then doubtless it seemed audaciously venturesome." By the mid-1870s, the Tribune and Western Union buildings not only went higher, they expressed their capacity to rise above the traditional city in their architectural treatment, particularly Richard Morris Hunt's Tribune Building with its tower. Yet the evolution of the skyscraper in New York remained slow. Schuyler could find no technical reason for the delay in moving beyond the load-bearing wall to steel-frame construction several years before it occurred. "Necessity," he remarked, "seems to have been singularly protracted."

This resistance of nineteenth-century New Yorkers to tall buildings, interesting in itself, has dimensions other than the aesthetic. Certain architectural ideas stressing horizontal, massive, and monumental forms seem to have preoccupied them, blunting their capacity to perceive monumentality in purely vertical terms. They assumed that a monumental civic structure would have traditional horizontal lines.

This nineteenth-century configuration of urban monumentalism probably reached its fullest development with Pennsylvania Station (1906–1913). While retaining the ideal of the nineteenth-century street wall, this massive and magnificent railroad station by McKim, Mead, and White extended over two entire blocks. In fact, it faced another civic structure, the new Post Office, which monumentalized an adjoining grid. Instead of giving elevated station to this architectural quality by placing the building at the termination of a diagonal avenue—as was done, for example, in late–nineteenth-century Paris—McKim, Mead, and White achieved their purpose by making the block itself a monument.

The nearly contemporaneous Grand Central Terminal (1903–1913) continued the architectural aggrandizement of New York civic space along horizontal lines, but it did not so much monumentalize a block in the grid like Pennsylvania Station as achieve its effect through creating a megablock structure that in certain ways anticipated Rockefeller Center. It moved beyond the limits of a block on a massive scale, but rather hesitantly. By placing the station astride Park Avenue, moreover, the planners created a dramatic vista on both sides of the station, which served to elevate the avenue itself as part of the monument and incorporate north–south movement of traffic through the city into it. The circumferential drive preserves the Park Avenue street flow, while allowing Grand Central Terminal to monumentalize a view of traffic flow north and south. While Forty-third Street is blocked, the municipal authorities insisted that the fenestration on the east and west walls be aligned so that, if necessary, a bridge could carry Forty-third Street traffic through the main concourse. Quite a similar effect was obtained in McKim, Mead, and White's contemporary Municipal Building, which stood in 1911 astride an arch that permitted a clear east–west vista along Chambers Street, once again underscoring the grid, even at the cost of creating a certain neoclassical oddity. The structure of Grand Central itself does not attempt to maintain the traditional five-story wall, but it saves the general principle, simply raising the height and maintaining a uniform cornice along Park Avenue. In this quarter of Manhattan, New York Central and its landholding company created in microcosm a fulfillment of the sort of urbanism one finds in the proposals of Garnier and Burnham. Both of them focus on the hubs of rail and street traffic as the sites to monumentalize. Modern technology makes it possible for the city to accommodate the railroad underground while monumentalizing a unified horizontal perspective above ground.

The lineage just traced from the Haughwout Building to Grand Central outlines the expansion of the horizontal vision of New York before World War I in its most primitive form. Other examples of neoclassical civic architecture could be cited and discussed, such as Richard Morris Hunt's Lenox Library (1870–75), which Schuyler rated when it was built in 1895 as unrivaled for its achievement of "monumental dignity." Hunt's East Wing of the Metropolitan Museum of Art is another, similar example. While the massive New York Public Library (1911) is also an obvious example of horizontal monumentalism, realized with commodiousness and liberality, a much smaller building, one called by Schuyler "a modern classic," emphasizes that it is not a mere matter of size that is at issue. The Knickerbocker Bank (1904), on Fifth Avenue at Thirty-fourth Street, by McKim, Mead, and White, was only three stories high, but according to Schuyler its very restraint in the matter of height gives it strength. With its tetrastyle front, the building was, in Schuyler's words, "ample in scale for purposes of impressiveness. Since it holds its own against the huge mass of the many storied Astoria, it is not likely to be put out of countenance by any succeeding erection."[14] Finally, the neoclassical uptown campuses McKim, Mead, and White designed for New York University and Columbia University in the 1890s are further examples of horizontal monumentalism.

At Madison Square, however, it is possible to trace a complicated pattern of development and perception that brings us closer to the tensions between horizontal and vertical lines in the development of New York's distinctive urban aesthetic. When the Fifth Avenue Hotel opened on Madison Square in 1859, it boasted the first hotel passenger elevator in the city. Yet it was architecturally and urbanistically of a piece with the old Astor House (1836) downtown, the hotel it replaced as New York's most fashionable place to shop and be seen. Architecturally, it remained within the five- to six-story street-wall tradition, and it faced the street. Both hotels were on Broadway frontage facing a triangular park, but such siting was clearly more comfortable for the Astor House, located as it was on Lower Broadway, before Broadway came into conflict with the grid imposed on New York in 1811. With the Fifth Avenue Hotel we begin to notice some of the complexity involved in imposing horizontal order on the New York grid (*Figure 40*). Not only is the façade broken, but the multiple lines of movement produced by Broadway, Fifth Avenue, the Park, and the streetcar rails produce not only an aesthetic tension in photographs and engravings, but also personal problems of movement and orientation in the city. This tension is multiplied further when one's view widens to include the curvilinear pattern of the paths in Madison Square.

Part of the success that was achieved at Penn Station and Grand Central Terminal was the result of responding to developments in transportation technology (i.e., electrification) that allowed rail transportation—both subways and trains—to be placed underground where it would not disrupt the grid. The triumph of the street-level grid over the underground technology in defining horizontal movement in New York is embodied in the names given the subway stations. The subway lines do not follow a grid pattern, but the system surfaces only at streets on the grid. In contrast to the Paris Métro, for example, which is "place" oriented (very few stations are named for streets; almost all for places, such as L'Opéra, L'Odéon), almost all Manhattan subway stops refer to streets. What could easily have been called the Madison Square station, for example, is called the Twenty-third Street station. This tension between surface and sub-surface legibility in New York underlaid the wide discussion and controversy over the introduction of a new subway map at the end of the seventies.

When the Fifth Avenue Hotel was opened, Madison Square was a major transportation node. The depots of the New York & Harlem and the New York, New Haven & Hartford railroads were located just off the northeast corner of the square. In 1873, after the first Grand Central Terminal was opened at Forty-second Street, P. T. Barnum transformed the property into a concert garden. In 1879, it was named Madison Square Garden, and ten years later the famous Madison Square Garden designed by Stanford White was constructed on the site (*Figure 41*). White's building is fundamentally horizontal, but it points to New York's distinctive skyscraper aesthetic. White, following the New York lead of Richard Morris Hunt's Tribune Building (1873–1875), placed an expressive tower, reminiscent of the campaniles in Italian city-states, on top of a blockish building. Twenty years later, McKim, Mead, and White would do much the same thing, though with the scale vastly increased, with the Municipal Building (1911), which went up across from Hunt's earlier Tribune Building. These developments, in effect vertical towers designed to enhance buildings of horizontal monumentality, contain the germinal aesthetic of the New York skyscraper. The Italianate campanile, ironically, was fully as characteristic of this new, modern structure as the steel frame. But we are moving too fast. Actual events moved much slower. Madison Square Garden was not perceived as a precursor of the skyscraper. It was an entertainment center built along the horizontal lines traditionally appropriate for monumental public architecture.

Ten years later, south of the square, another building went up. The Fuller, or Flatiron, Building (1901), designed by the Chicago firm of Daniel Burnham, is recognized for its height and for its steel-frame construction as one of the links in the evolution of the modern skyscraper. How does it fit the context of horizontal urban perception that we have traced? Part of the answer is contained in the most famous and compelling photograph of this building, taken by Alfred Stieglitz in 1903 (*Figure 29*). It is one of the few photographs that Stieglitz talked about, and it is worth quoting him:

> In the early months of 1903 I stood spellbound, during a great snowstorm, before the Flat Iron Building. It had just been erected on 23rd Street at the junction of 5th Avenue and Broadway.
>
> Watching the structure go up, I felt no desire to photograph the different stages of its development. But with the trees of Madison Square covered with fresh snow, the Flat Iron impressed me as never before. It appeared to be moving toward me like the bow of a monster ocean steamer—a picture of a new America still in the making. . . .
>
> Recalling those early days, I remember my father coming upon me as I was photographing in the middle of 5th Avenue. "Alfred," he said, "how can you be interested in that hideous building?" "Why Pa," I replied, "it is not hideous, but the new America. The Flat Iron is to the United States what the Parthenon was to Greece." My father looked horrified. . . .
>
> Later the Flat Iron appeared rather unattractive to me, after years of having seen even taller and more extraordinary skyscrapers—the Woolworth shooting into the sky, and then still others. . . . I no longer considered it handsome, nor representative of the coming age, nor was I tempted to photograph it.[15]

Many things about this passage are of interest: Stieglitz's father's abhorrence in 1903 of a vertical aesthetic, for example, and Stieglitz's almost mystical association of urban structure with national destiny. But his evocation of the ocean steamer is of particular relevance here. The image of a ship's prow as applied to the "edge" of the triangular building suggests a horizontal, not a vertical, thrust in the development of the city and, in Stieglitz's mythos, of American culture. His image is evocative of railroads crossing the continent, or of the streetcar lines crossing in front of the Flatiron Building. Ships' prows were high, especially since, in 1900, passengers and friends walked or rode right up to the bow of the ship at nearly the waterline, but ships moved horizontally. The cornice line of the Flatiron Building, from this perspective carries the eye of the viewer, and suggests a long and continuous horizontal structure behind it, hence justifying his speaking of the building as the leading edge of a progressive American culture.

In 1903, the dynamism of American culture and urban development, at least for Stieglitz, was horizontal. Later, after a perceptual shift, verticality rather than horizontality became central to imagining progressive advance. Once there were many taller buildings to be seen, the Flatiron Building was no longer that impressive. It was caught in the shift in urban aesthetics from horizontal to vertical. When it was the world's tallest building, Stieglitz still perceived it horizontally. Once viewers became attuned to verticality in taller buildings, the Flatiron was no longer tall enough.

A clearer idea of the evolution of the New York skyscraper and the accompanying perceptual shift can still be had in Madison Square by turning our attention to the Metropolitan Life Building and Tower, designed by Napoleon LeBrun & Sons (business block, 1893; tower, 1909; *Figure* 42) across the Square. The Metropolitan Life Building accommodates the tower by placing it on top of a horizontal business block. This strategy echoes the campanile characteristic of early Renaissance Italian civic architecture, and it was not new in New York in 1909; I have already mentioned Hunt's Tribune Building and White's Madison Square Garden tower. Such a treatment of bulk—often with Italian or French Renaissance architectural detailing—was a New York tradition extending back to the era of the Haughwout Building. And its pervasiveness explains Le Corbusier's remark upon first seeing New York's skyscrapers in the 1930s:

> It is an odd thing that the modern skyscrapers are the weak ones. The Italian Renaissance skyscrapers are of excellent quality, in contradiction with what I imagined before seeing them. For, prior to 1925, Brunelleschi and Palladio were in control. . . .
>
> In New York, then, I learned to appreciate the Italian Renaissance. It is so well done that you could believe it to be genuine. It even has a strange, new firmness which is not Italian but American. [16]

The monumental scale of the Metropolitan Life Building is impressive; it fills a whole block in the grid. It goes beyond the traditional five stories, yet the power of traditional perceptual categories is strong. The architectural treatment divides the façade into six units, thus modulating its break from nineteenth-century urban scale. It is worth noting, moreover, that it is oriented more to the grid than to the park, and its primary public face is the horizontal business-block façade on Twenty-third Street, rather than, as we might have expected, given our later aesthetic assumptions, the tower side facing the park.

Comparing the two pictures of the Metropolitan Life Building shown here, both taken from Moses King's *Views of New York*, one from the 1909 edition and the other from the 1915 edition (*Figure 43*), it is possible to see an important perceptual shift within the city, one that points toward the eventual acceptance of the tower as itself rather than as a campanile. The 1909 view from south of Madison Square emphasizes the business block and shows the tower behind it. The 1915 view, by contrast, is taken from north of the square, and the tower is in the foreground and dominates the picture. To judge from these pictures, in a period of six years, monumentalism had come to be more identified with verticality. By 1961, when the tower was renovated, it was visually separated from the business block, suggesting two structures rather than one. By then, the tower could stand alone. When those 1961 renovations were undertaken, the idea of a free-standing tower caused few aesthetic conflicts, but before about 1930 the dominant urban aesthetic in New York would not have accommodated such unabashed verticality.

In 1909 the Metropolitan Life Building and the Singer Tower that Ernest Flagg placed on top of a French Baroque business block represented the basic *form* of the New York skyscraper. They differed from the strong expression of uncompromising verticality that Louis Sullivan prescribed for the tall office building and that he achieved to a remarkable degree in his only New York building—the Condit Building (1898)—perhaps appropriately, in terms of our argument, hidden away on Bleecker Street on the "wrong" side of Broadway. What Sullivan prescribed in his famous essay "The Tall Office Building Artistically Considered" (1896), was alien to New York skyscraper architecture. Sullivan wrote:

> What is the chief characteristic of the tall office building? . . . [A]t once we must answer, it is lofty. This loftiness is to the artist's nature its thrilling aspect. . . . It must be in turn the dominant chord in his expression of it, the true excitant of his imagination. It must be tall, every inch of it tall. The force and power of altitude must be in it, the glory and the pride of exaltation must be in it. It must be every inch a proud and soaring thing, rising in sheer exultation that from bottom to top it is a unit without a single dissenting line. . .[17]

Cass Gilbert's Woolworth Building (*1913, Figure 37*), the building that Stieglitz mentions in describing his devaluation of the Flatiron Building, achieved a soaring exultation that no earlier New York building had achieved. But Gilbert achieved this effect in the context of the New York campanile tradition rather than in the manner prescribed in Sullivan's essay or exemplified in his Condit Building.

From Broadway today, the Woolworth Building appears to be a tower. We do not see, unless we approach it from the rear, the familiar New York business-block base that is prominent in pictures of it at the time it was completed. It is a massive version of the New York campanile: with a difference. Gilbert, for his "Cathedral of Commerce," as it was called during the opening ceremonies, used the Gothic rather than the Renaissance motif. If you want to soar, Gothic soars toward the heavens. The height of the horizontal cornice, as well as that of the tower, surpassed anything previously built in New York, but Gilbert's concessions to the nineteenth-century city are striking. Although the business block is higher than ever before, the architecture detailing continues to associate it with the traditional five- or six-story cornice line. There is an expanded base and cornice, and there are four intermediate horizontal divisions marked by architectural treatment. This decoration of the building may be read as a failure to achieve functional expression, or it may be seen as an intentional and comforting echo of the nineteenth-century urban building tradition. For a narrowly architectural history, the former explanation is appropriate. But for any urbanistic understanding of what Gilbert was doing, the latter explanation is compelling.

Until the mid-1920s, photographs and paintings reveal resistance to verticality. The most common and striking perspective of New York's tall buildings from the 1890s through 1930s was the view of the skyline across the water. Yet such views, it must be noted, do not really take advantage of the possibilities of verticality. Instead, they array the city's tall buildings along a horizontal axis. The city, in such views, is a mountain range; the ensemble is perceptually more important than the individual peaks.

It was not until the few years between about 1925 and 1931, particularly with the publication of the New York Regional Plan volume *The Building of the City* in the latter year, that the skyscraper-as-tower got its full aesthetic justification and its first examples, with the Radiator Building (1925), the Chrysler Building (1930), and the Empire State Building (1931). During these years, two extraordinary and visionary architects, Raymond Hood and Hugh Ferriss, along with Thomas Adams, director of the Regional Plan project, rejected the skyline as mountain range in favor of the portrayal of distinct towering peaks (*Figure 44*).

Hood seems to have been the one with the initial vision that was picked up by the other two, but whatever the precise pattern of influence among the three, they articulated a new vision of the city. And the two architects, by getting their vision incorporated into the proposals of the well-connected and powerful Regional Plan Association, insured for themselves a significant hearing. Hood and Ferriss offered visions of New York as a city of widely spaced towers. Hood proposed to place towers at express stops of subways, thus using the underground transportation system rather than the street grid to define the horizontal space of the city. Ferriss, in his book *The Metropolis of Tomorrow* (1929) contrasted the coming skyscraper city with the present skyscraper city that had been built up over the past fifty years (*Figure 45*). Acknowledging the visionary thinking of Hood, he wrote of the city represented in his drawings:

> . . . we are struck by certain peculiarities in the disposition of the towers now before us. In the first place, no two of them rise in close juxtaposition to each other. . . . Also, there is a certain degree of regularity apparent in their disposal throughout; while they are not all precisely equidistant, and their relation does not suggest an absolutely rectangular checkerboard scheme, yet it is obvious that they have been located according to some citywide plan.

The bases of these thousand-foot (or more) towers cover from four to eight city blocks. In between the towers, the "wide districts . . . which make up the greater area of the city—the buildings are comparatively low. They average six stories. . . ."[18]

With Harvey Wiley Corbett, designer of Number One Fifth Avenue, the dialectic evaporates and one finds a complete—and amusing—assimilation of verticality and beauty. Writing in the *Yale Review* in 1928, Corbett explained that the vertical is always more attractive than the horizontal; it provides an effect of slenderness that is more pleasing. "We have vertical stripes on our clothes because we think they add to our appearance. And, conversely, how are ugly clothes—clothes that we do not want copied, the uniforms of convicts—how are such clothes designed? They have broad horizontal stripes. No one would willingly wear anything so hideous. In his buildings, too, man has like lines that accentuate heights and carry the eye upward."[19]

Verticality had been accommodated into a new urban aesthetic. And photography could celebrate it in a way that Stieglitz did not and could not in 1903. The new fascination with verticality is apparent in New York photography of the 1930s, in the cropping done by Berenice Abbott in *Exchange Place,* or in the exploration of the vertical lines of the Empire State Building in *The Maypole* by Edward Steichen, or in the choreography and cinematography in the 1930s movie *Forty-second Street.*

Yet one should not exaggerate, even in the 1930s, how far New Yorkers had moved from the neoclassical civic vision of Burnham at the turn of the century. The New York Regional Plan, which incorporated the ideas of Ferriss and Hood, was a direct offspring of the Chicago Plan. The two individuals most responsible for the establishment of the plan in New York under the auspices of the Russell Sage Foundation, Charles Dyer Norton and Frederick Delano, had been actively involved earlier in the Chicago Commercial Club's sponsorship of the Chicago Plan. There are, it is true, more towers (Burnham and Garnier proposed one each in their plans, while the Regional Plan—and Ferriss and Hood—proposed many), but it is, like Burnham's, an attempt to express civic unity by producing a neoclassical urban form for the modern American city.

There is more to be said about the persistence of the horizontal civic tradition. If the Empire State Building is the premier example of the skyscraper as a block-filling tower, it is important to remember that its street wall is only six stories high, as the authors of the Forty-second Street guidelines remember in specifying the relation of tower to street they desire. And recall that the public or civic extension of Rockefeller Center's Promenade is flanked by the low-rise French and British pavilions that terminate in a six-story street wall. It was undoubtedly this historical low-rise horizontal tradition for civic architecture that Lewis Mumford was drawing on when he complained in the 'forties of the unabashed verticality of the United Nations Secretariat Building, comparing it unfavorably with the New York Public Library.[20] Finally, to mention a more recent example of New York civic architecture, the neoclassical horizontalism of Lincoln Center further underscores the persistent interest in horizontal monumentality. Indeed, the relationship of Lincoln Center to the street, the gridiron, and the transportation center at the convergence of Broadway and Ninth Avenue recall all of the tensions over the horizontal cityscape that marked Madison Square at the turn of the century.

The distinction between civic horizontalism and corporate verticality was recognized, in a strikingly paradigmatic way, in the Regional Plan in 1931. In the course of a discussion of New York's architectural distinctiveness, the authors of the plan presented two pages of pictures. The first portrays public buildings; the second, business structures. All of the former are horizontal, while all of the latter are vertical.[21]

Business has appropriated the tower as a means of expressing corporate power. The feeble but not yet extinguished expression of civic life continues to find limited expression at the street level. Indeed, the particular pattern of civic "contribution"—or retribution—exacted by the City Planning Commission (in return for allowing businesses to make their symbols—and profits—of "private" power higher) derives from the New York tradition associating civic purpose with the five-story street wall, horizontalism, and street access. When, for example, Citicorp sought permission to exceed the "as of right" height for its tower on Lexington Avenue, a variety of civic demands might have been put before them. But tradition (and, consequently, the zoning laws) restricted those options to civic amenities at the street level. The city got the "Market" and a street-level church, St. Peter's. The struggle for civic authority and public space in the city will not, one hopes, be fought in the streets, but, as Citicorp and other recent corporate towers indicate, it will be fought at the street level.

FIVE

Launching a Commercial Culture ·
Newspaper, Magazine, and Popular
Novel as Urban Baedekers

In the fifty years between 1880 and 1930, New York outdistanced other large American cities in the vigor and creativity of its commercial culture. No other city matched it for the range of entertainment, theater, nightlife, and other forms of recreation that were available in New York during these years. As in other cities, the wealthy élite in New York had established cultural institutions, clubs, museums, concert halls, and opera houses that provided links of shared speakers, performers, and exhibitions with élites in other cities. New York's large working population found expression for its political and economic concerns in union halls; ethnic, trade, neighborhood associations; and mutual aid societies. [1] In New York, however, a system of cultural production distinct from élite culture and from the culture of working-class politics flourished along Broadway and worked its way north from City Hall Park to Times Square as the period progressed. Moreover, this cultural marketplace soon began to attract the patronage of an increasingly wide spectrum of the city's population.

This chapter seeks to establish the identifying features of this commercial culture, to examine how it functioned, and to suggest the needs it served. Much of what historians have written about the origins of twentieth-century mass culture has located its emerging traits in the cultural activities of this earlier period. In their rush to find forerunners in the past, historians have overlooked the richness and complexity of what they have found. [2]

By focusing on the increasing centralization of cultural forms, and failing to take account of other changes taking place within them, these historical assessments have passed over the differing ways in which urban audiences patronized them. Some historians have assumed, mistakenly, that the public was sold entertainment that was sheer diversion and irrelevant to its needs. It seems obvious from other evidence that those who consumed popular culture were being provided with experiences that helped them make sense of the new urban environment. Cultural forms, in other words, provided road maps for a new, rapidly changing urban world. Viewed from the perspectives of its patrons, New York's new commercial culture was much more vigorous and varied than existing historical discussions of it might lead one to believe.

The Rise of a Commercial Culture

I employ the term "commercial culture" rather than the more common "popular culture" in order to emphasize the distinctiveness of New York's system of cultural production and consumption before the 1930s. Commercial culture began as the culture of the nineteenth-century street, where an astonishing variety of goods and entertainment offered by itinerant peddlers and showmen was consumed in a carnival atmosphere.[3] In such a culture, the city's streets functioned as both showcase and show. What began with itinerants and storefront theatricals soon became embodied in new cultural institutions that collected and displayed goods. The vehicles for this new commercial culture were exhibition halls, popular museums, amusement parks, vaudeville theaters, nickelodeon moviehouses, and a new kind of newspaper that became the verbal and graphic equivalent of the new cultural bazaars. These new cultural emporiums retained the stamp of their street origin, especially in their miscellaneousness, the strident pitch of their promoters, and their emphasis on consumption as "show."

The remarkable success of these cultural forms was due to their unique capacity to engage consumers in "reading" the city. Each new genre of commercial culture compressed a representation of city life into its format. These new genres had in common a seemingly random, potpourri organization that continued to dramatize the discontinuity, the kaleidoscopic variety, and the quick tempo of city life, as in the vaudeville revue. Their essence was to create, out of miscellaneousness, little self-contained worlds that were perceived spatially rather than narratively and over time. Like photographs, these pastiches were susceptible to varied interpretations. They were so attractive that markets for them quickly developed in other cities, where they lost certain features of their ethnic origin and local particularity, as had happened with minstrelsy and vaudeville.

After the 1920s, however, a quantum change took place in the degree to which New York produced commercial culture for a national rather than a local market. The feedback from audience to producer declined correspondingly, gradually changing the character of commercial culture itself.

By the end of the 1920s, national network radio, theater chains, centralized motion-picture distribution, and wire-service journalism had forever changed the previous half-century's close relations between cultural producer, cultural consumer, and the city of New York, transforming them into a new mass culture.

It is hardly surprising that this kind of commercial culture developed in New York, much as it had in London and large commercial centers elsewhere. Nineteenth-century New York's economic life descended directly from that of such Western trading cities as Venice and Amsterdam centuries earlier.[4] It shared with them an extensive sea trade, constricted land area, and the absence of the heavy hand of national government authority or official cultural institutions. This last characteristic, rare among major cities of the world, gave the mercantile and business classes in each city comparatively unchecked power to shape them, unlike their counterparts in metropolitan centers such as London, Paris, and Vienna, where the interests of other classes and official cultural institutions intervened. Moreover, New York was unique among major commercial cities in experiencing settlement, economic development, and urbanization as virtually simultaneous stimuli to growth.[5] A succession of disruptive changes thus shaped its development and left their mark on its physical structure during the nineteenth century.

The spatial organization of New York reflected the growing diversity and complexity of its commercial, social, and recreational activities. The most intense cultural commerce took place in and around the major axes or squares of the city, and the central focus made its way north along Broadway from City Hall Park in the 1840s and 1850s to Times Square by about 1910. By the 1890s, Madison Square had become the focus of the city's life, serving briefly as its public center. It was here, for example, that the memorial arch was constructed in 1889 to celebrate the victory of Dewey in Manila the year before, and here also that the vast parade in honor of Dewey came to a halt before the reviewing stand of the city's notables.[6]

Inter-class and Inter-Gender Contact

A localization of class life in this period tended to lock the wealthy, wage earners, and the impoverished into distinct areas of the city. By the 1890s, each had acquired a name and a recognizable mythos, much as the Bowery, whose reputation lingered on, had done in the antebellum period. New neighborhoods, characterized by distinctive types of housing such as the apartment house and the purpose-built tenement, made their appearance on a massive scale during these years, and tended to set off the style of working-class life from that of the middle and upper classes.

Meanwhile, a new set of élite cultural institutions made its appearance after the 1870s: museums, opera houses, clubs, and other exclusive social institutions. By the end of the century, universities had withdrawn in important ways from active engagement in the city's civic life to nurture the new academic disciplines, as Thomas Bender has suggested.[7] And cultural institutions had developed to market entertainment to the lower-classes: dance halls, burlesque houses, saloons, the various concessions of Coney Island, and, after the turn of the century, the new storefront moviehouses.[8]

By contrast, many new institutions brought New Yorkers of different classes together in novel ways. These new forms of inter-class orchestration sometimes involved actual physical proximity; at other times they were vicarious and perceptual, as in the consumption of print culture, architecture, or other shared visual experiences. The different classes in the city had always shared the principal streets and other public spaces, such as Broadway and the few unpaved, grassy areas like Battery Park, City Hall Park, and Union and Madison squares. The developing transportation system and its stations was probably the single most important locus of inter-class mingling. Ferryboats, elevated and street railway carriages, and, after 1904, subways caused different classes to rub shoulders on an altogether new scale.

Other new institutions brought different classes together on a more structured, hierarchical basis. The large hotels, theaters, and restaurants brought working-class people into subservient contact with others, but the growing numbers and increasing localization of such facilities changed the scale and quality of this contact. The new, large office buildings made possible by steel-frame construction, such as the huge Metropolitan Insurance headquarters in Madison Square, brought together a working population of considerable variety. In its elevators, dining rooms, and work areas, a population varying from managers to menials daily brushed shoulders. To minimize conflict and to assure order, enormous care was exercise by Metropolitan's management to segregate this work force of over three thousand men and women by function and gender. In only a few carefully supervised areas were men and women permitted to work together. Nonetheless, the sheer number of people working in these new office spaces opened further opportunities for mutual observation up and down the social scale.[9]

Much the same can be said of the new and larger department stores that appeared during these years. They segregated employees from clientele of all classes and imposed a rigid hierarchy from the management down the power scale to buyer, to floorwalker, to clerk, to cash boy. The customers, too, were of different classes, and bought different grades of goods. The most important feature of this new social promiscuity was that large and growing numbers of working-class New Yorkers participated in, or observed, the consumption of luxury products or the new forms of commercial entertainment. [10]

A large middle-class population also traveled on the city's elevated transportation system through working-class and ethnic neighborhoods they would not otherwise have seen. New forms of class interaction and reciprocal observation thus considerably tempered the "barrio" effect of the city's domestic localization.

To the people experiencing these changes at the time, the new institutions and practices that progressively brought the sexes together in the city on a radically different basis were dramatic changes. Distinct areas of the culture, most notably politics and management, remained male preserves, but the new presence of women was especially evident in such settings as office buildings and department stores. The elaborate steps taken to segregate divisions of the workplace by gender that were initiated by Metropolitan Life Insurance and other large employers underscored the acknowledged novelties of the scene. Despite official guidelines that prescribed a rigid dress code for women and that prohibited them from taking down their hair at work, men and women were still shown at recreation with one another in company publicity of the period. Clearly, despite regulations and codes, both sexes were still forced to improvise a decorum for these new encounters at work. These encounters were especially difficult where new gender arrangements were further complicated by differences in class and authority. [11]

Women of all classes were attracted to the new retail palladiums toward the end of the century, drawn by the alluring combination of bargains and luxury goods and by the increasingly luxurious amenities such as restrooms, parlors, and tea rooms that became available to women shoppers. [12] As a result, stores and office buildings became highly sexualized environments; each area of activity developed a distinctive folklore concerning the kinds of sexual encounters afforded by this new proximity and its new set of power relations between men and women.

During this period, the city also became a major leisure resource for middle-class women. [13] They arrived first during the last quarter of the century in the department stores, larger hotels, and at theater matinees. One could almost say that the era of commercial culture begins with the entrance of women into the cultural marketplace. After the turn of the century, in Broadway cabarets, roof gardens in summertime, and in places where dancing, dining, and entertainment were offered, middle-class women for the first time joined the nightlife of the city, sometimes even unescorted. A similar change took place in vaudeville and other forms of theatrical entertainment. In the 1870s, vaudeville houses like Tony Pastor's in Union Square had catered to a predominantly male audience. After the turn of the century, Florenz Ziegfeld's and George White's spectacles were performed to almost equal numbers of men and women. By the 1920s, white men and women, in pairs or unescorted, took part in the fashionable invasion of Harlem jazz clubs and engaged in other forms of "slumming" that had by then become a regular part of middle-class leisure and recreation. Prohibition further broadened the scope of permissible, if not fully acceptable, female behavior, as the élite mingled with the underworld in the speakeasies of Hell's Kitchen.[14]

The full spatial order of modern New York had emerged by the end of the 1920s, partly as a result of three other dramatic and almost simultaneous changes in the city: the rapid development of luxury apartment housing on Park Avenue during the 'twenties after the Grand Central railroad tracks were placed underground; the equally rapid concentration of office buildings in midtown, set off by the construction of Rockefeller Center; and the flowering of Broadway as a middle-class theatrical mecca under the genius of Ziegfeld and his imitators.[15] The new connotation of Park Avenue as the home of the "socialite" (to use a 1920s neologism), was understood by everyone by the end of the decade. Both Condé Nast and Ziegfeld maintained establishments there, which they used for lavish entertainment. The Rockefeller decision to develop blocks of office buildings in the 1950s brought about the concentration of publishing and communications industries in the midtown area, with the new RCA Tower as their focus.

The Culture of Pastiche

The new cultural forms that appeared during these changes in the city mixed many different elements of the city's culture. New York began to develop an elaborate commercial culture of pastiche, derived from its culture of the streets, as early as 1869, when Horatio Alger published his first novel about street boys, *Ragged Dick*. A street derivation marks the pastiche culture after 1869. The association of popular culture with the street is, of course, very old. In the sixteenth and seventeenth centuries, streets formed the principal arteries through which the mass of Europeans received print culture: religious proclamations (often read aloud), posters, broadsides, ballads, almanacs, chapbooks, and, in France, editions of classical writers, so called *livrets bleus* (for their cheap, colored paper), were hawked in the street by peddlers, or *colporteurs*.[16] As late as 1910, moreover, the same process continued in New York, as peddlers selling candy and seltzer dispensed editions of *David Copperfield* and *Les Misérables* (the reputed best-sellers) in Yiddish on the Lower East Side.[17] Street performance also continued to be a feature of popular entertainment, as pantomimists, jugglers, puppeteers, and other showmen set up shop wherever crowds could be collected.[18]

Almost every new form of popular culture or entertainment exhibits a preoccupation with reflecting this street experience in the broadest sense. Vaudeville, the penny press, Coney Island, and Tin Pan Alley, in their inclusiveness, variety, and pacing—as well as the pitch with which they were promoted—all derive from this older street-spatial tradition of entertainment. Radio, film, and television continued to exhibit some of these characteristics well after the 1930s. Whole new cultural genres have been created to give fresh expression to it. But the culture of pastiche, partly because of its street derivation, also evoked political and ideological controversy that resonated throughout the period and after, especially in a society that was energetically embracing domesticity and the values of familial order and that saw street life or anything deriving from it as representing various ugly forms of societal subversion. Getting things "off the streets" became a by-word of middle-class reform.

The press and the theater were, so to speak, just a step off the street. During this entire period, publishing and printing, followed by the construction trades, were among the city's largest industries.[19] Apart from general periodicals, printers ground out publications for every trade and self-defined group, for every special occasion. The volume of this material has rarely been exceeded, but the close tie between printing and building seems particularly unique to New York. Accounts of new buildings habitually filled its newspapers, and newspapers themselves were housed in some of the city's most distinctive structures.[20] It was no accident, therefore, that two of the principal axes of the city were named after newspapers—Herald Square and Times Square (originally, Long Acre)—nor was it coincidental that the first tall building with an Italianate tower was Hunt's Tribune Building of 1877 on Newspaper Row, off Broadway at City Hall Park. These two newspaper axes eventually performed additional functions in transmitting New York's urban modernity: Herald Square as a center of department-store retailing, and Times Square as the focus of theater and nightlife and as a center for large municipal celebrations.[21]

The fact that commercial culture, despite moral and aesthetic opposition, attracted a widening clientele drawn from almost every sector of New York's diverse population testifies to the important functions it served for those who lived through these years. It interpreted the city, making a new social world intelligible in the volatile and changing urban arena of New York. Indeed, cultural forms were invented to "read" the city in one way or another. The juvenile novel and the city guide of the 1860s and 1870s, the newspaper short story, the color comic, and the popular Tin Pan Alley song illustrate readings of cultural change in New York. All helped create new markets for popular culture, and attracted a diverse clientele that crossed social or generational boundaries. Their format, their tenor, their market success, can show how and by whom they were so avidly devoured.

Probably no aspect of popular culture or the history of journalism has been less carefully examined than the remarkable expansion of the so-called juvenile literature and magazines for "youth" in the two decades after the Civil War. [22] Something is known of the Horatio Alger and Oliver Optic novels, but the sudden mushrooming of this phenomenon is clearly ripe for further study. *Youth's Companion*, an older magazine founded in the 1820s, for example, rapidly increased its circulation under new leadership after 1869, until by the mid-1880s it surpassed the *Ledger* to achieve the largest circulation of any magazine then published— 385,000—outside the cheap mail-order weeklies. This success was obtained by surprisingly modern promotional methods of offering premiums—books, pictures, tools—for subscriptions and renewals. As a result, it could raise its advertising rates to $2.25 an agate line, well above the rate of *Harper's Monthly, Leslie's Popular Monthly, Century*, and *The Police Gazette*. [23] Horatio Alger's first, and most successful, novel, *Ragged Dick*, was serialized in the competing New York–published *Student and Schoolmate* in 1868, the year before its book publication, as were the serialized versions of the first Oliver Optic novels, written by the magazine's editor, William T. Adams. [24] Such fiction provides interesting evidence about how this new popular literature was consumed.

The association between youth and the city already had a history by 1869, in the volumes of advice literature counseling young men on how to obtain a foothold in the city. [25] The circumstances under which Horatio Alger found a much larger audience for this kind of story—it is estimated that *Ragged Dick* sold some 300,000 copies during the century—are therefore not without precedent. The eyes of a young man were seen as a revealing perspective from which to examine the new urban industrial world. In the "reading" it gave New York, this literature prefigured the adult guidebook that would appear much later.

At the narrative level, *Ragged Dick* recounts a homeless boy's progress from the city streets to well-furnished rooms in St. Mark's Place, and from bootblack to clerk in a countinghouse on Pearl Street. Contradictions or tensions of one kind or another resonate throughout the story. It is, first of all, a strange combination of boy's adventure story and moral tract. Although *Ragged Dick*, like Alger's subsequent novels, is preoccupied with inducing boys to abandon the life of the streets for middle-class respectability, it presents a much more attractive picture of the picaresque freedom and independence of street life than it does of somewhat grim, confining, joyless rise to success: a life of bathing, saving, praying, ciphering, and cautious investment. The only indulgence that Dick allows himself is the luxurious furniture in his rooms. He spends money in this way, the book stresses, only to encourage himself to stay at home and off the streets.

Youthful readers, by contrast, would probably have found good entertainment in the whirlwind tour of the city that makes up the first half of the novel, even if they had to deal in some way with the moralizing of the plot. Dick's city is described as a boy's paradise in his accounts of his former street life, his colorful street argot, his various encounters with criminal types, and the heroic rescues that take place during this tour. One chapter is even entitled "Dick the Detective," in the spirit of future juvenile fiction. All of this interspersed with moralizing and adult commentary. Similarly, although the novel officially accepts the social system that divides the city into rich and poor, there is more than a little of the irreverence of Huck Finn in Dick's bravado and his jokes about millionaires, fancy hotels, Delmonico's, or his Erie [Railroad stock] shares.

Then, too, although the novel endorses domesticity and, in the wealthy Grayson family, presents a model middle-class home, *Ragged Dick* presents a gender-biased picture of contemporary domestic values. With the exception of the Grayson episode, the novel is entirely about men and boys, fathers and sons, boys and boys. The only women are Irish landladies; the only married couple is a parody of matrimonial mismatching. The downtown New York of the novel is a city of men, as it largely was, but even the domestic arrangements portrayed in the novel are exclusively masculine, as thirteen-year-old Richard Hunter and his friend Henry Fosdick pair off and set up housekeeping, praying and sleeping together like husband and wife.

New York is thus seen through the eyes of boys. An adult New York almost fully equipped with contemporary moral geography emerges most forcefully in the book. Early in the novel, Dick gets himself hired as a guide to a young out-of-town boy who is staying at the Astor House. For an entire day, Dick shows his young visitor the sights of the city. The New York they see, the stories Dick tells his client, and the individuals and institutions Dick singles out for description are regular guidebook fair. Only the shadowy New York of sex and sin is omitted. The tour, for obvious reasons, does not stray from Manhattan's sunny midsection into its darker parts, but in other ways it follows the content of these guides almost chapter by chapter. In guidebook fashion, Chapter 6 is entitled "Up Broadway to Madison Square." Except for the Bowery Theater, Barnum's Museum, and the Newsboy's Lodging House over the *New York Sun*, the tour focuses on features of the city a twelve- or thirteen-year-old would neither know nor care about, any more than such a boy would care about ward politics, matrimonial mismatching, or the dangers of illiteracy. [26]

In short, *Ragged Dick* can be construed as a kind of anthology of different genres of narrative, full of oddly different kinds of details and commentary, each with its own separate appeal, and appropriate for family purchase and consumption—a species of pastiche culture characteristic of the period. No one "reading" of the city can be a universal interpretation, even during this early period. Degrees of acceptance, skepticism, and outright disbelief concerning the success ethic and the city's moral geography were probably quite compatible with enjoying *Ragged Dick* as a good boy's yarn. Conversely, the novel probably satisfied an adult reader's urge for an orderly, moral, and familial world with young boys safely off the street and put to clerical work indoors, while nevertheless permitting nostalgic glimpses of cherished childhood freedom, companionship, and adventure—and even a few sly digs at the injustice of the existing economic order in the city. It also gratified middle-class enviousness of the upper classes in its portrayals of the spoiled, indulged, and dishonest children of the rich.

Many guides to the city published in the early part of this period coincided with the appearance of the Alger and Optic serializations and performed a similar function for readers. They also seem to have been directed to similarly diverse audiences, each attracted for different reasons. The New-York Historical Society contains well over thirty such guides (depending on the criteria one employs in classifying them) published before 1900. Some of these guides went through numerous editions and obviously reached a wider audience than others. [27] Quite a number were written by clergymen or others with some definable religious or missionary intent. They form a distinct and recognizable genre with remarkably similar organization and content. They are, moreover, remarkably and interestingly different from guides to the city published in the twentieth century, such as the *WPA Guide* (1939) or W. Parker Chase's *New York, The Wonder City* (1932), though, surprisingly enough, some older moral and narrative characteristics do, in fact, linger on in Chase's book, different though it is in every other way. [28]

These guides clearly were not limited in their appeal to New York initiatives, nor to visitors from out of town. The premise behind their rapid growth and apparent popularity was the desire of a wide range of readers to know about the city in a way they could not, for various reasons, from personal observation. They were, in effect, little anthologies of essays on almost every dimension of city life, characterized by the widest possible appeal to different kinds of readers. Even the order of chapters, compared with modern guides, seems random and miscellaneous, with unrelated subjects following one upon the other. These guides, in other words, appear to present still another instance of the relationship between the city's physical variety and a developing culture of pastiche. They underscore how far this peculiar kind of pastiche penetrated respectable, genteel literature in the nineteenth century.

These guides did, however, retain a fairly consistent point of view. The authors underscored their consistently moral evaluation of urban behaviors at every turn. A pervasive tactic was to delineate the moral geography of the city. This tactic emphasized a connection between behavior and location within the city. Not only were crime, vice, political corruption, art, commerce, and great wealth assigned their particular neighborhoods, but each kind of behavior was metaphorically assigned an appropriate station in a color spectrum of light and shadow. This moral mapping of the city was, of course, nothing new to this period, and probably originated in a time when only respectable streets were illuminated.

What was new was the racy company this benevolent moralism began to keep after the Civil War. *Lights and Shadows of New York Life, or Sights and Sensations of the Great City* is, in fact, the title of a popular guide published in 1872.[29] It mostly represents the genre, including authorship by a clergyman, the Rev. James D. McCabe, Jr. The early chapters of the guide are consistent with a surviving civic conception of the city as a subject with chapters (in the order of their appearance) on the harbor, city government (including the Tweed Ring), the major polite streets and public spaces such as Central Park, the press, the police, Wall Street, and such public facilities as hotels, restaurants, streetcars, and ferries. A chapter on Horace Greeley, one of the many biographical sketches characteristic of these guides, conforms to this civic model for the city. But after this point, a jumble of miscellaneous subjects crowds its way into McCabe's account. Chapters called "Black Mailing" and "Female Sharpers" are sandwiched between chapters on Henry Ward Beecher and Jerome Park. A sketch of Commodore Vanderbilt is followed by a chapter called "Bummers," one on James Gordon Bennett by a chapter on drunkenness, and one on Peter Cooper by "The Heathen Chinee."

This long final section communicates an overwhelming impression of exploring terra incognita, an utterly new and different kind of moral space where older values, norms, and relationships no longer apply. This was not a society, furthermore, over which men of McCabe's stripe imagined themselves as exercising much control. On the contrary, a sense of class and moral disorientation pervades the text.

The anomalous character of this new city life frequently outran the expressiveness of ordinary English, reducing McCabe to listing the distinctive argot that pertained to crimes and various forms of vice, just as Ragged Dick delighted in passing on to Frank Whitney bits of slang, like what was meant by a "swell," to give him the flavor of street life and the kinds of skulduggery that characterized it. At one point, McCabe included an entire glossary of criminal terms.[30] At another, he quotes Brace's observation that boys came into the Newsboys' Lodging House without real names, known only as "Tickle-Me-Foot" or "Cranky Jim" or "Wandering Jew." Tenement-house life is deemed sufficiently peculiar to warrant a graphic illustration of a cross-section of such a domestic novelty, showing the astonishing variety of social life that can take place simultaneously in such a structure.[31]

These guides, in other words, had a multifaceted interpretive character shared with other kinds of popular commercial culture, such as architecture and photography. The many contradictions in the possible significance of these culture forms thus become comprehensible. For example, the pervasive evocation of light as moral metaphor—of darkness, shadow, and vice on the one hand; and of light, brightness, and virtue on the other—displays an almost Manichaean ambivalence about the new urban world. New York was wonderful, beautiful, the Paris of America, a paradise for women (middle-class, of course); yet it contained areas of unprecedented moral slime, abasement, misery, and corruption. Such contradictions seem merely confusing until we consider how they must have been read.

The superficially odd arrangement of chapter topics and illustrations, their miscellaneous substance, and their format invited casual browsing and dipping into for this or that detail or subject, rather than reading through from cover to cover, as in the seventeenth-century almanacs, chapbooks, and devotional books analyzed by Roger Chartier. Their length of 700 or 800 pages militated against such a sequential reading, as did the scores of short, choppy chapter headings. It would be a mistake, therefore, to consider the persistent moralizing in these volumes as reflecting the mentality of their readership or to assume a direct relationship between moral tone and audience response. Preachments apart, readers doubtless used these books as guides to the very vices they were being warned against. Moral rhetoric represented a threshold for entering into close scrutiny of many subjects. Moral condemnation, or at least cautionary prefacing, was the eye of the needle through which any consideration of sexual conduct was forced to pass.

After the 1880s, the daily newspapers, especially the evening and Sunday editions, provide the best examples of how this process worked. Without doubt, they became the single most innovative area of New York's blossoming commercial culture, far more fluid and responsive to change than juvenile literature or popular guides. No single figure had a greater impact on this process of cultural innovation and market extension than Joseph Pulitzer, publisher of the *New York World*. Pulitzer perceived with great clarity that a successful newspaper must acquire a readership in every class of the city and appeal to many different kinds of readers if it was to earn its share of the advertising bonanza that became available during this period.[32] By the end of the century, Pulitzer and William Randolph Hearst, who acquired the *New York Journal* in 1896, could both boast of daily circulations of close to a million, and a Sunday circulation approaching a million and a half or more. By one estimate, one out of six New Yorkers purchased a daily paper by 1900, and almost half the population purchased one on Sunday.

Other quantitative changes in newspapers created an equally important context for the expression of cultural change. The size of newspapers expanded enormously: from four pages in the 1870s to sixteen pages or more by the end of the century, with Sunday papers even larger. Advertising, rather than income from sales, became the basis of profitability, and the price of daily papers had dropped from three cents to one cent by 1900; the voluminous Sunday paper sold for five cents. Advertising boomed. The volume and rates in New York papers were by far the highest in the country. The actual amount spent on national newspaper advertising appears to have doubled every decade between 1870 and 1900, reaching an estimated total of $140,000,000 by the end of the century.

Equally evident changes in content, format, and promotion accompanied these quantum changes in market and help explain them. The *World* institutionalized features that had appeared elsewhere by devoting specific space or departments to items of interest to particular groups: sports reporting, fashion news, household tips for women, and other special features with wide appeal to readers. The *World* instituted polling as a basis for distinctive news reporting about changes in public opinion. In a bow to the city guides, an Episcopal minister was sent to live in Hell's Kitchen to report his experiences to the Sunday *World*. A New York shop girl was asked to review a play about a London shop girl; and Elizabeth Cochran (Nellie Bly), the paper's ace woman reporter, beat the record of Jules Verne's Phineas Fogg by circling the globe in 1889 in just over seventy-two days in a blaze of *World*-sponsored publicity.[33]

Dramatic changes in newspaper format were equally significant during the 1880s and 1890s. Multicolored ads, experiments in type size and color that led to banner headlines, and a front page that contained promotional stories in boldface type and other stories in boxes or in type of varying sizes were being used by both the *World* and the *Journal* by the time of the outbreak of the Spanish–American War, itself a newspaper event in New York. Along with the introduction of color and the variety of new graphic illustrations, these format changes visually transformed newspapers in this period.

By the end of the nineteenth century, the private corporations that supplied large cities like New York with a new kind of journalism had become of major economic interest. The process of chance could be characterized as going from community bulletin board to commercial billboard—exactly the characterization used by James Parton in the 1880s to protest the new style of illustrated, multicolor advertising. "Gentlemen," he exclaimed, "this is not advertising, this is billposting."[34] It was no coincidence that both Pulitzer and Hearst nursed political ambitions, since the *World* and the *Journal* had pieced together conglomerate readerships, drawn to their papers by one feature or another, in much the same way as political constituencies, those shifting coalitions characteristic of the period, were pieced together in campaigns. Pulitzer, who successfully ran for Congress from New York in the late 1880s, was especially clear about the analogy between journalism and politics. "I wish to address the whole nation," he once said of the *World*, "not a select committee."[35]

The question of how the readership made use of this journalism therefore becomes paramount. It would be easy to assume, as most historians have, that this strident new form of print culture dominated the thinking of increasing numbers of the city's population, setting trends in dress and entertainment, whetting the popular appetite for accounts of crime and sexual scandals, and setting the tone of political discussion—even fomenting war. Such an interpretation has the press by the 1890s feeding the appetites of semi-literate and newly literate ethnic and working-class populations with a kind of integrated "culture of compensation" that robbed them of class and ethnic consciousness by pandering to their curiosity and baser interests. Such an interpretation probably springs in part from the difficulty of showing that it may have been otherwise, as well as from the absence of the kinds of evidence historians are accustomed to employing. Most important, such a view is attributable to the naïve assumption that consumers read these papers from cover to cover and took the contents at face value.

By the 1890s, the Sunday *World* had become a remarkable example of New York's culture of pastiche: it offered something for almost every taste. It provided entertaining features that were subject to many interpretations by readers differing in class, age, and gender. As competition with Hearst heated up toward the close of the decade, the *World* added still more features and departments to hold its place in the market, and took the perilous step of reducing the price of its daily evening paper, the edition bought by the city working population, from two cents to one cent. A typical Sunday paper in this period would include a few pages of hard news; perhaps an editorial in boldface, large type, or boxed; crime stories; reports of sporting events; a society column; illustrated theatrical spreads; short fiction; a feature article on a famous literary or artistic personality; advice to working girls; household hints; and a discussion of manners. By the middle of the decade, the Sunday *World* began to include color comics in a section that rapidly grew from one or two to eight pages.

A close look at two new Sunday features, the color comic and the newspaper short story, may help us understand how this new kind of culture was consumed. Both genres were different from their closest antecedents and both evidently attracted a wide and expectant readership of a kind once attracted by serialized novels. Moreover, these features can best be explained by how they helped commercialize newly acquired leisure time in New York, rather than as part of a process of working-class indoctrination.

In 1894, Morrill Goddard, then Sunday editor of the *World*, introduced a comic color picture by Richard Felton Outcault, part of a continuing feature involving the adventure and antics of a group of slum kids, entitled "Hogan's Alley." There had been comic pictures and even primitive comic "strips" before, but the color pictures appearing in the *World* marked the beginning of a new era in serialized caricature, one that attracted wide and enthusiastic attention. Circulation figures reflected the success of this and other Goddard innovations, rising from 266,000 in 1893 to 450,000 in 1896.[36]

The central figure in "Hogan's Alley" was an urchin of toddler age with a vacant, toothless grin, always portrayed in a bright yellow dress. He quickly captured the public imagination, eventually giving his name, "The Yellow Kid," to the series and the designation *yellow* to the penny press in general. He was the first in a succession of picaresque children and childlike animal figures to enter the public domain and to take on a kind of life of their own.

The Yellow Kid and a succession of other comic figures, both in single pictures and, after 1897, in strip form, provide a case study of pastiche culture and how it must have been consumed. The key to success, it would appear, lay in creating a figure that was, first of all, socially prismatic, a figure whose behavior would have comic significance to those approaching it from different social perspectives. Ridicule of genteel middle-class convention, ethnic peculiarities, or mischievous violence against adults could be interpreted in many ways. Rudolph Dick's practical-joking "Katzenjammer kids," which began running in 1897 in the *Journal*, delighted children for a generation with their unruly manners and was regularly used by adults to point out a moral about the fruits of bad conduct.

Class interloping was another characteristic of color comics. Moreover, these comics were entirely preoccupied with leisure and public space. Almost no one works, any more than anyone goes home. Events take place on the streets. Leisure life, furthermore, is treated as the novelty it was for most readers. In the comics it is pursued with a new kind of energy and zest. The Yellow Kid of "Hogan's Alley" and Buster Brown, as well as their English "uncle," Alley Sloper, are always portrayed as "on the town," never in the slums. They go to, or turn up at, the fashionable city places and country resorts or, indeed (in the case of Buster Brown), travel to Europe. Despite the fact that the Yellow Kid is a toddler and Buster Brown only seven or eight, they get around the city unescorted. "Say, Tiger," Buster Brown exclaims to his dog in one sequence, "meet me at Herald Square at 5 o'clock. We'll go to a French restaurant, and then we'll go to the theater."[37]

These comics, in other words, provide still another reading of the city, one that consistently portrays it, often quite literally, as a kind of playground rather than the place of work it had been earlier to Ragged Dick. The attention focused on comic heroes clearly derived from their distinct individuality, even peculiarity, and their style in confronting the social world of the city (with admirable bravado, comic innocence, or foolish ignorance, depending on one's point of view). One appeal of the comics that enabled them to satisfy so many different kinds of appetites was the deft way they singled out the individual and energized his confrontation with mass society.[38]

The first single-paper color comics were clearly designed to be read in a particular way but not in any particular order. You could start anywhere, as with a newspaper itself, and stop anywhere without a sense of incompletion. In a particular episode from "Hogan's Alley," one could begin with the signboards in the background, which parody popular ads, or with the boxed "jokes" at the foot of the page, none of which associates in any way with the picture; or, indeed, one could focus on the baseball game with its comic disregard for the decorum of the diamond. Each picture contained jokes that were purely visual, and others that were purely textual, thereby allowing for varying degrees of literacy and appetite for English and for print culture.

Although more transitory than the color comic, the newspaper short story may provide even more revealing insights into the period. William Sidney Porter, who wrote under the name of O. Henry, almost single-handedly created the form of short story that flourished briefly after the turn of the century. No one after him practiced it with the same success. For a few short years between Porter's arrival in the city in 1902 and his death there of acute alcoholism in 1910, his stories provided a reading of the city that belongs to that historical moment in the same way that the *New Yorker* short story, created by John Cheever and others, belongs to the period around World War II.

City stories were the staple of Porter's New York years, although he continued to write about the picturesque criminal types in the Southwest that had first brought him attention. In his best stories, Porter's New York is not the city of the rich and established, nor even that of the apartment-dwelling middle classes. Upper- or genteel-class figures pop up as narrators and sometimes set the tone and voice, but his favored terrain was the bars, dance halls, and dives of Hell's Kitchen, the Tenderloin, the Bowery, and the seedy rooming houses on the lower West Side, or what he called "Brickdust Row," a world of the defeated and the transient. His central characters live on the fringe: losers, drifters; especially women locked into hopeless, humiliating, frustrating, and lonely lives.

Living semi-clandestinely as a kind of outsider in the city, Porter identified in a powerful way with its oppressed, the "little people" who held menial, tedious, thankless jobs, such as waitresses and laundry employees, and its large population of female clerks or "shop girls" (though he despised the term). Porter's stories are notable, furthermore, for their attention to people at work, especially women. So many stories touch on the plight of women working in department stores, for example, that Vachel Lindsay once referred to Porter as "the little shop girls' knight."[39] His city was one of hard work, fleeting pleasures, sexual vulnerability, and, for many of his characters, an ineluctable but unspecified fate. He could be seen as taking the moral geography of McCabe's guidebook and turning it upside down or inside out. His empathy for those who lived in McCabe's moral shadows and his contempt for those who victimized or exploited them produced a very different, if still ambiguous, reading of the city.

The evocative power of these stories gives them much of their present poignancy and literary interest. A succession of arresting images brings turn-of-the-century New York to life. In "The Unfinished Story," the ironic brilliance of Broadway at night looms over the weary figure of Dulcie as she walks home from The Biggest Store to her furnished room on the far West Side:

> The streets were filled with the rush-hour floods of people. The electric lights of Broadway were glowing—calling moths from miles, from leagues out of the

darkness around to come in and attend the singing school. Men in accurate clothes, with faces like those carved on cherry stones by the old salts in sailor's homes, turned and stared at Dulcie as she sped, unheeding, past them. Manhattan, the night-blooming cereus, was beginning to unfold its deadly, heavy-odored petals.[40]

In a litany, Porter lists the contents of a furnished room, things that have been left behind by a succession of defeated people, a kind of literary equivalent of the blues:

> A polychromatic rug like some brilliant-flowered rectangular tropical islet lay surrounded by a billowing sea of soiled matting. Upon the gay-papered wall were those pictures that pursue the homeless from house to house—The Huguenot Lovers, The First Quarrel, The Wedding Breakfast, Psyche at the Fountain. The mantle's chastely severe outline was ingloriously veiled behind some pert drapery drawn rashly askew like the sashes of the Amazonian ballet. Upon it was some desolate flotsam cast aside by the room's marooned—a trifling vase or two, pictures of actresses, a medicine bottle, some stray cards out of a deck.[41]

This aesthetic potpourri of New York's transient working population and their fleeting moments of pleasure—Masie in "Gents' Gloves" had twice gone to Coney Island and ridden the "hobbyhorses"—gives these stories an historical authenticity.

Even Porter's best stories bring a literary manner—voice, tone, and skill in the manipulation of plot—that develops in tension with his strong empathy for his subjects. They involve a complicated conflict between Porter's head and heart. Archness and cleverness are almost always at war with his sensibility and compassion. In many of his stories, these qualities tend to trivialize the lives of his characters by making them into marionettes dangling from the strings of his cleverness. His witticisms and mannerisms jar at times, undercutting what is humane in his vision of the city. Few modern readers will find his jokes funny, any more than they would be amused by those in color comics of the same period.

Something about the atmosphere of the time, the irritants, anomalies, and disparities that form the basis of a period's humor, has been lost to us. Porter's cherished "little people," the working population of the city, appear instead to be at once dehumanized and sentimentalized, as in his famous "Gift of the Magi," his surprise ending, his patronizing turns of phrase. On occasion, his working-class characters become the butt of upper-class "in" jokes, as when a flirtatious waitress is invited by a customer "to go to Parsifal" with him, and she virtuously replies, "don't know where Parsifal is, but not a stitch of clothing goes in the suitcase until the ring is on." On other occasions, a story exposes the terrible vulnerability of his characters like a raw nerve. In "The Brief Debut of Tildy," a homely Irish girl, unable to find an escort, takes an Italian boy to a dance, disguising him with an Irish name. Her humiliation comes when he pulls a knife in a fight on the dance floor and "everyone knew he was a dago." In another story, an unattractive waitress no one has ever flirted with, assumes, mistakenly, that a man has finally made a pass at her, and tells all her friends. This story, too, ends with disappointed humiliation.

In "Brickdust Row," Porter's last story in the Sunday *World*, a young "slum lord" wanders from his club and, out of boredom and curiosity, decides to visit Coney Island. On the ferry he meets a young woman whom he accompanies through the evening. As the night progresses, his impressions of Coney Island are transformed by his feelings for her. At first, he sees it as a tasteless pandemonium: "the mob, the multitude, the proletariat . . . shrieking, struggling, hurrying, panting, hurling it-self . . . into sham palaces of trumpery." Then, through his empathy, he sees it as he feels she must see it: "Here, at least, was the husk of Ro-mance, the empty but shining casque of Chivalry . . . the magic carpet that transports you to the realms of fairyland. . . . He no longer saw rabble, but his brother seeking the ideal."[42]

At the end of the story, he discovers that his companion of the night lives in one of his own tawdry brick row houses, "third floor back." He responds with a despairing shout the next day to his rental agent to do something about Brickdust Row: "Remodel it, burn it, raze it to the ground," he exclaims, "but, man, it is too late, I tell you, it's too late, it's too late." This story, perhaps better than most, suggests the social char-acter of Porter's fiction. His central character begins as a rich club member with the social and aesthetic views of James Huneker—who did in fact describe Coney Island in almost the same language—and leaves him, after his sentimental holiday, just where he began. His vague, sentimental embrace of Coney Island and the girl, like his brief outburst of anger and despair, shows neither real change nor the possibility of it.

These sentimental accounts of the relations between classes in the city have a specific historical meaning: empathy without political compassion. They reduced the scale of human suffering to what atomized individuals endured as their plucky, sad lives were recounted week after week for almost a decade.

How were such stories interpreted at the time? First of all, their senti-mental reading of oppression, class differences, human suffering, and affection helped create a new language for interpreting the city's complex society, a language that began to replace the threadbare moralism that New Yorkers inherited from nineteenth-century readings of the city. This language localized suffering in particular moments and confined it to specific occasions; it smoothed over differences because it could be read almost the same way from either end of the social scale. O. Henry stories demanded only a brief dispensation of emotion from their newspaper readers once a week and asked for little more. As many composers of popular songs soon learned, the sentimental was a miraculous form of social glue with a virtually unlimited national market.

Porter's stories appealed to the whole social spectrum. People like to read about themselves, just as they enjoy photography where their faces figure. The only place working people could read about themselves and find some understanding of their lives was in Porter's stories. They probably did not notice the lapses of tone or patronizing observations that we perceive. The self-conscious literary manner of these stories, their unintelligible or obscure references, must have given many readers a secure sense that they were encountering genuine literary culture. For readers in other classes, they satisfied a growing curiosity about the city's working-class and underworld populations, just as the guides to the city's shadowy areas had done earlier. In short, O. Henry stories offered a gratifying, innocuous form of slumming, sprinkled with interclass romances where millionaires marry working girls and take off into the sunset. These, too, would have appealed to either end of the social scale. The literary flaws detectable in these stories, then, help explain the breadth of their appeal. Their focus on the individual's plight, the absence of social or political implications, and their ideological neutrality, must have helped woo a wide range of readers who would have taken flight at anything resembling political partisanship or passion.

The same kind of crystal-ball universality characterized popular music. The world of popular songs written, published, and promoted after 1900 is a story in itself, and requires careful, separate analysis.[43] A few observations about Tin Pan Alley bring the analytical focus into final resolution, because the changes Porter and others initiated in reading soon permeated the music industry. Popular songs quickly became commercially formidable on a national scale unrivaled until the flowering of radio culture in the 1930s. Between 1900 and 1950, over 300,000 songs were copyrighted, the bulk of them before World War II.

The popular song was a perfect embodiment of the culture of pastiche emerging in New York. Song content was a miscellany of trivial, personal observations—"Where do they go, those smoke rings I blow?"—and as a genre could be read in almost any way. A melodic line could simply be hummed, or whistled, without words. One could be content with a single verse, or only snatches of lyric. References were almost entirely limited to romantic love. These songs soon became the most inter-referential of popular media. Songs about songs were not long in making their appearance. Popular music, therefore, spun the securest, most cocoonlike world of evocative emotion through an aura of romance and nostalgia that also limited its range.

"Bei Mir Bist Du Schoen" ("To Me You're Beautiful"), one of Tin Pan Alley's most legendary success stories, is a case in point. It was a Yiddish song sung and sold by Lower East Side peddlers in the mid-1930s. A bit later, it was "swung" by two appreciative black musicians, who sang it in Yiddish at the Apollo Theater in Harlem. Two Jewish musicians who heard it in the Catskills added English lyrics and therefore bypassed publishers' resistance to foreign lyrics. It was introduced nationally and made a hit by the then unknown Greek-American Andrews Sisters, who became, through the song's immediate success, the first female vocal group to sell a million records. By 1938, the song climbed to the top of "Your Hit Parade" and had become the theme song of a popular film about marriage, starring Dana Andrews.[44]

The story of "Bei Mir Bist Du Schoen" is, in other words, a microcosm of the cultural transformation that overcame New York in the succeeding quarter-century. Popular music after 1910, the year of Porter's death, was the single most important ethnic-group contribution to the city's commercial culture. It was almost exclusively the creation of the European Jews who had settled on the Lower East Side. An intricate network within this community recruited talent from piano-laden tenements and saloons with singing waiters, and promising young singers in local synagogues, and gave these singers a place in an expanding musical culture. What began on the Lower East Side, the Tenderloin district, and Harlem, became a national phenomenon.

The mushrooming of ethnic expression into national currency is underscored by the career of Irving Berlin, the dominant figure in Tin Pan Alley for almost fifty years. "Irving Berlin is American music," Jerome Kern once remarked.[45] Berlin arrived on the scene just as Tin Pan Alley was expanding into a vigorous national industry, and he participated in every phase of its development before he retired in the 'fifties. Tin Pan Alley from the beginning was built on market strategies that originated in New York—on "boomers" and "pluggers" whose business was to bring new songs to the attention of the public in music stores, dime stores, and on the streets. Even the exceptions to the Jewish origin of popular songs are instructive. Cole Porter, for example, was a Yale-educated Episcopalian, the son of a millionaire from Indiana, yet he once confessed to Richard Rodgers, when they met by accident in Venice, that early failures had taught him the secret of popular songs: "write Jewish tunes."[46] This irony has a further twist, since Cole Porter drew the melodies of romantic songs such as "My Heart Belongs to Daddy" from a Yiddish melodic tradition (featuring minor keys) in which romantic love played no part.[47]

The body of popular song created in New York by the 1930s subsequently formed part of a national culture that circulated over the radio and through Hollywood films. But it remained the product of New York culture at a particular moment, the moment when New York's immigrant Jews had little other access to recognizable forms of success; when "coon" songs, ragtime, and jazz emerged from the black ghetto; and when managerial and entrepreneurial talent arose from the Lower East Side. New technologies appearing at this moment made this cultural product generally and suddenly available, as the penny press had a generation earlier. However wide its circulation, this music never lost its New York flavor or its roots in New York's spatial arrangements and its commercial culture of pastiche.

The consumption of print, graphic, and other forms of commercial culture was only a part of the class life of New York's working population (to mention only one segment of the audience). Existing studies have emphasized the ideological intent of those who produced and distributed such culture and pointed to the narrowed options given to working-class consumers. From the consumers' point of view, however, these new cultural genres provided the least oppressive component of daily life. They may even have raised expectations, and hence fired demands, for a better life among those who regularly patronized them. The new newspapers, the popular songs, and the graphic and photographic art had an open and nonprescriptive format for consumption. For those who produced these cultural products, success in marketing them was the first concern. For the different groups within the city's population who consumed them, their plasticity and suggestiveness were the most important, since these qualities allowed for various interpretations. Varied interpretations meant broader markets and greater sales. At the same time, this seeming openness and the multiple options it provided readers was itself a product of the marketplace. The success of any particular genre or cultured product was wholly dependent on its profitability. What consumers received was therefore restricted to what sold.

The so-called mass culture that emerged after the 1920s did not wholly transform this older commercial culture; certainly not overnight. This probably explains why commercial and mass culture are typically confused. Historians and other students have ritually criticized mass culture as formulaic, culturally rootless, and trivializing. Much the same charges were made against commercial culture at the end of the nineteenth century; they have been repeated about the popular culture of almost every previous era. I contend, however, that the significance of commercial culture lies in how it helped consumers from across the social spectrum "decode" the city.

Commercial culture's vital and complex origins continued to characterize mass culture even as national markets incorporated locally created genres after the 1920s. Early films did not eclipse Broadway musical shows but drew upon and exploited their songs, dramatic material, and New York background. The comic style developed in early films by Charlie Chaplin and Buster Keaton rose above the standards of either the English music hall or the vaudeville stage. Since these later forms were produced for different audiences with different needs and a different relationship to their production, this evolving mass culture was based, one might say, on a different New York. It was no longer the city experienced by those who lived and worked there before the 'thirties, but one abstracted from history, a city for tourists, a city frozen in time, and hence part of a national mythology about big cities. But that is a different story.

In the era before the rise of mass media, New York's commercial culture operated, not as the instrument of one class's dominance over another, but as an arena where all classes could find some genuine, if fragmentary, representation of their experiences. As a pastiche of such new experiences, this commercial culture was a creature of the marketplace, like the culture of the street that preceded it, and was designed to be accessible, if not equally attractive and appealing, to all.

SIX

Times Square as a National Event

It is interesting to speculate about the significance of Times Square as a central entertainment district. Its location in the center of modern New York, its concentration of New York's entertainment activities, the striking visual impact that it had at its peak, and the equally striking character of the district in its decline raise interesting questions, not just about New York, but about urban cultures more generally. What, for example, underlay the centralizing tendencies in areas like Times Square? What more general changes in the society had to occur before such a cultural development could take place? Why did concentration take place when and where it did? What did this kind of development circa World War I mean for New York? for the rest of the country? What explains the national outreach of Times Square entertainment? What, finally, were the reasons for the decline of the area, and what consequences has this had for the city? To answer these questions is to relate a history that is necessarily both local and national. Basically it is, as John Agnew has said, the "story of the rise and fall of a distinctive American popular culture in the city,"[1] but it is also more than this. Americans have a tendency to isolate New York from the mainstream of national culture and to see its preoccupations as peripheral. It seems evident, on the contrary, that Times Square developed as an integral part of cultural changes taking place nationally; that it was a cause as well as an index of those changes.

What were the cultural signals sent out across the nation from the Square? A Broadway style including everything from neon lights and publicity hype to dress and a distinctive manner of speech had somehow, it seems clear, worked its way beneath our skin as a nation by some time in the 1930s. How did it get there? There are some fairly obvious answers. Broadway was the center of American theater during the first half of the century. For most of this period it was the center of a music industry, Tin

Pan Alley, that had serenaded American cities and towns with over a million songs since the turn of the century. Syndicated journalism, network radio, and Hollywood studios as national media began to use the entertainment district as a base of operations after the 'twenties. Broadway, as a result, was perceived almost everywhere as the hub of show business and entertainment generally. To put it in the language of advertising, New York had been "imaged" nationally as a kind of city of the night where the drumbeat of commerce never relents and the lights never go out.

It is amazing that it has taken cultural historians so long to get to Broadway as a national event, or chain of events, especially given the new work on urban cultures that has recently appeared. For those of us working singly, studies have necessarily been limited to particular facets and genres of urban culture. It may have required a collaborative study like the recently published *Inventing Times Square* to mount the assault.[2] Earlier studies of urban popular culture appear to have been more interested in indicting the mass media as manipulative forces than in understanding the process through which urban entertainment evolved, became centralized, and was later dispersed into mass media. It now seems important to understand the significance of the period in which mass media evolved from entertainment concentrations such as Time Square. In settling on such an inquiry we probably have the late Warren Susman to thank for reminding us that our cities hold a store of myths and folklore more germane to understanding our identity as an ethnically and racially plural nation than more frequently consulted rural myths and traditions. To interpret urban popular culture in this light is therefore part of a larger inquiry into who we are as a society.

Times Square, in fact, can be made to function as a kind of historical prism that refracts elements of a changing national culture. It seems clear now that many different kinds of initiative brought such a central entertainment district into being. Times Square did not just happen; it was invented. Deliberate tactics and strategies were employed to shape the cultural productions of the area. The bustling cultural scene of the 1920s and 1930s was not inevitable; it was contrived. It appears to have resulted from many different kinds of business decisions that, in turn, succeeded in giving the area its concentrated commercial energy and visual distinctiveness. Its colorful commercial character, too, was not predetermined. The *New York Times*, when it gave its name to the square upon arriving in 1905, foresaw its development as the city's public center rather than the gaudy entertainment center it soon became. We are reminded on New Year's Eve that another, competing idea of the area as a central public square still survives.

Structural changes in economics, culture, and religion had to take place in order to make Times Square possible. Changes in the economy, first of all, were crucial in bringing about the kind of concentrated consumption of entertainment provided by the Square. The emergence of a new interest in mass-produced goods and standardized consumption by the end of the nineteenth century, started things going.[3] The twentieth-century meaning of "consumption," in fact, did not even exist in 1900. The ensuing changes in production, distribution, and consumption style, fired by the unleashing of retail credit, created the first consumer culture during the 1920s. This new consumer world ran into a brick wall in 1929, only to resume its revolutionary development on a worldwide scale in the decades after World War II, finally bringing the blue-jeans revolution to Red Square itself.

The colorful segment of midtown radiating out from Times Square, with its concentration of entertainment, promotion, and display, became by the 'twenties an epicenter of these new promotional and consumption styles. This Times Square reflected the stepped-up pace of the advertising industry and of the service economy more generally. Brokering activities on Wall Street and the recent concentration of corporate headquarters, especially in the new advertising and communications industries, were helping shape the Square into an entertainment hub of the nation. This process was also enhanced by the increasing centrality of New York in world markets.

The appearance at a critical moment of the "broker" launched consumer culture. Brokers, through their intervention at all levels of the economy, were so successful in rationalizing the promotion and marketing of goods that by the 1920s they had helped create what one of them called "a staggering machine of desire."[4] Consumers, it appears, often without any conscious recognition, had been living in a heady atmosphere of promotion, advertisement, and enticement that must have penetrated into every corner of the culture and succeeded in altering the perceived reality of everyone who was exposed to these transforming new experiences.

The cultural changes required were equally drastic. A developing tourist industry, employing new marketing strategies of "tie-ins" between rail companies, hotels, and other purveyors, and offering discount fares and massive promotions, was able to target cities as attractive places to visit and vacation in, thereby helping reverse an older, nineteenth-century assumption that cities were pestilential, noisy, and unattractive—places to avoid rather than seek out. Picture postcards, in turn, helped single out distinctive urban sites worthy of a visit and in this way led to the creation of the kinds of urban Baedeker itineraries we take for granted in modern travel. The street became a center of attraction for those who came to find their recreation in observing the life of large cities. City residents inevitably followed suit. In a sense, the consumer revolution came to feed on itself, since the busy commercial areas of the modern city turned out to be among its principal tourist attractions.[5]

In these developments there was, for both visitors and residents, a marked enhancement of the visual, as opposed to the older moral, assessment of urban experience. More and more, in interpreting what they saw and felt, urban people were encouraged to believe their eyes rather than scripture. They therefore read the city in new and exciting ways. Besides printed ads, corridors of illuminated signs by night and colorful billboards by day created visual excitement throughout the city about products and locations so promoted. Strategies in advertising like the "tie-in," moreover, encouraged consumers to see products in relation to other desired objects or experiences.

Consumer products during the 'twenties began to assume their modern place in personal aspirations, personal dreams. Christian churches well into the nineteenth century had roundly condemned such aspirations for visual pleasures and worldly goods, dancing and entertainment, just as they had viewed almost everything about the commercial life of cities as little better than John Bunyan's Vanity Fair. Liberal churches at the end of the nineteenth century elected in a startling shift in direction to "take on" the world rather than reject it. The result was a gradual shift in perspective within Protestant churches that encouraged properly circumspect worldly recreation and pleasure.[6]

Why the headquarters and marketing center of theater and entertainment should have been located in New York and why and how this concentration of commercial entertainment became lodged in Times Square are important questions.[7] During the nineteenth century, New York became the marketing center of the nation and the largest *entrepôt* for overseas trade. As its commercial volume grew and heavy manufacturing moved west, New York retained its stranglehold on credit, banking, and market-sensitive manufacturing in women's clothing, luxury goods, fashion, and publishing. As a major center of publishing and market information and as the nation's largest seaport and the terminus of a national railway network, New York very early became an important destination for commercial travelers and a national barometer of what was fashionable, what was exciting, and what was new.

The process through which Times Square, or the area surrounding the intersection of Broadway and Seventh Avenue just above Forty-second Street, became the focus of commercial entertainment and nightlife is more complicated. Such concentrations earlier had been located successively off City Hall Park along Broadway in lower Manhattan, on the

Bowery, around Union Square, and, at the turn of the century, from Madison Square up Broadway to what is now Herald Square. Several things led to the rapid development of the area farther north that we have been calling Times Square. The development of a transportation network between 1900 and 1920 was a major factor. In particular, a major rail terminus in the vast new Grand Central Station at Forty-second Street and Fourth Avenue concentrated commercial activity in midtown, and the construction of a subway system after 1904 eventually funneled movement both north and south through Times Square. The existence of a large garment district just to the north of Thirty-fourth Street led entertainment entrepreneurs and other developers associated with such activities to skip over the intervening blocks just to the north of Herald Square and concentrate their efforts on the stretch of Broadway on either side of Forty-second Street and in surrounding side streets.

One should not leap to the conclusion that the concentration of entertainment in Times Square was predestined. A sequence of risky and unorthodox decisions by theatrical producers and others set off midtown development from previous real estate transactions in New York. The development of Times Square revolutionized the real estate market by substituting commercial prospects for moral character as the new measure of value.[8] Times Square thus became a threshold of modernism in the real estate market and a harbinger of much that was to follow, especially in the speculative redevelopment of other deteriorating neighborhoods.

It is this midtown area that for convenience I have been referring to as "Times Square." Strictly speaking, "Times Square" refers to the open spaces created by the convergence of Broadway cutting diagonally across Seventh Avenue in front of the new Times building that was constructed in 1905 at Forty-second Street. Once known as Long Acre Square, it was not a "square" at all, but an important commercial axis resembling the junction a few blocks to the south, of Sixth Avenue and Broadway at Thirty-fourth Street, that, after the location there of the *New York Herald*, became known as Herald Square. Both areas became important commercial districts; Herald Square, finally, for department-store retailing and Times Square for entertainment.

Historically, this area around Forty-second Street has gone by many different names, and its parameters have changed correspondingly. The New York theater district was called the "Rialto" even before it moved uptown from Union Square, probably in reference to the Venetian Rialto and its prominence in Shakespeare's *Merchant of Venice*. In the opening decades of the century it was known simply as "Broadway," the designation that appears most often to have carried the area into song and myth. "Times Square" was the name given to the subway stop, at the insistence

of the *Times*, when the subway was brought in. Not many locals adopted
the name, preferring "Broadway" for the stretch of Broadway between
Thirty-seventh and Forty-second streets that contained the largest concentration of theaters and related activities. Few habitués called it Times
Square, preferring such labels as "The Main Drag," "The Main Stem,"
or, for Forty-second Street itself, "The Deuce."

The extent of this territory is also in dispute. Those principally concerned with theater and vaudeville tend to limit the focus of their attention to the area that contained the largest concentrations of theaters and
their support institutions, from just south of Forty-second Street up Broadway through the forties into the fifties. For those with more musical
interests, it extended from the original Metropolitan Opera House on
Thirty-ninth Street to Carnegie Hall on Fifty-seventh. The sporting scene,
on the other hand, was centered after 1925 near the new Madison Square
Garden at Eighth Avenue in the block between Forty-ninth and Fiftieth
streets. The music industry was more widely dispersed, but a major center
after its completion in 1931 was the Brill Building at Broadway and Forty-
ninth just to the east, with Irving Berlin's office a block to the south.
Nightlife was even more widely dispersed, with the largest clubs, cabarets,
and speakeasies slightly to the north of the theaters in a district reminiscent of the old Tenderloin, an area of cheap and seamy bars, dives, and
rooming houses located at the turn of the century in west midtown. It is
probably more instructive to visualize Times Square as a hub centered at
Broadway and Forty-second Street with axes radiating in all directions
than it is to try to conceive of it as a precise area.

It was the commercial dynamic of this entertainment district that assured its popular outreach and its persisting challenge to propriety and to
authority, as well as its seemingly unshakable grip on the imagination. No
figures demonstrate the power of this dynamic better than Irving Berlin
and Damon Runyon, two brilliant entrepreneurs who tapped the linguistic resources of the area and in the course of doing so brought Broadway national and international fame.

Irving Berlin arrived on the Broadway scene just as the sheet-music
business was beginning to expand into a booming national industry. His
career embodied almost every imaginable role in the history of Tin Pan
Alley, from plugger and boomer and singing saloon waiter promoting
popular songs by others, to composer and lyricist, musical publisher, and
theatrical producer. By 1915, he had invented the generic form of popular
song that was to characterize the music industry for almost half a century.
Berlin songs were characterized by the short line, ragged meter, and a
slangy, often comic, phraseology drawn from the city. Born in Russia of
Jewish parents and brought up on the Lower East Side, he had worked

saloons in Chinatown and Union Square before he moved his operations up to Times Square from Twenty-eighth Street just as the area was booming. He soon acquired the Music Box as a theater for staging musical drama. He so thoroughly institutionalized popular music that, as Furia shows, he finally set up separate offices for handling sheet music, compositions for Broadway shows, and his Hollywood musical scores.[9]

Damon Runyon arrived in New York in 1911 as a seasoned journalist from the West and, after his Broadway years writing for Hearst's *American*, left for a new career writing and producing films in Hollywood. Runyon's years as a reporter working the area brought him in touch with the volatile linguistic world surrounding Times Square, a "language funnel" for the special argots that had developed in the area. The sporting world (especially horse-racing and boxing), bootlegging, the underworld more generally, and the worlds of vaudeville, carnival, and show business had all developed rich and expressive argots by the 'twenties.[10]

Journalists like Runyon, Ring Lardner, and Jack Conway of *Variety*, I try to show in Chapter 9, were quick to exploit the vitality of these languages in forging new journalistic styles for themselves. In doing so they were in the vanguard of the creation of an American slang that rapidly spread through the local, then national press, in magazines like the *Saturday Evening Post*, which published Runyon's Broadway stories, and finally, during the 'thirties, through national network radio and through Hollywood films to the rest of the country. Walter Winchell, writing for *Vanity Fair* in 1927, included a list of slang expressions from the area and called New York "the slang capitol of the world." Ten years later, the list of slang expressions he included had, thanks to the work of Runyon and others, become part of a national slang that was quite generally employed. A whole cast of Broadway characters out of *Guys and Dolls* with their colorful monikers and vivid speech had found a place in some national dramatis personae. The authority challenged by his softhearted gangsters and gamblers was less the law than the formalities of written English and Emily Post, the same authorities challenged in Irving Berlin's lyrics. One revolution that Times Square had helped bring off was a revolution in vernacular speech, a revolution that a sometime habitué of the area, H. L. Mencken, had labored to track in the various editions of *The American Language*.

Meanwhile, theatrical activity in the area evolved into a large-scale national business based in, and operated out of, Times Square. By 1915, both theater and vaudeville were on course toward their peak of expansion in the 'twenties. Some fifty theaters were producing over a hundred and fifty new shows. The full range of support institutions, such as costume, wig, and scenery makers, as well as hotels, restaurants, and cabarets, was then in place and expanding. The big, splashy musical revues put on by Florenz Ziegfeld and others had begun to make their appearance. Road companies were touring successful plays through chains of theaters across the country. Motion pictures, which were to dominate entertainment in the area after the Depression, had only begun to make their appearance.

Theater, in fact, taking its cue from the economy at large, proved to be a very lucrative investment in this period. This expansive vitality was largely the result of a new breed of theatrical producer who, seeing a market opening, mobilized and organized the industry and thereby succeeded in attracting the capital necessary for expansion.[11] The role of B. F. Keith's United Booking Office is central to understanding the kind of vaudeville circuitry that developed within the city itself and, more extensively, on a regional basis around the country. It seems to have been the adoption of modern corporate management by the Shuberts that enabled them to win out over the theatrical Syndicate, which had employed the pool as a less flexible way of accumulating venture capital.[12]

The adjacent commercial culture of the city had an even more pervasive influence on the development of theatrical entertainment. The fact that American theater was unsubsidized, unlike most European national theaters, meant that success depended entirely on the volume of tickets sold. Market forces therefore encouraged an ever-widening appeal to fresh audiences. Broadway theatrical entertainment throughout the 'twenties was therefore not unlike prime-time television programming today. The number of new productions expanded through the peak year of 1927–28, when 264 shows were produced. Every effort was made to entertain and satisfy this broadening audience for theater. In an earlier period, vaudeville had succeeded where legitimate theater had failed through the age-old vaudeville device of tailoring acts to local audiences. Theater expanded its appeal, like vaudeville, by recourse to the "road"; but it also was forced to limit theatrical repertory to the sure thing. Theatrical fare on Broadway during the 'twenties therefore strikes us today as formulaic and repetitive, tailored to the moment and the need to be constantly entertaining and undemanding. Controversial and serious themes were seldom aired.[13]

Meanwhile, what modern marketing was referring to as the "tie-in" turned out to be a built-in feature of the Times Square area. Theater both formally and informally spilled over into the surrounding blocks every night.[14] Stars of Oscar Hammerstein's shows made a late-night appearance at his Roof Garden; Ziegfeld's *Midnight Frolic* included stars from his *Follies* downstairs. Later, during the 'thirties, Ziegfeld dancers made regular appearances at the large clubs run by Niles T. Granlund, Billy Rose, and others. Certain hotels, restaurants, cafés, and informal hangouts were also theatricalized by the frequency with which they entertained celebrities from the stage. In other ways, too, they appear to have operated as extensions of Broadway theater. By the thirties, Billy Rose, adopting marketing techniques then in use, used discounts and special arrangements with hotels and conventions in the city to fill large clubs like his Diamond Horseshoe, which could provide 700 patrons with a show and a five-course meal nightly.

The 'thirties and the revocation of the Volstead Act brought many other changes besides the introduction of the huge dinner clubs. Most striking perhaps was the rapid decline of legitimate theater, especially on the stretch of Forty-second Street that once contained the principal theaters. No new theaters were built after 1929, and most of the existing ones stood vacant, lent out as radio studios or converted to cheap "grinder" moviehouses that ran continuous showings. Only the New Amsterdam was the scene of regular theatrical production, and four out of five theaters stood vacant.

In the 'thirties, crowds still thronged to Times Square for entertainment. The movie palace and the motion-picture premiere replaced the theatrical "opening" as the signature activity.[15] The Palace, once the capital of vaudeville, had been made into a movie theater. For a decade during the 'thirties, burlesque proved to be a major attraction in the area. The Minskys and others, reworking an old tradition of "naked dancing" for audiences of sporting males, struck a very different note from the sophisticated follies of Ziegfeld, George White, and Earl Carroll. Outside of entertainment, different tastes also prevailed. Fancy restaurants and luxury hotels went into permanent decline during the Depression, replaced by cheap eateries, peep shows, taxi dance halls, penny arcades, and dime museums—a series of related changes that turned the area into a midtown version of the classic midway.

As early as 1905, there had been indications about where Times Square was heading as an entertainment center. There is no better indicator than the opening in April of that year of Fred Thompson's vast Hippodrome, which occupied an entire block between Forty-third and Forty-fourth streets along Sixth Avenue. Thompson, the architect and entertainment entrepreneur who had created the immensely successful Luna Park in Coney Island the previous year, attempted with the Hippodrome to redirect the course of show business in the area. Thompson conceived of his Hippodrome as an immense machine for entertainment of "the masses," which he called, in a reference to new large-scale retailing, "a department store in theatricals." Encompassed in one building was to be everything in the way of entertainment the ordinary citizen could want and at prices (from twenty-five cents to a dollar per seat) most could afford.[16]

At the center of this palladium of fun were to be huge spectacles like the opening *A Yankee Circus on Mars*. Thompson's credentials went back to the Midway of Chicago's 1893 Columbian Exposition and included several amusement parks before the opening of Luna Park. With the Hippodrome he clearly hoped to open an entertainment beachhead in a city center, a midway-as-theater and a theater-as-midway, or, as the advance publicity put it, "a city within a city." Its amusement-park lineage was apparent in everything from its block-long electrified billboard façade to the intricate technology of the inner working of its machinery for moving staging areas. As it turned out, it was an idea ahead of its time, and Thompson was to lose control of his creation after a bare fourteen months. The Hippodrome, nonetheless, provides a brilliant premonition of an entertainment future that was to depend increasingly on catering to an expanding popular appetite for amusement and employ ever more striking visual fare in the effort to do so.

What these changes were to mean, culturally, apart from a rejection of older, élitist notions about entertainment and decorum, is one most interesting questions raised by Times Square. Clearly something important was happening, had happened to ideas of recreation and entertainment, fun and enjoyment. It would appear that older religious conceptions of recreation as rational and instructive were giving way to notions that derived from sensory pleasure and astonishment. Americans had traditionally kept delight and astonishment at a distance through their association of them with childhood. Toward the end of the century, adults were given furtive opportunities to experience these emotions, but through the eyes of children. At the circus, in the growing volume of children's literature, and in the new amusement parks, new forms of what was once thought to be childish pleasure and delight were experienced by adults. A classic instance from the new juvenile literature with this ambivalent appeal is Huck Finn's innocent astonishment at the antics of a circus clown as described by Twain. As the impresario of amusement parks, Fred Thompson appears to have embodied this childish quality in his own imaginings. Thompson was characterized by contemporaries as a Peter Pan, "as the child who never grew up," a description that goes a long way toward explaining both his successes and his failures.

There is probably no better benchmark of such a shift in values than the extraordinary success of L. Frank Baum's *The Wizard of Oz*, which became a long-running Broadway show soon after its publication in 1900. That a book by a former department-store window-display designer could become such a theatrical success is testament to the widespread acceptance of a new commercial aesthetic of color and light, and supplies important evidence of its provenance. The sudden appearance of color, glass, and light in commercial displays worked an arresting revolution that not all Americans welcomed. [17] Thorstein Veblen, for example, saw in all this the usurpation of religious iconography for mercenary ends. Transformed by new technologies in illumination, Times Square became "the white light district" and "the Great White Way." It is estimated that over one million Americans daily raised their eyes to take in the half-a-block-long sign of the Dodge Brothers mounted on top of the Strand Theater in the center of the square.

Indoors as well as out of doors, the art of display underwent a dramatic change between 1900 and the end of the 'twenties. Another part of the process through which new technologies in illumination and a fresh interest in color were refined into a new commercial aesthetic is illustrated in the career of Vienna-born Joseph Urban.

It would be hard to think of two figures in the world of commercial culture farther apart than Fred Thompson and Joseph Urban. Thompson, a manufacturer's son from the Midwest, was self-taught, while Urban, from the Hapsburg court and enjoying the personal patronage of Emperor Franz Josef, was trained at the Viennese Academy of Art. Thompson's milieu was the incandescent midway; Urban's, the cooler medium of the musical stage and the sophisticated urban drawing room. The first sought to astonish and delight, the second sought the gratification expressed by the archly lifted eyebrow. Together they defined the outer limits of the new commercial aesthetic. The influence they exerted, moreover, illustrates a point that has been made by Gregory Gilmartin about an evolving commercial aesthetic. [18] Commercial art has difficulty innovating from within like other art, since market pressures tend toward homogeneity and what Thorstein Veblen called "marginal differentiation." Significant changes in a commercial aesthetic therefore are obtained only through a process of cannibalizing ideas and forms from the world of art and architecture outside the commercial sphere. For Thompson, the area to raid was the rich store of design implicit in the forms of the new industrial technology; for Urban, it was the cooler vision of European modernism with its utopian *Jungstil* dream of redesigning everyday life.

Urban, trained as an architect and designer in the spirit of craft, had acquired a varied background in design and especially in stage and production design by the time he arrived in New York in 1915. He soon became associated with Florenz Ziegfeld and the *Follies*. For the next seventeen years, until Ziegfeld's death in 1932, he functioned as the "eye" of the *Follies*, designing everything from costumes and sets to the interior and exterior of theaters. Beyond this work, he served as the personal architect and interior designer for Ziegfeld. He designed houses, nightclubs, and hotels for Ziegfeld and his friends in and around Palm Beach and in New

York. His success lay in his ability to bring to society the same sense of sophisticated theater and drama he had introduced to the *Follies*. The linear, stylized aesthetic that Urban brought from the fringes of European modernism to American commercial design revolutionized musical theater on Broadway.[19] For a generation, Americans appeared unwilling to carry their newly acquired taste for modern design beyond the musical stage and its cabaret environs. The next generation of European-trained designers, such as Raymond Loewy, succeeded in carrying this same aesthetic revolution into a much wider sector of modern consumer life. By such a reckoning, Broadway becomes the American threshold of modernism in architecture and design a generation before the arrival of the more authentic Bauhaus structures in the 1940s.

Something resembling a blind taste test must have brought Urban from the supervision of the Imperial Jubilee of 1908 and the patronage of Count Carl Esterhazy, for whom he had built a hunting lodge in 1904, to Florenz Ziegfeld and his circle. Urban's move and comfortable relocation in the latter milieu underscores the analogous "aristocratic" power exercised in America by the leading figures in the new world of commercial entertainment.

A number of historians have recently called attention to the political implications of a move after the turn of the century to redefine the boundaries of propriety and respectability. Whatever one chooses to call the *ancien régime*, older moral conventions governing behavior in the city changed rapidly as the century progressed. In this move to redefine boundaries, the interests of those who dominated commercial entertainment were a formidable, if often contested, factor.

No one would have disputed the fact that these moral boundaries by the time of World War I were in disarray. Nightlife of the kind that had been developing in Times Square was an obvious factor in the breakdown of the social conventions that had governed the behavior of middle-class Americans. There is a solid basis, in fact, for the association of theater, night, and vice that had governed earlier standards of behavior. There was a close proximity of theater life to brothel life throughout the nineteenth century. The two activities were closely coordinated in the move uptown from the Bowery and Union Square to their adjacent locations in Times Square and in the Tenderloin district directly to the west, which had become the center of brothel life by the turn of the century.[20]

Prostitution by the end of the nineteenth century had a recognized place in the life of the city and operated as part of a "semi-public economy of vice and amusement." The brothel world was a gender-specific one of sporting male patrons employing the services of prostitutes. During much of the century it operated openly if discreetly in the rows of brownstones lining the side streets of the area, largely tolerated by city officials and the police, who shared in its profitability. Income from vice and gambling was, in fact, a major source of funding for political machines. A succession of changes put strains on this older state of affairs. The appearance of large numbers of women in public—first in the new department stores and at matinee performances of the theater and, in the years immediately before the war, escorted at night in the lobster palaces, cabarets, and other places where the new craze in ballroom dancing could be enjoyed— challenged convention in a way that was bound to bring resistance.

This resistance came initially, not from government authority, either state or local, but from what has been characterized as "a private state." Voluntary organizations and committees of citizens such as the Society for the Suppression of Vice (SSV) and the Society for the Prevention of Cruelty to Children took it upon themselves to bypass existing authorities and exercise power. During the nineteenth century, the power of the private state was often exercised directly and was immediately influential. Increasingly after the turn of the century, the private state surrendered its responsibilities to enhanced public authority, state and local, with organizations such as the State Liquor Authority rather than the SSV superintending the moral character of the area. Committees like the powerful and long-lived Committee of Fourteen, whose tenure lasted until 1932, became powerful agents of reform. The rationale and objectives of these groups reflected the objectives of Progressivism in the country at large.[21] Their agenda was largely one of making the city safe for the new commercial culture and making commercial entertainment safe for the city.

In the struggle between vice and propriety, the major entrepreneurs of commercial entertainment like Ziegfeld appear to have played a mediating role. Their undertakings thrived on probing the boundaries of what was acceptable, packaging and repackaging sexuality in forms that expanded its acceptance as well as its market. European sophistication of the kind embodied in the very conception of the *Follies* and fortified by the stylized elegance of Urban's designs was one of many ways of reaching into the population for an enlarged nightlife clientele.

The effect on the area of this regulation by the private state was not a suppression of sexuality, but a shift from participation to what Laurence Senelick has called "spectation," from the flesh-peddling of prostitution to various forms of refined and not-so-refined voyeurism in commercial entertainment and other forms of nightlife.[22] Even prostitution, which seemed to have nearly disappeared by World War I, soon resurfaced as part of a large and increasingly complex sexual underground in the city.

How such a sexual underground is organized and functions in the city—the politics of sexuality, so to speak—is suggested by the ways gay men as one criminalized minority created social space for themselves in the Times Square area after World War I. The many-layered world of homosexuality in the area, the social and geographical divisions within the gay world, the places and ways of meeting, communicating, coding, and decoding, have recently been described by George Chauncey.[23] He has pointed to the particular forms of entertainment, like the concerts, later, of Judy Garland and Bea Lillie that drew gay men and created a sense of collective responsiveness. A highly organized street culture governed male hustling and other forms of sexual exchange in public. It becomes clear from Chauncey's analysis the degree to which an underground can exist almost invisibly, as in his example of gay clients occupying one side of the Astor Hotel bar unbeknownst to most of those sitting around them.

By the 'thirties, surveillance in places selling liquor was regularly exercised by the State Liquor Authority on the premise that gays as "undesirables" were a disorderly element. The responsibility for constraint rested with those who managed commercial entertainment. Market forces acted in both directions with gay clients, acting against their "obvious" behavior in peak hours and acceptingly, even invitingly, in slack times when their patronage added to profitability, as it did after midnight in the local Automat or in the local Childs restaurants.[24]

By the end of the 'thirties, the groundwork had been laid for the civic revulsion that underlies current efforts to restructure the area. An old élitist neighborhood built by the Astors had gone through a series of transformations that had carried it from a silk-hat brothels district discreetly serviced by carriages and cabs, through a period as a glittering center of legitimate theater and vaudeville, through its reign as the center of a gaudy carnival of popular show business and a greater and greater array of commercialized sexual entertainment. Burlesque, for example, arrived late and spread rapidly, as the Depression had taken its toll on theater, as one way of filling empty houses. The "rough trade" of male hustlers along Forty-second Street, memorialized in John Schlesinger's *Midnight Cowboy*, was another fallout from the Depression when unemployed men from the West took to hustling as a way of surviving hard times. The layered and complex social organization of the Times Square world was capable of accommodating and providing protective coloration to a varied population, from inside and outside the area, with different stakes in its economic and entertainment life.

Beyond such changes, the invention of Times Square points to a striking transformation—one could call it a revolution—in the spatial arrangement of cities. Historically, the center of the city had always been either city hall or the central market, the forum or the agora. Times

Square, located in the transportation hub of New York, was neither. The *New York Times* had hoped in 1905 that its new tower would preside over the Square as a civic presence, a kind of journalistic *hôtel de ville* or *rathaus*, rather than look down on a center of misrule of the kind that eventually developed.

The modern commercial city as represented by New York had developed an unanticipated inclination to locate its entertainment and amusement industries where they were most accessible—and conspicuous. These commercial activities, in the full rein they gave to urban society's appetites and fantasies, by their very nature challenged and defied the norms of behavior that prevailed elsewhere in the city. Cities historically had contained districts that served similar needs, but these districts did not occupy the city center. Their influence on the general population, moreover, was muted by the discretion and reticence that surrounded them. The modern city was unique in its convergence on such commerce in recreation at its very core. It was also unique in giving the site of such commerce center stage in a national cultural marketplace.

The historical model provided by New York of a great metropolis radiating such cultural signals from its inner core required a timing and a unique configuration of institutions that cannot be reimposed upon the city today. Changes in theater and in other popular forms of entertainment have delivered a fatal blow to such a central entertainment district. Wig makers, costume and scenery production firms have fled the high rentals in the area, along with other support institutions that once made up the complex overlay of theatrical activities. The newspapers, so vital to creating the legendary Broadway, no longer play their former role. Hollywood studios that once provided a visual and musical conduit to Broadway for the rest of the nation have long since turned their attention elsewhere. Tin Pan Alley, along with other changes, has lost its heart to Nashville. Gone, too, are most of the structures and visual effects that once gave Times Square its distinctive appearance. The trophy for brilliant nighttime illumination has passed to Tokyo's Ginza district.

Because the historical Times Square was a creature of its time, in other words, no imaginable redevelopment of the area could bring back what was once there. Given the high value of midtown real estate, it was inevitable that developers would move in to pick up the slack created by deteriorating nightlife and the encroachment of cheap sexual entertainment that had moved in after the heyday of theater and prime moviegoing. Efforts by developers that purport to restore the past—or even a feeling of the past—have led to farcical results: office buildings displaying neon ribbons reminiscent of the "Great White Way," as Ada Louise Huxtable has recently pointed out.[25] The *Times* campanile that once provided a visual center to the Square has been "deconstructed" into what she describes as "junk architecture." The bulldozer revolution that swept away the large hotels and the one- and two-story surrounding structures with their lacework of massive signs has ushered in a generation of dull new hotels and unimaginative skyscraper towers whose sheer bulk has forever altered the scale, the daytime exposure to sunlight, and the overall feeling of the area.

Times Square, as Huxtable describes it today, was never a site of great architecture. Interesting touches could be found here and there. An Italian campanile for the *Times*, for example, or the mansard roofs on the two large hotels, here and there emblems of French Renaissance design, and ornate, riotously eclectic historicist interiors provided an architectonic background for those who cared to peer behind the glitzy baubles. In an eloquent tribute to five towers rising several blocks north of the square, Huxtable has succeeded in pointing to still another and final irony in the history of the area. Times Square in redevelopment has finally found architectural distinction, not in theaters, hotels, or other structures associated with its vernacular entertainment past, but rather in sleek, modern office towers. These towers, presumably soon to be occupied by a substantial portion of the city's legal profession and by brokerage houses that have decamped from Wall Street, herald a new and different future for the area under redevelopment. . . . *Plus ça change.*

SEVEN

Walter Lippmann in *Vanity Fair*

On the last day of June, 1914, an unlikely trio traveled out from Manhattan to spend the evening at Coney Island. The trio consisted of Learned Hand, already a federal district judge; Francis Hackett, former book editor of the *Chicago Evening Post*; and Walter Lippmann. All three were guiding spirits of the just-created *New Republic*. What the first two thought of the visit is not known, but Lippmann, who had just begun to keep a diary, set down his own somewhat contradictory reaction. "Hand, Francis and I . . . *did* Coney with much exhilaration. The place lacks sexual interest. As Alfred[1] says, it is carefree because it revives our infantilism."[2]

Already a prodigy at twenty-five, Lippmann was about to embark on a career in journalism and public affairs that was to take him, by the age of thirty-four, to the prestigious position of editorial director of Pulitzer's *World*. The *New York World* was probably by the 'twenties New York's most respected paper, "our paper" to members of the Algonquin Round Table. Lippmann by this time was already an established member of a youthful cohort, including such Harvard classmates as T. S. Eliot and John Reed, that was to bring distinction to new parts of the culture. Through his books, his services to the Wilson administration, and the ties he cultivated with English Fabians and such prominent Americans as Bernard Baruch, Thomas Lamont, and Bernard Berenson, Lippmann was soon to acquire the cachet of a new kind of celebrity. When he traveled after the war, he traveled in style, was sought out for advice by heads of state. His was a name, to quote a colleague on the *World*, "that would open any door."[3]

For Lippmann, the 1914 Coney Island excursion was only an early brush with what was to become a lifelong preoccupation: the world of commercial entertainment that Coney Island symbolized for men of Lippmann's class and generation. Its crowds, its fantastic architecture and illumination, the movement and excitement of its rides, the atmosphere of loosened restraints, symbolized for Lippmann the new urban masses at play or what he called "the clamorous life of cities." Like Broadway, it had come to evoke values that were central to his idea of the modern city: a complex culture of commercial entertainment characterized by show-manship, sensationalism, and other forms of non-rational appeal.

Throughout his life, Lippmann remained a regular if selective patron of commercial entertainment. He frequently attended the theater and major Broadway shows and, with his first wife, Faye, dined out in the city's restaurants. Such activities became, in fact, part of a lifestyle of high consumption not unlike that of other prominent journalists of the day. He even, to judge from his correspondence, courted such popular entertain-ment figures as Chaplin, Irving Berlin, and George Gershwin. During the 'twenties he carried on an extended relationship with the magician Harry Houdini and attended private exhibitions he gave, including one parapsy-chology experiment at Houdini's house.[4] Now and then, as in the case of Houdini, he wrote about these matters on the editorial page of the *World*. In what was probably his largest commitment to commercial culture, Lippmann contracted in 1920 to do a series of articles on public affairs for Condé Nast's glitzy magazine of entertainment and culture, *Vanity Fair*, an activity he continued into the 'thirties. As an author of successful and sought-after books, moreover, and as a paid consultant to publisher Alfred Harcourt, he remained, in other ways, actively in the literary mar-ketplace, as of course he was in his newspaper work as well.

If Lippmann's involvement in the commercial culture of his time is clear, his attitude toward this side of his life is less so. It also underwent an important change by the end of the decade. While he was an avid and admiring consumer, he tended in what he said about these experiences to keep them at a distance and to employ them as metaphors for mass society, as he had done with the Coney Island episode. Excessive puffery, anything blatantly vulgar or smacking of sham, brought instant condemnation. More and more as the 'twenties progressed, he singled out Broadway and show business as a symbol of what had gone wrong with the democratic process, where sensationalism and thrills had replaced rational appeal.

By 1927, Lippmann was forced to concede that the contagion he called "blazing publicity" had come to characterize the press and other media fully as much as it characterized Broadway and Hollywood.[5] The world of entertainment and the world of publishing seemed for a brief time all of one piece. When the *World* ceased printing, he turned down other edi-torial options and withdrew to the comparative seclusion of a syndicated column. After 1931, Lippmann no longer helped run newspapers; he simply wrote for them. It seems evident, moreover, that he never con-fronted his darkest thoughts about the journalism of the 'twenties but wrote thereafter with blinders on.

It was Lippmann's objective working as a journalist during that decade to function as a critic and reformer within commercial culture. As early as *Drift and Mastery* he had pinpointed the problem of American democratic society as essentially a cultural predicament. Americans lived in a society that was rootless, rudderless, and transient. Everything about America, he reported, had a cheap and improvised character. The modern urban American was an immigrant at heart, regardless of class or origin, with the tastes of the *nouveau riche*. "The evidence is everywhere," he said.

> The amusements of the city, the jokes that pass for jokes; the blare that stands for beauty, the folklore of Broadway. . . . We make love to ragtime and we die to it. You have only to study what newspapers regard as news to see how we are torn and twisted by the irrelevant. . . ."[6]

Like his Harvard contemporary Van Wyck Brooks, Lippmann perceived a nation divided between Harvard and Broadway, between what Brooks labeled "highbrow" and "lowbrow," abstract theory and "catchpenny opportunism," to use Brooks' phrase for it. Lippmann had early assigned himself a mediating role between these two worlds.[7]

It was some such rationale that, in addition to the money it brought in, appears to have led him to take on the work for *Vanity Fair* and to accept increasing editorial control of Pulitzer's *World*. His rise to power at the *World* was considered meteoric and seemed an obvious channel for his talent. It brought immediate gratifications—power, wealth, social lionizing—and was everywhere, outside radical circles, acclaimed as a coup. At least to some of Lippmann's friends, the decision to write for *Vanity Fair* was more puzzling. *Vanity Fair* by 1920, as an interesting study by Cynthia Ward has shown, had established itself as a new kind of magazine catering to a select clientele of wealthy urbanites, mostly New Yorkers.[8] Condé Nast, whose great genius lay in advertising, had designed it as a platform for the display of luxury goods. Though its circulation remained comparatively small, it reached an affluent audience. A full-page ad for Tiffany's began each monthly issue, and generous editorial attention, in addition to ads, was devoted to fashion and motoring. Frank Crownin-shield, hired by Nast to edit *Vanity Fair*, brought with him a sure sense of the audience from his previous editorial experience on *Munsey's* and the *Century*. Under his leadership, *Vanity Fair* soon offered its readers the cultural credentials of modern urban life. Each monthly issue became a guide to sophisticated taste and behavior and laid before the insecure a glossy guide to what was going on culturally in the city. The appeal to cultural insecurity was especially evident in *Vanity Fair's* promotions. "Are you a conversational half portion, an intellectual side dish?" ran one.[9]

Lippmann was one of the group of gifted young writers that Crownin-shield brought on the magazine to meet such expectations. At one time or another, Edmund Wilson, Robert Benchley, John Peale Bishop, Sherwood Anderson, Robert Sherwood, Dorothy Parker, and many others fed such monthly departments as "The World of Art," "The World of Theatre," and the department in which Lippmann's own pieces appeared as lead articles, "The World of Ideas."

Most of Lippmann's articles were informal but careful exegeses of political developments: a valedictory to the departing Woodrow Wilson, the significance of Warren G. Harding's nomination and election, Al Smith's candidacy, and, at least initially, such issues as war reparations. Lippmann developed a keen nose for detecting the atmosphere that surrounded political events, using just the right anecdote, the mini-profile, and the deft verbal strokes to characterize the mood in the country. Thus the nomination of Harding, while troubling, was ascribed by Lippmann to a country weary of war, homesick like a weary, affluent tourist. "There comes a time," he commented, "when all the Ritzes of Europe seem unpalatable in comparison with Child's. . . . Show him another cathedral and he will scream, another masterpiece and he will perish."[10] Here was a successful translation of politics into the cultural patter of *Vanity Fair!*

But if the format of *Vanity Fair* remained much the same, the mood quickly changed. The drift was clearly toward a deeper pessimism about the prospects of democracy and toward the views embraced in his two important books of the 'twenties, *Public Opinion* (1922) and *The Phantom Public* (1925). Thus, already in January of 1921, in a discussion of Harding's election, he observed, "Anyone who likes to believe that the voice of the people is the voice of god is free to engage in the jolly task of explaining the last election."[11] In writing about the shift in the British view of war reparations a year later, he argued that it was hard to believe "that any of us can, while he sits at the breakfast table, arrive at useful opinions about so complicated a matter. . . ."[12] More and more he was inclined to conclude that to depend on some kind of mandate from the public was a hazardous political tactic at best. By the mid-'twenties he had concluded that the public as an organized body of opinion was a fiction—a dangerous one.[13]

Lippmann was soon confronted with a dilemma. In a society where the public was passive and evasive and only a few insiders had sufficient knowledge of any issue and few others seemed to care, what was the journalist to do? One can only infer what Lippmann's answer would have been. One tactic he used was to flay the system of cheap promotion and the kind of publicity that was deflecting public attention from serious political issues. In such indictments, Broadway and Hollywood came to symbolize the forces that were undermining democracy. In *The Phantom*

Public it was, in fact, a metaphorical reference to the theater that best expressed his new impatience with popular audiences. "The public," he observed, "will arrive in the middle of the third act and leave before the last curtain, having stayed just long enough to decide who is the hero and who is the villain of the piece."[14]

Just as noteworthy, I believe, was the comfortable fluency with which these pronouncements flowed from his pen, despite what might have seemed the compromising situation of holding a position of power on a major metropolitan newspaper, in the thick of the very thing he seemed to be condemning. From his pinnacle in the tower of the *World*, he seemed to find the distance and perspective he was seeking, walled off from the clamor on the floors below. On *Vanity Fair* he began to reach the kind of audience whom he discovered he felt comfortable with. The 'twenties for Lippmann was thus a period of groping for such an affluent-class clientele and toward an appropriate style and idiom. It was probably the recognition that he had found a clientele and idiom that sped his departure from editorial responsibilities in 1931.

In private correspondence throughout the decade, Lippmann complained to Felix Frankfurter and other friends of the difficulty of presenting complicated issues to the public, as he had earlier tried to do with that of war reparations. As the years passed he tried to explain such matters less often. More and more he seemed to opt for a kind of mood music and a more general characterization of events and personalities. Thus, the opposition around the country to the presidential candidacy of Al Smith, he observed in December 1925, was "inspired by the feeling that the clamor of life in the city should not be acknowledged as an American ideal."[15]

The Sacco and Vanzetti trial provided Lippmann with a recognized problem. It was clearly an issue of the first importance, yet complicated and divisive. Lippmann wrote not a word about it in *Vanity Fair*, though, of course, the *World* editorially took a stand. When Frankfurter questioned him about his handling of the trial, he responded characteristically,

> In thinking about it, bear in mind the great difficulty in discussing the details of the evidence for a newspaper audience that has no background in the case. . . .
> I should despair of being able to educate any considerable number of our readers about the testimony taken in trial.[16]

In fact he stated in an editorial on Sacco and Vanzetti, "we do not question and we never have questioned the rectitude of the Government and its advisory committee." Lippmann clashed with Heywood Broun over the subject (Broun's columns were cut and omitted and he was eventually sacked) in a series of editorials that took on the character of opposing standard-keepers in a battle of liberal positions.

Again and again during the 'twenties Lippmann struck out at the Broadway ethos as a corruptor of public discourse. *Vanity Fair* in June 1928 had printed a piece critical of King Vidor and his war film, *The Big Parade*. The article made disparaging remarks about film critic and playwright Lawrence Stallings, author of the anti-war play "What Price Glory?" and a Lippmann friend and classmate. Clearly angry, Lippmann wrote to Crowninshield, wondering

> whether you haven't inadvertently been made the victim of some Hollywood movie politics. . . . The whole article seems to me altogether out of key with *Vanity Fair.* It's a boost of the blatant publicity man type, without perspective, without style. I feel very distressed about it and I should be greatly distressed if I thought *Vanity Fair* was going in the direction indicated.[17]

In a unique move in 1924, Lippmann devoted an entire editorial to blasting a new play by David Belasco entitled *Ladies of the Night.* "It is perhaps as dishonest a play as has been produced in a long time," Lippmann wrote. "Its purpose is to go just a little bit further than any other manager has gone in presenting the dirty accompaniments of vice. . . . It is a bottle of bad hooch,"[18] he concluded.

His most explicit attack on the Broadway ethos came in 1928 with his retort to theater critic George Jean Nathan, who had written in the February *Vanity Fair* that his sense of humor was too highly developed to permit him to take an interest in democratic politics. This witticism, coming as it did from a critic known for his coverage of the Broadway scene, was too much for Lippmann. Lippmann shot back in the next issue:

> A man who can endure all that Broadway has to offer, who can make a life work talking about Broadway theatre, is neither so humorous nor so delicately attuned, but that he could endure the grossness and stupidity under a democratic form of government.[19]

According to Lippmann, the moral atmosphere of Broadway was no better and no worse than that of city politics. Both dealt in false façades in the effort to create stars with public appeal.

The role of cultural policeman, however, began to have its limits for Lippmann. He was beginning to feel like a lonely cop on the beat, as he confessed to Learned Hand. Meanwhile, changes in the delivery of news through the media had begun to pose a serious problem for him. By 1925 he was already giving voice to such worries. In a letter to *New York Times* publisher Adolph Ochs in December of that year, he tried somewhat apologetically to justify remarks made the night before about the "tyranny" and "benevolent despotism" of the Associated Press. In controlling what news was selected for wire transmission, AP was determining what the rest of the country would know about what was happening in New

York. Thus a New York story that was deemed locally important could be side-tracked by an arbitrary decision at AP in favor of some more colorful but less significant piece of news. The AP offering, Lippmann pointed out, was made all the more tempting by the fact that its stories arrived already edited and brightly packaged for immediate printing. The AP was in this way undermining the authority of influential newspapers in every city. Nonetheless, Lippmann assured Ochs, it was a problem created by what he called the "mechanics of transmission," and AP as such was blameless. "It is a fault of the conditions, the remedy for which I do not pretend to know."[20]

The writer's loss of control over the production of his work continued through the decade to preoccupy him, as it did other artists and writers. In New York, journalists were everywhere making the discovery that they were part of a capitalist system that was coloring the character of their work and limiting their independence.[21] This recognition carried many of them to the Left. On Lippmann this discovery had the reverse effect. He became increasingly absorbed in addressing those in power. Yet his preoccupation with controlling the disposition of his own work continued.

In 1927, Lippmann took the critical step of breaking his long professional association with the publisher Alfred Harcourt. Harcourt had been publishing Lippmann's books; as a consultant on an annual retainer, Lippmann had played an important role in building the Harcourt list by bringing in such influential English authors as Lytton Strachey and John Maynard Keynes. The increasingly commercial character of the Harcourt list and the kind of publicity that went into the publication and promotion of such bestsellers as Sinclair Lewis's *Elmer Gantry*, however, clearly violated Lippmann's idea of a publisher's proper role. He switched to the more staid, British-based Macmillan, but not without a blast at his old friend. "I am satisfied," he wrote to Harcourt in a somewhat testy letter, "that the attention of the firm is almost entirely preoccupied with the conspicuous books on your list."[22]

Lippmann's darkest pessimism about publicity and the media came in "Blazing Publicity," an article published in *Vanity Fair* that September, two years after his tightly argued, grim deconstruction of the idea of the public in *The Phantom Public*. The article was directed at utopian visions of the media's potential. It was perfectly true, he observed, that new inventions like photography, film, and something he called television—especially given the capacities of the news-gathering organizations—promised a world in which everything that happened anywhere could be known everywhere simultaneously, almost as it occurred. The effect of such a development, however, was not to flood the world with light. On the contrary it is like the beam of a powerful lantern that plays capriciously upon the course of events, throwing now this now that into brilliant relief, leaving the rest in comparative darkness.

Such a news delivery system was based, Lippmann concluded, "on the theory that a population under modern conditions is not held by sustained convictions and traditions, but that it wants and must have one thrill after another." As he had put it earlier in the article, "The machine itself is without morals or taste of any kind."[23]

Nothing that Lippmann subsequently said about the media matched these perspicacious and pessimistic observations of 1927. Two statements about the press he made on the occasion of leaving the *World* in 1931 seem platitudinous by comparison. In an article that appeared that year in *The Yale Review*, Lippmann professed to believe that the public would ultimately weary of sensationalism and hunger for some new kind of factual journalism.[24] In March, Lippmann gave a speech at a dinner held in his honor by the American Academy of Political Science and hosted by an old friend, financier Thomas Lamont. Some five hundred dignitaries, friends, and former colleagues, including such figures from his past as Colonel House, former advisor to President Wilson, and Learned Hand, assembled at the Astor Hotel in Times Square. He spoke on the subject of journalism and the liberal spirit. The speech was still another valedictory to Progressive reform, but with a new note. The problem of the press was no longer that of mobilizing public opinion, but rather that of encouraging America's corporations to undertake internal reform. The most important audience for the journalist was no longer the masses but the likes of those seated before him:

> For us the problem is to civilize and rationalize these corporate organizations. . . . It is vain to suppose that our problems can be dealt with by rallying people to some crusade that can be expressed in a symbol, a phrase, a set of principles or a program.[25]

The Astor Hotel dinner was probably the moment of Lippmann's greatest public prominence. That week's issue of *Time* ran a cover story on him. News that the *World* had stopped publication in February brought job offers from everywhere, including a professorship of government at Harvard. The most tempting offering came from Ochs, who invited Lippmann to take over the *Times'* Washington bureau. Instead, Lippmann chose an offer from the *New York Tribune* to write a regular column. The prospect of independence as a maverick Democrat on a Republican paper had great appeal.[26] Now he had the further prospect of speaking to a national élite through the newspaper's syndication services, which would bring his columns over the wires to newspapers across the country—opinion from New

York, predigested and ready to print. A few months later, when he began work for the *Herald-Tribune,* he had become part of the problem he had so shrewdly analyzed six years before in his letter to Ochs. A new era of mass culture had arrived, and Lippmann, like it or not, was part of it.

The role that *Vanity Fair* had played in bringing Lippmann to this point probably needs to be underscored. Ronald Steel, in his recent biography of Lippmann, sees this experience as a kind of lighthearted holiday from the phlegmatic atmosphere of the *New Republic.* Its effect on Lippmann, according to Steel, was chiefly stylistic. "The magazine," he concluded, "brought out a side of his character—irony, a gift for character analysis, intellectual playfulness, and even a romantic idealism that had been dampened at the ponderous *New Republic.*"[27] It would be a serious mistake, I think, to see such a shift as simply a change in literary manner. In retrospect it seems to provide a better indication than anything else of where Lippmann was heading. *Vanity Fair* brought Lippmann his first taste of writing for a wealthy élite, and the experience was clearly liberating for him. In a sense, the style that Lippmann adopted at *Vanity Fair* was the message: it signified Lippmann's comfort with the distance he had placed between himself and those "masses" to whose service he had dedicated himself as a college student.

As an uptown German Jew, Lippmann had never been comfortable with the Jewishness of the Lower East Side, as Ronald Steel has pointed out. At Harvard he had been stung by his rejection by élitist "final" clubs because he was Jewish. ("Final" clubs like Porcellian [FDR's club] were the ultimate social goal at Harvard, reached after a lower tier of "waiting" clubs like Hasty Pudding.) The liberation of his style while at *Vanity Fair,* therefore, had a deeper significance because it had been brought about by his tacit acknowledgment of class and by his own gratification by the experience of class acceptance. For *Vanity Fair* writers of collegiate background like Edmund Wilson and Robert Benchley, by contrast, it was precisely this comfortable class relationship, stylistically, that had to be examined, disavowed, or, in the case of Benchley, travestied. Major studies of French symbolism and Marxism for Wilson and a comic career on the stage and in Hollywood for Benchley logically followed their *Vanity Fair* work. The *New York Herald-Tribune* offered Lippmann the prospect of continuing this comfortable relationship on a national scale. Accepting the offers from Hearst or Scripps-Howard would have meant continuing in an obsolete tradition of popular journalism, a journalism of thrill and sensation.

There is a certain irony, finally, in his pronouncing his farewell to popular journalism where he did, in the Astor Hotel in Times Square, in the center of New York's commercial culture. The Depression had brought to a close the extraordinary economic growth of the city's theater life, and the center of the entertainment industry was about to shift to Hollywood. Popular journalism had undergone changes brought on by the growing wedge that had been driven between most Americans and those in his audience at the Astor Hotel that night. The takeover of the *World* by Scripps-Howard was evidence of such change. Lippmann's distance from Depression America is symbolized by a vacation he took a few days later that could have been composed from the advertising copy of *Vanity Fair*—a long, leisurely voyage through the Greek islands on Thomas Lamont's private yacht.

EIGHT

The Power of the Word ·
Greenwich Village Writers and
the Golden Fleece

In 1916, Djuna Barnes, later of avant-garde and expatriate notoriety, was
still a working journalist—and a very good one—in New York. In an
article entitled "Greenwich Village As It Is" that she wrote for *Pearson's
Magazine* that year, she began with a question: "Why has Washington
Square a meaning, a fragrance, so to speak; while Washington Heights has
none?"[1] No one today would put the question in quite these terms (or, in
any event, would mean something quite different by "fragrance," certainly). In 1916, Washington Heights did not have its bridge or most of its
residents, and Washington Square was in the center of "the Village," as it
was called. As she goes on to explain, its "fragrance" derived, at least in
part, from the picturesque contrast in class life between the north and
south sides of the Square, between rich and poor, old American and
immigrant Italian:

> Here on the North Side are stately houses, inhabited by great fortunes, the
> Lytigs and Guinnesses and all those whose names rustle like petticoats, and on
> the other side a congeries of houses and hovels passing into rabbit-warrens
> where Italians breed and swarm in the sun as in Naples, where vegetables and
> fruits are sold in the street as on the Chiaja and ice-cream is made in the
> bedrooms and spaghetti on the cellar-floor . . . and here is the row of houses
> whose inhabitants provide the Woman's Night Court with half its sensations.
> Satin and motor cars on this side, squalor and push carts on that, it is the
> contrast which gives life, stimulates the imagination, incites to love and
> hatred.[2]

There is clearly more to this passage than the social contrast being
described. "Spaghetti on the cellar-floor," indeed. The portrayal of immigrant squalor does not come from Barnes as a Village neighbor describing
the Village "as it is" but from literary convention, an old convention or set
of conventions for describing the poor that goes back to Dickens and other
nineteenth-century urban pioneers. What is new here is the literary space

between rich and poor that, Barnes asserted, is occupied by writers and artists like herself. "The greater part of New York is as soulless as a department store," she continued, "but Greenwich Village has recollections like ears filled with muted music and hopes like sightless eyes straining to catch a glimpse of the Beatific Vision."[3] Clearly, we are in literary territory.

Literary territories are treacherous to define, and Greenwich Village is no exception. In one important sense, however, the Greenwich Village that established its reputation as a literary refuge, as the first American Bohemia for writers and artists, was the invention of the prewar Villagers like Djuna Barnes, who departed from her otherwise matter-of-factly lighthearted description to strike this note. This Greenwich Village was less a place than a state of mind. Its inventors shared literary and political convictions, personal aspirations and animosities, and a style of life that was designed to place a boundary between them and the middle-class world they came from.

Writers had lived in the Village before and, especially, after these years, many of them better known today than the prewar Villagers. John Masefield, later England's poet laureate, had worked in the kitchen of O'Connor's Saloon at Christopher Street and Greenwich Avenue at the turn of the century. e. e. cummings, Ernest Hemingway, John Dos Passos, Malcolm Cowley, Edmund Wilson, Edna St. Vincent Millay, and Willa Cather all lived in the Village during the 'twenties. As a group these later Villagers were less clannish, less militant than the older Villagers, and, though some of them embraced the Left with fervor, they lived in an easier relationship to midtown commerce and the publishing establishment. For them the Village was less a separate world, less a collective experience than it had been for the older generation. In their reminiscences they emphasized that it was a cheap place to live and socialize in at the start of a literary career, and they carefully set themselves off from older survivors of the prewar Village. "We came to the Village without any intention of becoming Villagers," Malcolm Cowley recalled in *Exile's Return* (1934).[4] For him the older Villagers seemed out of touch. They were "aesthetes" who wore capes and painted their floors black.[5]

Even during the prime teen years there were writers who lived in the Village but were not of it. Marianne Moore moved with her mother to St. Luke's Place in 1918 to edit the *Dial*, but her detachment from the Village literary scene is suggested by her reference to the Provincetown Players as the "Plague Players." Theodore Dreiser, who lived at Tenth and Broadway, liked to eat and drink at the Villagers' hangouts, The Brevoort on Eighth and Fifth avenues or Polly's on MacDougal Street. Sinclair Lewis spent the summer of 1918 on Cape Cod with the Provincetown

Players and, when he worked uptown as an editor, sometimes turned up at Villager parties, but both appear to have been drawn less by literary or political affinity than by the aura of sexual freedom that surrounded Village women. Whether or not you were a Villager, at least in these years, was less a question of where you lived than whom you knew and what you believed.

The true Village, the Village that started a half-century of literary contagion, was the village of *The Masses* and the Provincetown Players, of John Reed, Mabel Dodge Luhan, Max and Crystal Eastman, Hutchins Hapgood and Neith Boyce, Floyd Dell, Susan Glaspell, and George Cram Cook, among others. It may be said to have begun around 1912 or 1913 when a number of events signaled that a new crowd had made the scene: in 1912, Max Eastman became editor of *The Masses* and began to overhaul and revive it; Henrietta Rodman broke with a group in Gramercy Park over admitting black members and founded the Liberal Club on MacDougal Street just south of the Square; in 1913 came the Paterson Strike Pageant in Madison Square Garden, organized by John Reed and Mabel Dodge, and the highly publicized and much-discussed Armory Show of post-Impressionist art, in which the Villagers had a propulsive hand; finally, in 1916, the theater group that had been producing plays in a wharf warehouse in Provincetown for two summers began regular productions on MacDougal Street.

This Village, considering its importance, had a very brief lifespan. In the eyes of these Villagers, the end came with abruptness four or five years later with the arrival of the subway and the coming of war. By 1920 they commonly acknowledged that the great days for the Village were over. Mabel Dodge, whose weekly salons had provided Villagers with a town hall, had long since departed for Taos and D. H. Lawrence. Prohibition had brought uptowners in great numbers to the Village at night. The Provincetown theater had been taken over by professionals and was no longer engaged in searching self-portraits of Village life; and its moving genius, George Cram Cook, had resigned and moved to Delphi in Greece. *The Masses* had been silenced by the Creel Commission for its opposition to the war and never recovered. Hutchins Hapgood by then was complaining that the attractive small-town quiet and isolation of the Village had ended, that the area was overrun by sightseers and had sprouted too many tourist attractions, too many nightspots. During the 'twenties, the focus of Village life shifted westward beyond Sixth Avenue to the area around Charles and Bank streets, and Washington Square lost its central place in its activities. By then two things were clear: an era had ended, and a Greenwich Village myth had been launched.

There is no single document that better illuminates the spirit that went into this myth than a poem written in 1913 by John Reed. At the time he wrote the poem, Reed was on the verge of a career as a journalist in Mexico and Russia that was to bring him worldwide recognition. The poem, entitled "A Day in Bohemia," comes from a small volume that Reed published that year at his own expense and distributed to his friends.[6] What is immediately striking about the poem is the way it resonates with the highjinks of a college humor magazine rather than the classical Bohemia of gypsy extraction popularized by Henry Murger in France.[7] Its tone is closer to parody than to protest. It begins with a mock-heroic invocation to the Muse to "buckle to it" to memorialize,

> . . . . . . Those unknown men of genius
> Who dwell in third-floor-rears gangrenous
> Reft of their rightful heritage
> By a commercial, soulless age.[8]

There is another game going on here. The space Reed occupies here is the poetic space of the heroic couplet, a merry rhyming space with echoes of Alexander Pope, irony, and satire. The movement of the poem is to extend this poetic space geographically over Greenwich Village and to claim it, rhetorically, for literature.

> Twixt Broadway and Sixth Avenue,
> And west perhaps a block or two,
> From Third Street up, and Ninth Street down,
> Between Fifth Avenue and the Town,—
> Policemen walk as free as air,
> With nothing on their minds but hair,
> And life is very, very fair,
> In Washington Square.[9]

By the end of the poem, the literary conquest of the Village is complete, with every hangout, every important denizen hauled into couplets, its literary and artistic life memorialized in verse. The local character of this original Village is evident from the references in the stanzas that follow. The eating places mentioned were all within a few blocks of the Square. The Brevoort Hotel at Fifth Avenue and Eighth Street and the Lafayette across the Square on University Place, both hotels, were important Village hangouts for many years. Every spring a dinner honoring Walt Whitman, New York's first Bohemian, was held in a private suite at the Brevoort. The poem continues:

I challenge you to tell me where you've et
Viands more rare than at the Lafayette
Have you forgot the Benedick,—the Judson,
(Purest of hostelries this side the Hudson)
The Old Brevoort, for breakfast late on Sunday,
The Crullery, where poor men dine on Monday?
You don't remember Thompson Street? For shame!
Nor Waverly Place, nor, (classic, classic name!)
MACDOUGAL ALLEY, all of stables built,
Blessed home of Art and Mrs. Vanderbilt. [10]

In what follows, the relationship of the Villagers to midtown commerce becomes a major theme, though the larkish spirit continues—Reed initially refers to the contrasting sides of Washington Square described by Djuna Barnes, but the target of the satire quickly widens to include the uptowners heading south each morning to Wall Street,—the "Jasons" passing "fleeceward" in their motor-cars:

Lives there a man with soul so dead, I ask,
Who in an attic would not rather bask
On the South Side, in lofty-thinking Splendor,
Than on the North Side, to the golden ladle born,
Philistine, suckled at a creed outworn!
Unnumbered Jasons in their motor-cars
Pass fleeceward, mornings, smoking black cigars—
I smoke Fatimas but I ride the stars. [11]

It is hard to know how to take this playful contrast between the cigar-smoking Jasons with dead souls and creeds outworn and those "who bask . . . in lofty-thinking Splendor." Clearly Reed here intends satire rather than serious protest. His target is intellectual mediocrity, not capitalist oppression.

The next stanza lists the jobs the Villagers have in the uptown commercial culture: one works as an advertising copywriter, another works on the Sunday supplement of a paper, another teaches art at a school, another is a journalist in the city room, and the last draws works as a commercial artist drawing illustrations for clothing catalogues.

Despite this economic subjection to what Reed calls "Uptown," the poem continues the original playful assault on intellectual mediocrity:

Yet we are free who live in Washington Square,
We dare to think as Uptown wouldn't dare,

Blazing our nights with arguments uproarious;
What care we for a dull old world censorious
When each is sure he'll fashion something glorious?
Blessed are thou, Anarchic Liberty
Who asketh nought but joy of such as we![12]

The first line of the poem is the nub of the Greenwich Village myth. To be "free" in Reed's terms is to be freed from dullness, censoriousness, and those qualities that restrict individuality and personal distinction. We are reminded of the aspiration to "ride the stars" in the earlier stanza and to "fashion something glorious" in the last. "Anarchic Liberty," clearly, is invoked to legitimize personal aspiration rather than social rebellion, to say nothing of revolution. One thinks of Reed three years later trotting off to interview Pancho Villa dressed in a bright yellow corduroy suit, more dandy than proto-revolutionary.

The Village enemy responsible for mediocrity was commerce, personified for this generation of Villagers by the business life of midtown and the cultural activities like Broadway theater that were associated with it. It was commerce that was swallowing up talent and turning sharp minds into dull mediocrities. It was a capitalism of dullness rather than social oppression. Villagers had attacked commercial culture from the outset. In this earlier period, those around the Provincetown Theater reiterated their detestation of the Broadway theater and all it stood for. Other objects of this kind of scorn soon materialized: the daily press, the "slick" magazine one or another worked for. In a sense, *The Masses*, the vehicle for the attack on capitalism and commercialism, drew heavily on its enemies' methods in its format. Colorful illustrations, cartoons, and caricatures reflected the Villagers' ambivalence toward commerce and toward capitalism generally.

This kind of attack on commerce by Village rebels like Reed presents us with something of a puzzle. Why was this freedom from mercenary taint so central to their sense of who they were? Why did dullness and mediocrity pose such a threat? Why did it lead this particular group of New York writers and intellectuals toward radical stances of one kind or another; toward socialism, various forms of radical feminism, and a lifestyle as self-styled Bohemians and outsiders?

At least on the surface they followed an itinerary in reaching New York that is not very different from that followed by writers like Damon Runyon and Ring Lardner who made fortunes from their work as newspapermen, sportswriters, and fiction writers for the midcult magazine press. Like the commercial writers uptown, they arrived in New York from small towns and cities across the country: Hutchins Hapgood from Alton, Illinois;

George Cram Cook and Susan Glaspell from Davenport, Iowa; Crystal Eastman and Max Eastman from Marlborough, Massachusetts, and Canandaigua, New York; Floyd Dell from Barry, Illinois, and Davenport, Iowa; Carl Van Vechten from Cedar Rapids, Iowa; and John Reed from Portland, Oregon.

What, one wonders, brought them to New York? At the base of Reed's claim "we are free" lies the assumption that these Villagers had not been drawn eastward by the same magnetic force that had provided New York with the vast cultural workforce recruited from the same towns and cities that was manning New York's theaters, newspapers, publishing houses, advertising agencies, and other producers of commercial culture, and that they were impervious to its attractions. It is important to remember that New York since the mid–nineteenth-century had been the national center for printing and publishing of all kinds. It therefore had exercised a powerful attraction on anyone bent on a writing career. Its reputation as a center of theatrical entertainment had a similar effect. Its newspapers, too, offered opportunities and salaries that gave them a free hand in attracting and recruiting promising journalists like Runyon, Lardner, and Ben Hecht from across the nation.

New York's prosperous newspaper industry appears to have been an important attraction for this first cohort of Villagers, a surprising number of whom came with extensive experience as working journalists. Susan Glaspell, for example, the most talented playwright except for O'Neill to work with the Provincetown Players, began her career as a staff writer for the *Des Moines Daily News*, achieved a by-line as "News Girl" before moving on to writing fiction for *Harper's*, *The Ladies' Home Journal*, *Women's Home Companion*, and other national magazines. She arrived in New York in 1913 at the age of thirty, the same age as Runyon, who had been born in Manhattan, Kansas, and had worked on half a dozen Midwest papers before coming to New York and beginning work for Hearst. Floyd Dell, like Runyon, had worked on a succession of Midwest papers before reaching New York: the *Davenport Times*, *Davenport Democrat*, the *Chicago Evening Post*. Hutchins Hapgood had served as drama critic for the *Chicago Evening Post* and the *New York Globe* before moving on to write features for the *New York Advertiser*, then edited by Lincoln Steffens. Carl Van Vechten had written for the *Chicago American* before coming to New York and writing for the *Times* in several capacities. Even John Reed, the youngest of them, had worked on the *Harvard Lampoon* and *Monthly* and, fresh from college, had gone to work for *American Magazine*. Reed, who adopted Steffens as his mentor, made the most distinguished mark of them all in the next few years as a journalist for *Metropolitan Magazine*.

Yet none of their similarities to uptown writers like Runyon and none of these ties to uptown commercial culture account for the stance the rebels took. The Village myth of freedom expressed in Reed's poem takes for granted that you could work and earn your living in the midtown commercial culture without in any way sharing its values; that you could work as a journalist, advertising copy writer, stage designer, or magazine editor without being touched by the values that pervaded the expansive uptown world. What was there about them that gave them this conviction of their immunity?

This generation of Villagers was, as they insisted, different from their counterparts uptown; but it is important to understand just how they differed from other writers who, like them, earned their living from the commercial culture of the city. This was a fact that Malcolm Cowley was to underscore in 1934 as he looked back on the Village experience. In each case, something in their experience must have turned them away from the kinds of careers they might have aspired to elsewhere in the city. Each of them at some point must have made a conscious decision to reject conventional uptown success.

What this touchstone of rebellion was seems to have varied from one to another. For most of this first generation of Villagers, "Greenwich Village" began far from New York City. Something close to home usually sparked the rebellion. Every American city of any size appears to have had a live cell of Bohemia by early in the century. Each provided an oasis from the mediocrity of town life and a temporary resting place for those on the move. For Susan Glaspell the oasis was a group in Davenport, Iowa, called the "Monist Society," which met to discuss literary and philosophical ideas and seems to have launched her in rebellion. For Margaret Anderson growing up in Indianapolis, it was the response to a letter she had written to a columnist for *Good Housekeeping* with the suggestion that she read Edmund Gosse's *Father and Son*. For Anderson a second stage was ignited by the group in Chicago around Francis Hackett, literary editor of the *Chicago Evening Post*, the nub of what became the Chicago Renaissance. Floyd Dell's rebellion had been fueled by the same group when he served as assistant to Hackett on the *Friday Literary Review*. Chicago, both the university and the city, seems to have played an important mediating role in directing the careers of several other Village rebels of this first generation, Hutchins Hapgood and Carl Van Vechten among them. Once they were on their way, the word seems to have spread among them that Greenwich Village was another and better haven, both a cheap place to live and an exciting "literary" place to be.

These experiences—glimpses of a Bohemia of individual self-expression—of those who worked as journalists distinguished them from others like Runyon and Lardner, who went on to uptown journalism and commercial success. There was no group for whom such a Bohemian utopia had more significance than it had for women, especially the cohort of college women attracted to New York in these years when college-trained women were a rarity. The prominence of women in the Village group, the central place of feminism of one kind or another in the rebellion, is underscored by everything we know of them. But American colleges and universities played an important role in providing an oasis for both men and women. The first Villagers were all, except for Dell, college graduates, and a number of them had advanced degrees, some more than one. Glaspell graduated from Drake; Max Eastman from Williams; Crystal from Vassar (with an M.A. in sociology from Columbia); Van Vechten from Chicago; Cook, Hapgood, and Reed from Harvard. Cook held a degree from Heidelberg as well, and Eastman earned a doctorate working under Dewey at Columbia.

It is unclear exactly what this experience of higher education meant. This particular cohort of early college graduates appear to have nursed a sense of themselves as pioneers exploring new terrain. For more of them, college was their introduction to intellectual excitement experienced among peers apart from the society. It seems to have awakened in them a desire for self-expression, a hunger for intellectual recognition and originality. The college women, moreover, quickly came to see that college had not brought them the same access to self-expression away from the academy as it had their male classmates. Their association with other college women, moreover, appears to have fostered the notion that women had perspectives and values that their male cohorts with college training did not seem to share. [13]

One of the important Village institutions for communicating this kind of perspective was the group of radical feminists in Heterodoxy, the female debating group that began meeting for lunch every other week in the Village in 1910. We are only beginning to understand the importance of this group in shaping the course of prewar feminism and reform. Heterodoxy contained feminists of every class, stripe, and occupation, from Emma Goldman to writers and actresses like Glaspell and Ida Rauh, from openly lesbian couples to conventionally married women. In their discussions and later in the organizations members of Heterodoxy founded and supported, they took drama, reform, and feminist politics in new directions. [14]

College had convinced the women that they were the equals of their male cohorts. College had also made them self-conscious and instilled an appetite for self-expression. Reading social theorists and major thinkers such as Sigmund Freud and Henri Bergson gave them an almost theatrical sense of human society and experience. Lectures by Bergson and William

James, given at Columbia in the spring of 1913, were signal events in the shaping of the rebellion.

The men, too, were drawn to many of the same interests, partly through the influence of the women, but even more through the romantic personae they appear to have developed, a sense of themselves as mavericks and explorers that emerges uniformly in their memoirs. The willingness of these women to form unconventional sexual ties with men, to cut themselves adrift from the mores of middle-class America, was a great attraction, one the men had some difficulty in comprehending. Dell, Hapgood, and Cook all converted to a kind of circumspect feminism, although all of them complained at one time or another about the female "clubbiness" that seemed to accompany feminism. In Dell's case, conversion came early with his book, *Women as World Builders*, published in 1913.

This questioning of gender roles in the society was an important part of the Village rebellion. Many of the major women's organizations, such as the Feminine Alliance, were rooted in the bimonthly debates and discussions among members of Heterodoxy.[15] In the plays produced by the Provincetown Players, written by Glaspell, Neith Boyce, and others in critical 1910s, questions of gender roles were dominant. Susan Glaspell's feminist play *The Verge*, in fact, became a minor classic for small theater groups around the country.

All of these developments contrast sharply with the masculine monopoly of midtown commercial culture. The Broadway scene in which Runyon, Lardner, and other journalists figured, like the adjacent theater, music, and sporting worlds, was exclusively male terrain. Women figured only as objects of sexual conquest, observation, and jest. The slang that developed in the Times Square area, rooted as it was in the argots of boxing, horse-racing, and gambling, was a distillation of male experience. Its creators and propagators coined such terms as "bimbo" and "ball and chain" (for "wife").[16]

Nonetheless, despite these important differences from uptown writers and their own often-repeated rejection of everything commercial, the Villagers appear to have been driven by an appetite for personal, individual distinction that was the particular creation of their times and very similar to that which propelled some of those working in uptown commercial culture. It was this appetite, once they had recognized it for what it was, that took them out of their hermetic middle-class families, their small cities with limited means for venting their ambition and imagination, and brought them finally to New York and the Village.

The means for obtaining public visibility had immeasurably increased during the twenty years preceding the Village revolt, in such a way as to create a new era of self-amplification. It was in this period, for example, that Times Square was establishing itself as the center of commercial cultural production. Hand-in-hand with this new style of production was a promotional style from which it was inseparable. Its bywords were illumination, visibility, celebrity. Broadway chose the sobriquet of "Bright Lights," but there were other ways of achieving the same promotional results, the same amplification of self, as Reed was to demonstrate during the rest of his career as a journalist. Individuals performing in the new entertainment media of national theater and vaudeville networks, those writing exposés in the expanding tabloid press, and many ordinary people caught up in highly publicized events had experienced wholly unexpected degrees of fame and celebrity. One thinks of the poet Harriet Monroe reading poetry to an audience of thousands at the Chicago Columbian Exposition in 1893.

The literary critic Philip Fisher, commenting on the novelty of these new forms of public visibility, observed that the "years between 1890 and 1910 [might be described] as a series of experiences in the modeling of a highly visible structure of identity under the new circumstances of performance."[17] It was in the area of public performance that the new searchlight of celebrity was most evident. This searchlight, according to Fisher, transformed performance and performance spaces in the same way that it amplified the reputation of individuals. Presidential politics, theater, journalism, and literature were never afterwards the same. It was in this heady air of emerging star systems that the future Villagers were reared. Like Carrie in Theodore Dreiser's 1900 novel, they appear to have arrived in the city with a hunger for fame and the new forms of power that went with it.[18]

Assessing the activities of these first Villagers in this light helps explain what drove them in the directions they took. In the Village the intellectual and artistic aspirations, their desire to express themselves that they had nursed in private, became exciting matters of public interest. Their reminiscences are striking, coming from writers and artists, in their emphasis on the social and public. One would think, to read them, that the vitality of the Village lay in eating, drinking, and talking. Everyone who wrote about the Village in this period remembered it for its hangouts and its talk. It was clear that for this group the joy of finding like-minded souls, all wanting something similar and unconventional, overshadowed almost everything else. Mabel Dodge, writing twenty years later, recalled that it seemed "as though everywhere, in that year of 1913, barriers went down and people reached each other who had never been in touch before; there were all sorts of new ways to communicate, as well as new communications."[19]

Greenwich Village as a new public arena for achieving self-expression and celebrity had something of the character of a small town made up of the nation's village atheists and town criers. What Mabel Dodge meant by "new ways of communicating" and "new communications" is evident from her own activities in the first months after her arrival home from Florence, Italy. One such instance of novel theater was the extraordinary spectacle staged in Madison Square Garden in May of 1913 to dramatize the plight of striking Paterson silk workers. Nothing in Times Square could have rivaled the sight of red searchlights projecting the letters "IWW" on the sky above the Garden as lines of workers from Paterson, twenty-eight blocks long, waited to enter; nor the dramatic re-enactment of the strike that followed. Dodge and John Reed had worked tirelessly with other Villagers in the weeks preceding, but it was Dodge who was singled out by Hutchins Hapgood as the originator of the idea. In an article in the *Globe* he explicitly linked her achievement to that of the business world. "We are familiar in America with promoters in business, in land speculation, in philanthropy, but not so familiar," he added, with what was called "'Promoters of the Spirit.' "[20] It seemed clear to Hapgood that the Paterson Pageant was of a piece with Dodge's other major promotions: the Armory Show of post-Impressionist art, and the salon she had established in her Fifth Avenue house, an institution that brought together figures from labor, the arts, and radical politics. "I imagine her real purpose in coming here," he commented, "was to advertise, exploit, and promote, what she thought was a new and important form of art. . . ."[21]

The revolution, as one might call it, that she and her contemporaries had helped bring about involved what was made visible, what she and others succeeded in bringing out of the shadows into public space. The process of bringing previously private or suppressed experience into high visibility takes place in every age. In our own age, for example, mental illness and drug addiction have been brought out of the closet to confront us on our streets, in a way that would have been unimaginable even ten years ago. In the same way, the period before the first World War was characterized by a succession of revelations and exposés of corporate greed, urban corruption, and what was called "vice"—prostitution and other forms of packaging and marketing sexuality.

The Villagers added their own contributions to what was to become public and "out there" to be seen. Mabel Dodge, in an interview conducted in June of 1913, had stated her belief that the printed word would soon be replaced by live speech, and she added that she herself was trying "to loosen up thought by means of speech to get at the truth at the bottom of people and let it out."[22] The Paterson Strike Pageant, for example, had been an effort to bring class conflict into the realm of what was visible and make labor strife into theater. In this case, the social tensions surrounding industrial conflict were literally made into theater. Under the editorship of Max Eastman, *The Masses*, with its colorful graphics by Village artists, expensive "slick" paper, and handsome format was still another excursion into making politics into theater, of moving political and economic thought and revolutionary dogma from verbal abstraction into visible public space. The object of these theatrical manoeuvres was to seize public attention in a new way. John Reed's promotional epigraph for the January 1913 issue would have done honor to J. Walter Thompson: *The Masses*, Reed wrote, is "a free magazine; frank, arrogant, impertinent, searching for true causes; a magazine directed against rigidity and dogma wherever it is found, printing what is too naked or true for the moneymaking press. . . ."[23]

The Village revolt was an attack on the media of commercial culture that succeeded in an eery way in anticipating in its use of media where the media were heading. The Villagers themselves, as we read them, seem to have been caught up in the excitement and intoxicated by the power they experienced as they forged and witnessed these changes. In doing so, they seem closer to the commercial world they condemned than they must have realized. Through the voices of Mabel Dodge, John Reed, and other Villagers, one can hear the prophetic voices of Marshall McLuhan and Henry Luce simultaneously.

There is still another and final point to be made about what the prewar Villagers had attempted. Their objectives, it should be evident, went well beyond the dramatization of politics. Mabel Dodge's Wednesday evenings were nothing less than attempts to bring the American culture of her own time in its entirety under a single roof and expose it in microcosm, to bring out into the open all of the secrets that people in their isolation withheld from one another; to create, one might say, a laissez-faire economy of ideas. As she listed those she wanted present— "Socialists, Trade-Unionists, Suffragists, Poets, Lawyers, Murderers, Psychoanalysts, Birth Controlists, Clubwomen, Clergymen"[24]—it becomes clear how widely she was willing to range. It also becomes clear how close in its emphasis on inclusiveness such language comes to mimicking the lingo of the contemporary marketing theories employed by the new department stores.

Other Villagers extended this range even further. Susan Glaspell, in a succession of plays that she wrote and produced for the Provincetown Players after 1916, created a theater of the most private emotions. The stage became a means of bringing to light the inner reflections of women, the tensions between men and women in marriage, the onset of violence in marriage, the masculine bias in the legal system (a women is held for the murder of her husband), the ways women fail one another, the silly sides of feminism, and the naïve and glib ways contemporary women made a fad of psychoanalysis. She dramatized, as O'Neill was later to do, dimensions of the human psyche that had not previously been seen on the American stage.[25]

It is difficult, living as we do in the wake of such cultural changes, to recognize the revolutionary, even shocking, character these initiatives had at the time. It is necessary to remind ourselves that this first cohort of Villagers had succeeded in theatricalizing social realities long before radio, film, or television had made such revelations into clichés; just as they had introduced their peers to the intimate life of the emotions as visualizable experience before the cinema close-up and, later, the small screen had begun to do so. The Village world itself, capes and black floors included, had after all been an effort to dramatize the artist's life and the life of the mind and to provide them with a space, a home, a stage set off from the middle-class world, before our colleges and universities had begun to do so in a systematic way.

NINE

The Man Who Would Say (Almost) Anything · H. L. Mencken, New York, and the Great Opinion Factory

One horse-laugh is worth ten thousand syllogisms.[1]
   H. L. Mencken, 1924

I have made a living for many years by thrusting myself upon the attention of strangers. I have written and printed probably 10,000,000 words of English, and continue to this day to pour out more and more. It has wrung from others, many of them my superiors, probably a million words of notice, some of it pro but most of it con. In brief, my booth has been set up on a favorable pitch and I have never lacked customers for my ballyhoo.[2]
   H. L. Mencken, 1939

This holy terror from Baltimore is splendidly and contagiously alive. He calls you a swine and an imbecile, and he increases your will to live.[3]
   Walter Lippmann, 1927

THEODORE DREISER   Well if it isn't Anheuser's brightest boy out to see the town.

H. L. MENCKEN   Certainly, my father is the richest brewer in Baltimore, and he makes the best beer in the world. See this gaudy tie and these yellow shoes? Every jack-dandy and rowdy-dow in Baltimore wears them. What else do you expect of me?[4]

This odd exchange between Mencken and Dreiser took place during Mencken's first recorded appearance on the New York scene in 1908. In the light of Mencken's subsequent career in the city, it is a tableau worth recalling. Fresh off the train from Baltimore, a journey he was to make hundreds of times in the next forty years, he apparently had made his way brashly into the offices of the *Delineator*, prompted by an invitation from its editor to drop around "next time he came to town." Dreiser, who had somehow heard of Mencken's medical penchant, had asked him to do some articles on medical subjects for the *Delineator*. Mencken always read widely in medical literature and, to judge from his letters to Carl Van Vechten and other friends, he was a legendary hypochondriac who was seldom without the early symptoms of one or another of the major illnesses.[5] Mencken, meanwhile, had caught Dreiser at a distinctive point in his own life, the three years he worked as a high-salaried editor of a slick women's magazine put out by the Butterick dress pattern house.[6]

At the time of the conversation, Mencken was twenty-seven years old and had been writing for Baltimore papers for almost ten years, but to Dreiser, ten years his senior and by then an established New York journalist, he appeared much younger and greener. Dreiser, clearly impressed by the encounter, took the trouble to record it in some detail. Mencken came into the office, Dreiser remembered,

> like a small town roisterer or college sophomore of the crudest yet most disturbing charm and impishness who, for some reason, had strayed into the field of letters. More than anything else, he reminded me of a spoiled and petted and possibly over-financed brewer's or wholesale grocer's son who was out for a lark.[7]

Dreiser's take on Mencken was in a way prophetic. Mencken superficially was, of course, none of these things. He had never seen the inside of a college, and Baltimore, where he had grown up, was anything but a small town. Mencken, moreover, was not a roisterer, nor was he spoiled, petted, or over-financed. He was a hard-working reporter, an omnivorous reader with strong interests in music and literature, still living at home with his mother, and no doubt, despite the shoes and tie, operating on limited means. Nonetheless, Dreiser had caught the essence of this extraordinary visitation. He caught the swagger, the poise, and the hint of defiance that were to be lifelong traits. It seems clear that Dreiser read Mencken as a literary character and saw in him an odd mixture of dandy and classic New York Bowery Boy, the artisanal butcher-boy on a spree. He seems to have seen the show Mencken put on, moreover, for the bright and daring dramatic bit that it was. His performance, Dreiser noted, "bristled with a gay phraseology and a largely suppressed though still peeping mirth."[8]

By 1908, this scene would suggest, the influences of Edgar Allan Poe, Oscar Wilde, and especially of his mentor, bohemian music critic James Huneker, were already making themselves felt. But Dreiser also caught in Mencken that hint of vulgarity and puffery he later noted in his editing of the *Smart Set*, which Dreiser felt was too "Broadwayesque," its contents "like a diet of soufflé."[9] Beneath it all Dreiser had seen in Mencken the mark, however dandified, of the German burgher. It was probably this shared German strain that helped forge the close bond that soon developed between them, and also left them both permanently somewhat alienated, always with a feeling of being outsiders in the literary world, even at those moments when they were receiving the greatest critical recognition.

By the mid-'twenties, Mencken had probably become the American writer best known to the American public. Long before his death, he had become the subject of a vigorous industry organized around his adulation. Biographical sketches and studies of his writings had appeared regularly in magazines and newspapers since the 'twenties. By the 'fifties, re-issues of his books, anthologies, compilations of his writings, biographies, and bibliographies were crowding the shelves of libraries.

His whole literary career is resonant with ironies. Whimsical, irreverent, abusive in what he wrote, he personified one whole segment of the New York commercial press, yet he always insisted he was neither mercenary nor a New Yorker. A reactionary and a lifelong foe of what would become known as Progressive reform, he succeeded as editor and writer in placing himself in the vanguard of modernism and of the literary and cultural rebellion that followed the war. As editor of the *Smart Set*, he tutored a generation of college intellectuals in the sophisticated and sexually liberated ways of the literary world, yet he himself was not a college man and, by most standards, neither sophisticated nor sexually liberated. A doctrinaire determinist who believed that individuals counted for little in the calculus of change, he became the very embodiment of assertive, masculine individuality.

Over the next two decades, Mencken developed much the same contradictory relationship to New York itself. Although Mencken's trips to New York after his 1908 meeting with Dreiser were so regular and so extended that he once described himself as a "commuter," he never moved to the city and always spoke of Baltimore as home.[10] Mencken over the years had a difficult time settling his accounts with the city. He could never decide whether he liked it or detested it. It became for him a great gaudy marketplace with all the attractions and all the perils of Bunyan's Vanity Fair. Throughout his life he argued back and forth within himself the qualities, good and bad, he found in New York; sometimes speaking for the city, more often attacking it as cold and soulless. It was a citadel of the rootless, a vulgar marketplace, the stronghold of the mercenary and all who were out after "the old *mazuma*." "He is a vagabond," he wrote of the New Yorker in 1926. "His notions of the agreeable become those of the vaudeville actor."[11] "There is little in New York," he wrote the next year, "that does not issue out of money, but what issues out of money is often extremely brilliant, and I believe that it is more brilliant in New York than it has ever been anywhere else. A truly overwhelming opulence envelops the whole place, even the slums." Or, a bit later in the same essay, "it has a glitter like that of the Constantinople of the Comneni . . . the Baghdad of the Sassanians."[12]

It was the spectacle of the city, especially at night, that repeatedly elicited his most poetic tributes. In an essay entitled "Totentanz," written in 1927, the spectacle of New York became a Strindbergian dance of death:

> The spectacle of New York remains—infinitely grand and gorgeous, stimulating like the best that comes out of goblets, and none the worse for its sinister smack. The town seizes upon all the more facile and agreeable emotions like band music. It is immensely trashy—but it remains immense. Is it a mere Utopia of rogues, a vast complicated machine for rooking honest men? I don't think so. The honest man, going to its markets, gets sound value for his money. It offers him luxury of a kind never dreamed of in the world before—the luxury of being served by perfect and unobtrusive slaves, human and mechanical. It permits him to wallow regally—nay, almost celestially. . . . Nor is all this luxury purely physiological. There is entertainment for the spirit, or for what passes for the spirit when men are happy. There were more orchestral concerts in New York last year than in Berlin. The town has more theaters, and far better ones, than a dozen Londons.

Even its ugly features attracted him, he conceded:

> There are more frauds and scoundrels, more quacks and cony-catchers, more suckers and visionaries in New York than in all the country west of the Union Hill, New Jersey, Breweries. In other words, there are more interesting people.

Even his attempts at praise, however, were qualified by digs of one kind or another:

> I hymn the town without loving it. It is immensely amusing. I see nothing in it to inspire the fragile and shy thing called affection.[13]

When he came to New York on magazine business, usually for a few days every other week, he stayed at the Algonquin and lived the life of an out-of-towner, dining, often with his fellow editor George Jean Nathan, at Luchow's near Union Square or at the Café des Beaux Arts at Fortieth Street and Sixth Avenue.

Fascinating as New York was for Mencken, Baltimore was "the secret sharer" in his life. Without some familiarity with his childhood and young manhood in that city, he is almost indecipherable. The large German-American community of Baltimore in which Mencken was raised continued to play an important role in his life. German-Americans during

Mencken's youth were scarcely a small minority in a city of some 400,000 in which they made up a quarter of the population. As the oldest son of the oldest son of Burkhardt Mencken, who had emigrated from Saxony in 1848, Mencken, before he jumped ship and became a journalist, had been in line to become the family's head, or *stammhalter*, and, it would seem, there was something of the suppressed *stammhalter*, something presumptuous and hegemonic, in everything he subsequently did.[14]

The Mencken family always claimed for itself an elevated status in German-American Baltimore. As prosperous merchants and free-thinkers proud of their ties to high academic and professional forebears in Germany (they even boasted of ties to Otto von Bismarck), the Menckens had always held themselves aloof from most German-American activities and organizations in the city. The family deviated from other German-American families in another way that had an important bearing on Mencken's subsequent development. His grandfather had married a Scotch-Irish woman from Jamaica who had made English the language of the family. Both Mencken and his father grew up speaking English, and Mencken, one is led to believe, spoke only halting German. His wide childhood reading in English literature also resulted in part from this circumstance.[15]

From his father, whom he greatly admired, he inherited the strongly conservative views of a successful businessman: a belief in hard work, hard currency, prompt payment of bills, avoidance of debt; a distrust of labor and unions; and a political philosophy that condemned anything radical, liberal, or smacking of reform. From a very young age, he had been tutored by his father to assume the direction of the family tobacco business. Through this experience he acquired the business sense and management skills that later served him well as an editor. Photographs of him over the years suggest that he also acquired a lifelong taste for good cigars of the kind manufactured by his family. He also retained some of his father's somewhat arrogant feelings toward his Baltimore neighbors. He early internalized the family's sense of superiority, further strengthened by his study of Darwin and evolution, and came to hold most of his German compatriots, especially the Catholics among them, in almost the same disdain that he reserved for other immigrant groups.[16]

Mencken's mother had, if anything, an even more dominant and lasting influence on his life. He continued to live with her on Hollins Street until her death in 1925. When he spoke of the importance of returning each week to Baltimore from the hubbub of New York, his feelings toward the city seem unconsciously to have been colored by his feelings toward her. Returning home to Baltimore, he wrote in 1926, "is like coming out of a football crowd into quiet communion with a fair one who is also amiable, and has the gift of consolation for hard-beset and despairing men."[17] It was only after her death, he later acknowledged, that he took full account of the central place she held in his life. "I begin to realize," he wrote in a letter, "how inextricably my life was interwoven with my mother's. A hundred times a day I find myself planning to tell her something or ask her for this or that. . . . The house seems strange [without her] as if the people in it were deaf and dumb."[18] This strong maternal attachment overshadowed his whole life and appears to have deeply complicated his feelings toward other women. When his wife died in 1935, Mencken returned to live out his life in the same family house on Hollins Street where he had lived with his mother.

While he never fully eradicated his ties to German-American Baltimore in the coming years—the war was to strengthen them, in fact—something, by the time of his meeting with Dreiser, had already jarred him from the track of his *stammhalter* destiny. His early life in Baltimore had been directed toward equipping him to follow his father into the family tobacco business. He graduated from the local Polytechnic at eighteen and, without apparently any serious thought of attending college, went to work at once in the family's cigar factory. The routine and tedious character of this work, however, soon proved uncongenial to him, and he stayed on only until his father's early and sudden death in 1899 made a long-desired move into writing and journalism possible.[19]

How he decided on such a vocation is something of a mystery. His bookish interests began in childhood. During the years before he joined the *Smart Set* as book editor in 1908, he portrayed himself in his reminiscences as an autodidact in the mythic Benjamin Franklin mold, one of the many masks he adopted in an effort to conceal or obscure his inner workings. He reports studying writing, for example, through a correspondence school, reading randomly and voraciously, hearing about Henrik Ibsen from a ship captain on a return from a business trip to Jamaica, getting word of G. B. Shaw from a former New York drama critic who had moved to Baltimore, and learning to play the piano and joining a "Saturday Club" of amateur musicians who met regularly to play and discuss the classical repertory. He speaks of dreaming of becoming a composer, a dream he relinquished with regret. His true sense of vocation came even later, several years after he had begun to write for newspapers, as he gradually abandoned writing poetry and fiction on the strength of his evident talent in sharp and colorful opinion.[20]

Meanwhile, he experienced great success as a young newspaperman. He began reporting for the *Morning Herald* in 1899, and by 1905, at the age of twenty-four, he had risen to managing editor. During these years when he worked on assignments of every kind, he came to feel that he had thoroughly imbibed "the old-time journalist's concept of himself as a free spirit and darling of the gods, licensed by his high merits to ride and deride the visible universe." He had already acquired a reputation as an ace reporter, an occasional satirist and versifier, as well as a forceful editor. When the *Herald* went under in 1906, he accepted a job as Sunday editor of the prestigious *Baltimore Sun* in order to give himself more time for intellectual pursuits. The *Sun* thereafter became a working home to Mencken. Before his health took him out of action in 1948, he had made the full transition from reporter, to editor, to manager and, finally, to director of the *Sun* company—all in all, a career characterized by a kind of entrepreneurial success his father would surely have admired.[21]

In the spring of 1911, three years after he had started doing a book column for the *Smart Set* in New York, Mencken, in an effort to revive the editorial page of the *Evening Sun*, officially began another phase of his career as a social and political satirist. In May of that year he began to write a by-line column entitled "The Free Lance," in which he derided town reformers and "visionaries" and satirized local activities that he found ridiculous.[22] The columns that began to appear initiated his signature activity as a writer. Although these first satiric efforts pale beside the work of his abusive virtuosity a few years later, he had clearly moved his exertions from the city desk to the opinion factory and, despite his professed residency there, from Baltimore to New York.

The role of verbal curmudgeon, of David to the Goliath of tradition and propriety, appeared to come naturally to him. He seemed during the next few years to have discovered in himself the suppressed mirth that Dreiser had detected in 1908, and he appeared to positively revel in his new work. He had discovered along with many others that opinion, especially clever and abusive opinion, sold more brightly than the news. It was no accident that the masthead declared that *Smart Set* was "a magazine of cleverness." It was "cleverness," as contemporaries construed the term, rather than any great power of mind or critical penetration, that was to make Mencken's fame and fortune.

What Mencken set out to do was in 1911 a timely initiative. The vogue enjoyed by those who provided readers with idiosyncratic, often outrageous opinions was one important by-product of the kind of objective news reporting that evolved rapidly after the 1890s.[23] As Michael Schudson has shown, the kind of objectivity that newspapers began to demand of their writers early in the century put heavy and sometimes noxious restraints on those who did the reporting. This new idea of objectivity went beyond the simple need to get one's facts straight. The idea of objectivity that emerged in this period reflected the new scientific conception of taking the self out of reporting, as distinct from simply getting it right. The perceived danger was not just bias or inaccuracy but the tangle of subjectivism brought on the scene by psychoanalysis and new scientific studies of human behavior. Mencken recalled that, as a young reporter working for the *Sun*, he and his fellow reporters felt "hobbled by their paper's craze for mathematical accuracy." "Immense stress upon accuracy," he recalled, was demanded by city editors who counseled reporters to take nothing at face value, to double-check and verify everything. The result, Mencken felt, was reporters, drained of personal perspective and affect, who "tended to write like bookkeepers."[24]

This new discipline of the newsroom, nonetheless, proved seductive, even to those who bristled at the restraints. Veteran reporters, while they found ways to circumvent the mindless impersonality of the new objective reporting, never forgot the chastening experience of having their early stories torn apart. This new and demanding standard of accuracy, moreover, became something to push against as they sought to develop other forms of newspaper writing that offered greater freedom of expression and imagination. Shrewd practitioners like Mencken quickly perceived that the new fixation on objectivity opened a gap in news reporting and therefore created a market for those who traded in lively opinions.

The move in these years to other forms of writing from the practice of news reporting is less surprising than it might at first seem. A striking number of writers in the early part of the century—James M. Cain, Ernest Hemingway, and John Dos Passos, among others—gravitated from reporting news to writing fiction, as Shelley Fishkin has shown.[25] The new concept of objectivity, moreover, proved to be an effective schoolmaster for reporters. Hemingway, as Fishkin shows, learned from the style sheet of the *Kansas City Star* to describe a scene with verbs instead of adjectives. Press style sheets and the city editors who enforced them helped relieve news reporting of its fatty rhetorical excess and encouraged a new, lean prose style, even as it helped filter expressions of opinion from news reporting. These steps served to give opinion by-line prominence in other parts of the paper. Editors, far from abandoning opinion, simply repackaged it, often for the Sunday editions that became so popular in this period.

Quite a number of writers, Mencken among them, retained an attachment to the newspaper, even though their work often took them far afield. Ben Hecht, Ring Lardner, and Damon Runyon continued to see themselves as newspapermen. Runyon, for example, continued to seek assignments as a reporter, while he branched out as a sports writer, a comic feature writer, and, eventually, as an author of popular, slangy magazine fiction. Plays and movie scripts followed. Yet he continued to take news assignments that interested him, almost to the end of his life. It is easy to see parallels between Mencken's career and the careers of these others. Before he found his niche after the war as a colorful, often abusive critic of life and literature, he had tried just about every genre of commercial writing available.

Between 1908 and 1914, when Mencken and George Jean Nathan became co-editors of *Smart Set*, Mencken wrote a monthly book column for *Smart Set* and regularly reviewed books for the Baltimore Sunpapers and for other magazines and journals. For Mencken these were years of frantic and unfocused activity in the literary marketplace. By his own estimate, he somehow hacked his way through 1,831 books in this period. In addition, he reviewed Baltimore theater for the *Sun*, and translated and published plays by Ibsen. He also translated writings of Nietzsche. In addition to all this, he undertook hackwork of various kinds, even ghosting a book on baby care for a Baltimore physician and concocting under the pseudonym "Owen Hatteras" (which he shared with Nathan) various confections—epigrams, comic sketches, and stories—to fill the pages of the *Smart Set*. For Dreiser's magazine, the *Bohemian*, he provided a novelette about marriage, an article on "the psychology of kissing," and something entitled "The Bald-headed Man." Some time during this period Mencken and Nathan acquired two sleazy pulp-story magazines, the *Parisienne* and *Saucy Stories*—"boob bait" and "louse magazines" Mencken called them, although they brought in, for a time, more money than anything else he did. They were later sold. In the midst of all of this, he managed two extended and closely reported trips to Europe and sustained a voluminous correspondence with an ever-widening circle of writers, editors, and publishers such as Alfred Knopf, whose friendship he energetically courted.[26]

The key experiences for Mencken during these years were in his work as a book reviewer and drama critic. Theater and book columns in magazines and newspapers were the cradle during the prewar years where a new abrasive style of criticism was nurtured. Previously, book reviewing and drama criticism had been little better than advertising. Mencken's generation discovered the excitement and interest they could generate with sharp criticism that derided existing commercial standards in publishing and theatrical production.

Mencken appears to have further honed his craft by watching his co-editor, George Jean Nathan, who wrote a theater column for the *Smart Set*. Nathan, like Mencken, came from an established business family, but his trail to Broadway led from the Midwest through Cornell University and summers with his father in France. He began writing theater criticism for the *New York Herald* in 1906. He was soon writing his distinctive style of punishing criticism for half a dozen other New York periodicals. Nathan's style was that of the ultimate urbanite. He lived for most of his life in the Royalton Hotel near the Algonquin and detested the country, which he once characterized as the place where cherries for Manhattan cocktails were grown. His aloof, arch posture as a critic made him an important and feared figure on the Broadway scene; "the Dean of Broadway," as he was later called.

This new style of criticism provided the backbone for a kind of magazine catering to sophisticated urban audiences. By the 'twenties, a generation of critics known for their scathing cultural reportage was in place. Nathan wrote for *Judge* as well as *Smart Set*, John Peale Bishop for *Vanity Fair*, Alexander Woollcott for the *New York Herald*, and Dorothy Parker and Robert Benchley, who began on *Vanity Fair*, for the fledgling *New Yorker*.

Magazine journalism in New York before the war had been a volatile sector of the literary marketplace. Mencken and Dreiser between them experienced it fully. Magazines changed titles, editors, and character almost overnight, and their fortunes changed accordingly. One factor in this volatility was the proliferation of magazines aimed at a specifically urban clientele of prosperous middle-class readers. *Puck, Judge,* and *Life,* all founded in the decades after the Civil War, were joined by *Vogue, Vanity Fair,* and *Smart Set* around the turn of the century. Different as they were, by the prewar period all of these magazines were giving expression to what might be called "the new urbanity." That is, they all in one way or another engaged in lively explorations of New York's cultural milieus and regularly included articles on theater, fashion, and the comic vagaries of Democratic politics. These explorations were financed by the swelling coffers created by new genres of specialized advertising specifically beamed at prosperous urban residents. *Puck, Judge,* and *Life* began as comic weeklies in the 'seventies and 'eighties. Lurid color lithography, anti-Tammany caricature, and political satire and nonsense verbal humor—"the pun is mightier than the sword," *Life* once quipped—were their trademarks.[27]

Vanity Fair, Vogue, and *Smart Set* had, to be sure, different origins and developed different emphases. They nonetheless came to have a similar urban, middle-class appeal. *Vogue* commenced publication in 1892 as a weekly magazine devoted to the doings of New York high society. Its editors were members of the exclusive Calumet Club, and its stockholders were in the social register. Its relatively small circulation of about 25,000 was predominantly made up of those with an interest of one kind or another in this small world. Its greatest coup in these early years was to obtain details and pictures of the trousseau of Consuela Vanderbilt before her marriage in 1895. For thirty years, Walter C. Robinson, himself a clubman, published a column entitled "As Seen by Him" that ruminated on the leisure pastimes of New York society and discussed "proper clothes, proper manners, amateur sports, and entertainment." After 1900 it gave extensive attention to the rapidly growing interest in bridge. Robinson's columns were a celebration of what he called "the metropolitan spirit" that he believed had been awakened in New York.

Vogue's raison d'être was summed up years later by the jesting question of one of its later editors: "Now that the masses take to bathing every week, how is one to distinguish the gentleman?"[28] After he purchased the magazine in 1907, Condé Nast, who had made his reputation as advertising manager of Collier's, gradually steered Vogue out of its New York society backwaters toward being the large-circulation international arbiter of fashion and manners that it had become by the early 'twenties. In doing so, Nast placed himself and New York in the center of a literary social swirl that gave us the terms "sophistication" and "socialite." Vogue became the keystone of a magazine empire that was based, among other things, on the highly profitable mail-order dress pattern business generated out of Vogue.

Vanity Fair, before it was acquired by Nast in 1913, had a wholly different history, one that illustrates a kind of evolution relatively common in this period. Publication had begun in 1890 as the Standard Quarterly. The Quarterly was a ten-cent "naughty picture magazine" on the model of the popular barbershop perennial, The National Police Gazette. Its concern with fashion went no further than the garter belt. While its transformation into the ultimate New York magazine of sophistication and fashion did not take place overnight, it was accomplished in less than a decade. Under the knowing editorship of slick collegiate Frank Crowninshield, it, too, became a kind of cultural guide for young college intellectuals. Edmund Wilson, not long out of Princeton and starting a literary life in the city, became one of its early managing editors in 1922. John Peale Bishop, Robert Benchley, and Dorothy Parker, at one time or another, wrote theater criticism.[29]

Smart Set had been founded in 1900 by a Colonel D'Alton Mann, the shady publisher of Town Topics, who had built a small empire around society gossip and financial tips. Mann specialized in inside knowledge about society life, so much so that he was rumored to have been engaged in blackmail. He had originally hoped to publish a magazine for polite society that was actually written, like Vogue, by society figures. Failing in this, he sought out those who could give a character of what he termed "cleverness" to the magazine, a word that found its way into the magazine's subtitle. Neither Mencken nor Nathan was completely happy with the motto "A Magazine of Cleverness," but they were never able to agree on a substitute. Mencken once listed the other options they had at one time or another considered: "A Magazine That's Read in the Pullman," "A Magazine of Caviar for the General," "A Magazine for the Modish," "A

Polite Magazine for Polite People," "An Amusing Magazine for Amusing People," "We Don't Buy Names, We Make Them," "A Magazine That Other Editors Read," "Alla Moderna," "A Magazine for the Civilized Minority," and "The Aristocrat Among Magazines."[30] They were probably wise to stay with "cleverness."

Cleverness was a key concept at the turn of the century, near kin to what would soon be referred to as "sophistication." In a traditional hierarchy of kinds of intelligence, cleverness probably ranked well down the list below wisdom, and even below wit. As it was used at the time it seems to have denoted a skill in coping, in manipulation, and a ready capacity to get quickly and readily on top of things. It was to the world of ideas what success was to the marketplace, and it is therefore not surprising that it emerged as a positive quality in the journalism of this period.

It was clearly one badge of "the new urbanity." City people were clever, for example, and knowing. Cleverness was especially thought to be the property of the College Man. The original *Life* had been founded in 1892 by three former editors of the *Harvard Lampoon*, and many of the editors of these early humor magazines were veterans of college literary magazines (although it is interesting to note that none of the three most successful editors of such magazines—Mencken, Frank Crowninshield, and Harold Ross—had even attended college). College men in particular had learned that it was clever to laugh at oneself, just as it was clever for society people, without yielding an inch of status, to joke about the foibles of polite society, its customs and pretensions. It was also clever to see one's own manners as provincial and to look elsewhere for cues to what was smart and fashionable; to know about the world. One such earmark of cleverness in the *Smart Set* was the regular publication of stories written in French.

It was into this kaleidoscopic world of magazine journalism that Mencken made his way in the years after 1908, without college and without any pedigree better than that of the industrious and somewhat whimsical burgher that he was. He had become something approaching de facto editor of the *Smart Set* before he officially assumed the title in 1914. The previous editor, Wilbur Huntington Wright, a young protégé brought on at Mencken's urging, had pursued the best young writers in American and England, but his penchant for cultural rebels and what was thought to be harsh fictional reality had lost readers for the magazine and incurred what the publisher considered extravagant costs. A large drop in circulation led to Wright's resignation, the sale of the magazine, and the installation of Mencken and Nathan as editors.[31] The new editors assumed their positions with strict orders to economize. They also recognized that to survive they would have to tilt the contents of the magazine more toward mainstream readers, "the fat women trying to keep awake in Pullman cars after heavy greasy meals" that Mencken once complained of writing for.[32]

For the next six years the *Smart Set* was at best a marginal enterprise. Faced with little money to solicit good writing and with a declining circulation, Mencken and Nathan were forced to write much of the content of each issue under pseudonyms. (Mencken took a fancy to the *nom de plume* "Duchess of Boileau.") Sometimes they were forced to go without salaries themselves. It is easy to see why Dreiser found the magazine cheap and commercial. *Smart Set*, given its somewhat shady past as a magazine known for sensational hackwork, had a long way to go to reach any kind of intellectual respectability. Wright in 1913 had clearly under-estimated the task of turning it around. It seems remarkable, in fact, that Mencken and Nathan were able to make headway in this task by the beginning of the 'twenties, especially during the astringent circumstances imposed by the war.

To judge from the existing correspondence, Mencken's editorial wit and sharp business sense were the principal factors in this achievement. He seemed to come naturally to the art of locating good writing and soliciting it on the cheap, tasks he was able to perform from his home in Baltimore. He unhesitatingly provided well-known writers with topics for articles he thought would have more general appeal. Some of these suggestions now seem ludicrous, and many of them were promptly rejected by writers to whom they were offered. He once, for example, urged Carl Sandburg to write love lyrics instead of more paeans to Chicago. Nonetheless, he appears overall to have known what he was doing. The magazine became more successful and controversial, more focused on issues that concerned him with each year. "In the days before the war," he later recalled, "my *Smart Set* reviews got steadily increasing notice, and it came to be a sort common assumption that I was the chief fugelman of a new criticism, principally aimed at overturning the old American idols."[33] Before Mencken and Nathan left the magazine in 1923, the *Smart Set* had achieved avant-garde panache by introducing its readers to James Joyce, and printing some O'Neill and several Fitzgerald stories, not to mention selections from Flaubert, Stendhal, and Goethe.

As the years passed, Mencken and Nathan settled into the collaborative routines that would carry them into the 'twenties: Nathan ran the office, appearing every morning for an hour or so, and Mencken when in town turned up for editorial meetings at the *Smart Set* office at 45 West Forty-fifth Street[34] or, as often as not, over food and drink at one of their favorite haunts, such as Roger's Chop House at Sixth Avenue and Forty-fifth Street.

This first period as editor, however, proved costly to Mencken intellectually. He complained constantly of the stupidity of the demands made upon him. During this whole time he wrote only about a dozen essays out of the volumes he composed that he was willing to acknowledge and rework for republication in his *A Book of Prefaces* (1917) and *Prejudices, First Series* (1919). These two works, and similar collections that were to follow almost yearly, established him as a literary force that, according to Edmund Wilson, brought *Smart Set* to the attention of young collegiate intellectuals like Wilson himself.

During his lifetime Mencken acquired a considerable reputation as a literary critic and savant, so much so that he was widely referred to as "the Sage of Hollins Street." These collections, which had such impact then on young intellectuals like Wilson, do not bear up very well under examination today. They are remarkable more for the unconscious tactical genius they exhibit than for their qualities as literary or cultural criticism. How aware he was of the tactical character of his writing is hard to say, but Mencken's achievement in these two books, whatever his conscious intentions, was to position himself as a leader of the cultural rebellion that had begun before the war. "It was the war," he wrote in 1923,

> that really broke down the old tradition. The bald fact that the majority of that old tradition were violent Anglomaniacs, and extravagant in their support of the English cause . . . , was sufficient in itself to make most of the younger writers inclined the other way. The struggle thus became a battle royal between fidelity to the English cultural heritage of the country and the advocacy of a new national culture.[35]

Mencken must have sensed that the *Smart Set* was not the best vantage point from which to launch such a campaign. Bolstered by the success of his assault as a critic on commercial publishing, he therefore sought to show that his insurgent fringe of the literary marketplace was somehow a legitimate arbiter of literary worth. He must have worried that his values as a magazine editor might be confused with those of commercial publishing in general. Deliberately or not, he soon undertook a clever and damaging attack on what he called "the middle layer" of commercial publishing, by which he meant "the literature that fills the magazines and burdens the book-counters of department stores . . . that pays like a bucket-shop or a soap-factory, and is thus thoroughly American."[36] Mencken's "middle layer" was clearly the prosperous mainstream of publishing that included the major book publishers and large circulation magazines like the *Saturday Evening Post*.

He also seems to have recognized that he must demolish the competition. No group provided Mencken with greater incitement than the coalition of Progressive intellectuals and reformers then active in New York. This alliance of clergymen, secular reformers, academics, and women's groups—with its neighborhood associations, settlement houses, and other reform causes, in those years often funded by German Jewish philanthropy—was destined to trigger Mencken's fury. By early in the century this group had achieved a prominent place in New York journalism with representatives on many New York newspapers and magazines. To name them is to suggest the dominant place they occupied: Lincoln Steffens of *McClure's*, the *American*, and *Everybody's*; Hutchins Hapgood of the *Commercial Advertiser*; and Walter Lippmann of *The New Republic*, to list only the most prominent.

The New York opinion factory in the prewar years, in other words, was riven down the center. When Mencken entered the scene, it seemed clear enough that the Preachers and Forward-Lookers and Purveyors of Uplift had the upper hand. Earnest, idealistic, often German-trained, they had injected into their reporting a new spirit of scientific objectivity and openness about the city that found a ready market in New York readers. Mencken found the tone of these new Progressive journalists preachy, self-righteous, and offensive. Their belief that the society could be engineered, that the flood of immigration could be accommodated, and that an enhanced government could eventually eliminate social injustices and urban pathologies seemed to him sentimental nonsense.

When Van Wyck Brooks published *America's Coming-of-Age* in 1915, Mencken classified it as one of those "hortatory and pontifical books . . . [that] instruct the rest of us in our opportunities in the manner of *The New Republic*." It was unusual for Mencken to turn down a writing assignment, but when *The New Republic* invited him that year to write an article on Dreiser, he promptly rejected the offer and reported to a friend that there was "no more oleaginous and forward-looking gazette in These States."[37]

At the same time Mencken launched his lifelong war against "the Professors," by which he meant mostly professors of English, those who, in his eyes, had been responsible for reducing literary criticism to the exercise of moral censorship. The tendency of Professors was to repress the expression of passion, especially sexual passion, and to trivialize literature by treating it "as an academic exercise for talented grammarians, almost as a genteel recreation for ladies and gentlemen of fashion—the exact equivalent, in the field of letters, of eighteenth-century painting and German *augenmusik*."[38]

He also commenced a parallel assault on the Greenwich Village avant-garde. The Village had acquired a reputation as a haven for socialism, free love, feminism, and literary experimentation—all anathema to Mencken, who boasted that he never went below Fourteenth Street. Mencken always claimed that Village writers in their obsession with technique all sounded the same. In short, the Village was a place, he insisted, full of frauds, fakes, and impostors. "As a result," he concluded, "the Village produces nothing that justifies all the noise it makes."[39] In any event, he once noted, practically everything Villagers wrote came to him at the *Smart Set* for eventual rejection.

Most important of all, he seems to have recognized that he would have to provide his rebellion with a fresh and compelling set of values by which to measure intellectual vitality, and a canon of writers who exemplified them. *A Book of Prefaces*, because it takes uncertain steps in this direction, is more of interest than the first volume of *Prejudices* published in 1919. A similar problem, however, vexes both of these books, as well as the similar collections that soon followed. All of Mencken's critical writings on literature and society aimed their invective *seriatim* at targets of opportunity. No doubt they were at the time seen as fostering a rebellion against tradition. Today, however, they have a scatter-shot quality, and, despite Mencken's reference to a new "national culture," his critical articles do not appear to emerge from a coherent social or aesthetic perspective. At the same time, their colorful abusiveness apart, they have a disturbing sameness. While Mencken in the reviews and essays he wrote ranged over a broad expanse of American and Continental writing, his tendency was to see all literary work in terms of his own freshly experienced alienation and to read his own version of *fin de siècle* inner despair and nihilism into every work he admired.

It is interesting to speculate about what gave Mencken the credentials for such leadership and what he individually had to offer the rebellion besides a ready and acid pen. Middle-aged, more straitlaced, and without the collegiate or patrician polish of the other rebels, he nonetheless succeeded in making himself into a leader of the assault on convention and tradition. To his protégé Willard Wright, Mencken struck a new and much-needed virile note in literary criticism. Wright wrote in the *Los Angeles Times* in 1910: "He is one of those rare immoralists, who care not a whoop for reverence or precedent. By his brutality, his assertive masculinity, his walloping rages, he has done much to quash the effeminacy which for half a century has devastated our literature."[40] At the same time, unlike so many of the others who joined in the attack, Mencken never abandoned the bastion of the middle class. He seems, indeed, to have been an odd kind of immoralist. His writings abound in praises of home, propriety, and the bourgeois comforts. Instead he fought the battle of the books from his class ramparts, asserting his establishment values even as he assailed them.

Up until the war, Mencken had succeeded in holding the two parts of his life—his Baltimore world and the New York literary marketplace—in precarious balance. By the time the war ended, his was a house thoroughly divided against itself. It was not simple alienation he came to feel, but what appears to have been alienation coupled with rage at his own alienation.

To say this, of course, is to infer a kind of knowledge about him that few contemporaries felt they possessed. The intense privacy with which Mencken cloaked his inner life was well known among his friends, and few felt they knew what he concealed behind the comic mask he wore in public. The polarities within him, nonetheless, seem endless: his Baltimore world of mother, *Sun*, and burgherdom, and the glitzy commercial swirl of carnal indulgence that he found in New York; the domestic propriety of his Hollins Street home against transient quasi-bohemian existence of the Algonquin and Luchow's; Scottish grandmother and the English language against the Germanic in parents and grandparents; puritanism against prurience; heterosexuality against the male bonding of the publishing world; inner Kaiser against victim of tyranny; to name but the most obvious conflicts he seems to have felt.

The result for Mencken seems to have been a heightened and tortured alienation that in his writings took the form of caricature. He became in a sense a verbal cartoonist of the attack on tradition and convention. After the war, in his incisive derision of everything American he delighted as only a master of caricature, a Nast, a Buchwald, or a Trudeau, can delight. He was relentless and devilish in what he wrote because he knew at first-hand the values of the bourgeois world he was attacking. He was unsparing at least in part because he himself was unspared.

The model artist for Mencken in these years was Joseph Conrad, whose novels he examined in the opening section of *Prefaces* (1918). From Conrad and other European writers he admired, he had pieced together a view that, as he put it, "human life is a seeking without a finding, that its purpose is impenetrable, that joy and sorrow are alike meaningless."[41]

For reasons that are unclear, Mencken seems never to have nursed the meliorist and utopian dreams that were so common among his contemporaries. His vision of modernity, to judge from remarks made here and there in this period, appears to have embraced a dark, determinist universe he had conjured up, a world that consisted predominantly of men sweating and toiling without respite or effect until they dropped from fatigue, disease, or inner dissolution. What he hopefully offered young readers was a world without hope and without joy where the only pleasures were brief outbursts of Dionysian lust and the only refuge seems to have been the recessive security of home. Such a world view, he felt, "you will see writ largely in the work of most great creative artists." And he went on to list the figures to whom he thought this philosophy applied: Beethoven, Shakespeare, Turgenev, Ibsen, Dostoyevsky, and Zola among Europeans, and Twain, Crane, Norris, and Dreiser among Americans. To penetrate to such a truth was the mark of a superior mind, one that could shake off the shallow veneer of optimistic individualism and sentiment that was suppressing creativity. This philosophical attainment was especially rare in America, where he believed such dark strains of naturalism were held in check by puritanism, Comstockery, and especially by feminine domination of the literary marketplace.

Mencken's critical method, apart from some shrewd attention now and then to stylistic concerns, was to examine all writing ideologically with some such correct view of the human struggle in mind. Using such a measure sometimes led him to exaggerate the worth of writers such as Edgar Saltus who are now virtually forgotten, and to underestimate the importance of major intellectual figures such as William James, John Dewey, and Thorstein Veblen, whom he treated dismissively, along with Progressive intellectuals like Lippmann. Ironically, such a method was little different from that of the Professors, like Stuart Sherman, whom Mencken condemned for applying Christian ethics wholesale to literature. When he proceeded at this level of analysis, he seriously distorted or obscured the qualities of the writings he used as a model.

His critical essays, for example, are interspersed with rules of thumb for determining quality. "Character in decay," he notes at one point, "is thus the theme of the great bulk of superior fiction. . . . In nearly all first-rate novels the hero is defeated. In perhaps a majority he is completely destroyed. Each protagonist is a new Prometheus, with a sardonic ignominy piled upon his helplessness. Each goes down a Greek route to defeat and disaster, leaving nothing behind him save an unanswered question."[42]

The result was a tendency to homogenize all good writing and all bad writing by scoring it against such a black-and-white scale of literary virtue. A procedure of this kind inevitably led him to overlook distinctive qualities in the new American writing he examined in his rush to judgment. Thus we discover that at Mencken's hands Dreiser emerges looking for all the world like Conrad. "Substitute the name of Dreiser for that of Conrad," he concluded in the second essay of *Prefaces*, "and you will have to change scarcely a word."[43] This kind of categorization is a far cry from the critical credo that Mencken cited admiringly in an essay on his co-editor, George Jean Nathan: "The doctrine . . . that every work of art is, at bottom, unique and that it is the business of the critic, not to label it and pigeonhole it, but to seek for its inner intent and content, and to value it according as that intent is carried out and that content is valid and worth while."[44]

Many of Mencken's shortcomings were noted by critics at the time, and Marius Bewley, in a discerning essay in *The Complex Fate* (1952), issued what amounts to a death warrant on his critical reputation, one that does not even spare his work on the American language. "If Mr. Mencken has sometimes corrected and enlarged his erudition," Bewley concluded, "there is little evidence that he has ever deepened his sensibility."[45]

Mencken's popular reputation in the country at large, however, was based less on his literary criticism than on the pungent and provocative cultural criticism that he published in the years immediately after the war. Most of the barbed insults he is remembered for were the product of a period of three or four years. His most stinging attacks on women were produced at this time, too. There was a male macho cast to most of his derision, which struck out at the tender, sentimental, and charitable character of contemporary Progressive reform as well. It was then that he came forward with his ridicule of what he called the "Booboisie": the Yokels and Hayseeds, Schoolmarms, Y.M.C.A-ers, 100 Percent Americans, Comstock Censors, Methodist Preachers, Forward Lookers, Uplifters, and other despised types that made up his cast of comic-strip Americans.

Mencken's dramatis personae of comic types played very well before the new urbanites who by the 'twenties were devouring magazine literature of the kind published by *Smart Set*, *Vanity Fair*, and kindred publications. White, urban, middle-class, and heavily collegiate, they must have delighted in the punishing blows Mencken delivered to figures from small-town rural America, much as they delighted in Mencken's protégé, Sinclair Lewis. In a decade that included the Red Scare, Prohibition, and Comstockery, they also would have found much that the government stood for and did laughable. They therefore must have welcomed his vehement stands against Prohibition, sexual repression, and the matronly domination of the culture. As white, predominantly Protestant Americans in cities filled with newly arrived immigrants, many of them would also have responded to his clever, insinuating assaults on Jews, Catholics, ethnic minorities, and Democratic machine politics. Mencken's attacks on Harding and Coolidge were carried out in a decade when politics, both national and city, were perceived by these same urbanites as comically inept. Mencken's clever dismemberment of Harding's language, "A Short View of Gamalielese," which appeared in the *Nation* in 1921, found a wide and appreciative audience among urban sophisticates, who found they enjoyed political *opèra comique*.

Beginning in 1918, insult had followed upon insult. "The government of the United States, in both its legislative arm and its executive arm, is ignorant, corrupt, and disgusting." "The administration of justice in the Republic is stupid, dishonest, and against all reason and equity." American foreign policy was "hypocritical, disingenuous, knavish, and dishonorable." Finally, "the American people . . . constitute the most timorous, sniveling, poltroonish, ignominious mob of serfs and goose-steppers ever gathered under one flag in Christendom since the end of the Middle Ages, and they grow more timorous, more sniveling, more poltroonish every day."[46] In 1922, Mencken and Nathan, in a summation of what appears to be Mencken's looking-glass political philosophy, published their editorial credo:

> Both of us are opposed to all such ideas as come from the mob and are polluted by its stupidity: Puritanism, Prohibition, Comstockery, evangelical Christianity, tinpot patriotism, the whole sham of democracy. Both of us, though against socialism and in favor of capitalism, believe that capitalism in the United States is ignorant, disreputable, and degraded, and that its heroes are bounders.[47]

In this statement as in most of the others from this period, it is sometimes impossible to determine the perspective from which Mencken judges an issue.[48] Again and again he engaged in reason-by-invective. In this passage, it is a little clearer why democracy is a "sham" (presumably because Puritanism and all the other following items have the effect of suppressing public opinion) than it is to see what exactly is wrong with capitalism in America or why capitalist heroes are, of all things, "bounders" (a strange word indeed for someone of Mencken's intensely Anglophobic views).

Intellectuals on the Left, such as Edmund Wilson, who relished Mencken's attacks on the establishment, failed to note that his heart went out to no one. Unlike so many of his intellectual contemporaries, he showed little interest in the celebrated cause of Sacco and Vanzetti,[49] which did so much during the 'twenties to build a literary Left. He wrote as though he were utterly detached and contemptuous of the entire society. Asked once why he chose to remain in America and did not become an expatriate, Mencken remarked "Why do I go to the zoo?"[50] In an essay written in 1922, he systematically ticked off the defects of each ethnic group in the society. Italian immigrants, for example, "have brought no more of the essential culture of Italy with them than so many horned cattle." "The Scandinavians are even worse [than the Germans]. The majority of them are mere clods." His sharpest barbs were reserved for American Jews: "They changed their names to Burton, Thompson, and Cecil in order to qualify as true Americans, and when they are accepted and rewarded in the national coin, they renounce Moses altogether and get themselves baptized in St. Bartholomew's Church." The Anglo-Saxon owed his dominant place to one fact alone: "those newcomers are even more clearly inferior than he is."[51]

His own heroes were the supreme skeptics like himself who populated his tiny "civilized minority," that élite of the stubborn and the cussed that

"Winter, Fifth Avenue," by Alfred Stieglitz, 1892, Fifth Ave. and Thirty-fourth St. The Metropolitan Museum of Art, gift of J. B. Neumann, 1958.

"The Terminal," by Alfred Stieglitz, 1892. Courtesy of The Art Institute of Chicago.

"The Hand of Man," by Alfred Steiglitz, ca. 1902. The Metropolitan Museum of Art, The Alfred Stieglitz Collection, 1949.

4

"The Madonna of Ellis Island," by Lewis Hine. The Metropolitan Museum of Art, gift of Clarence McK. Lewis, 1954.

"Breaker Boys," by Lewis Hine. From the collection of the International Museum of Photography at George Eastman House.

5

6

"Forty-Year-Old Woman," by Lewis Hine. From the collection of the International Museum of Photography at George Eastman House.

"Family in New York Tenement," by Lewis Hine. From the collection of the International Museum of Photography at George Eastman House.

7

8

"Slum Negro Dying of Tuberculosis," by Lewis Hine. From the collection of the International Museum of Photography at George Eastman House.

"Newsies at Skeeter Branch," by Lewis Hine. From the collection of the Library of Congress.

9

10

"Little Negro Orphan, Washington, D.C.," by Lewis Hine. From the collection of the International Museum of Photography at George Eastman House.

"Steamfitter," by Lewis Hine. From the collection of the International Museum of Photography at George Eastman House.

11

12

"Man at Dynamo," by Lewis Hine. From the collection of the International Museum of Photography at George Eastman House.

"Boilermaker," by Lewis Hine. From the collection of the International Museum of Photography at George Eastman House.

13

"Down and Out in New York City," by Lewis Hine. From the collection of the International Museum of Photography at George Eastman House.

"Empire State Building," by Lewis Hine. From the collection of the International Museum of Photography at George Eastman House.

New York City skyline photo, 1977. Reprinted with the permission of New York Times Pictures.

Bird's-eye view, New York City (from the roof of the RCA Building), by Samuel Chamberlain. Courtesy of Rockefeller Center. © The Rockefeller Group.

18

Night pattern, New York City, November 16, 1933, by Samuel Gottscho, from *The Columbia Historical Portrait of New York*, John Kouwnhoven (New York: Doubleday, 1953), p. 492.

"London After the Fire of 1666," engraved by Frederick de Wit. Courtesy of Weinreband Douwma, Ltd., London.

19

"New York from Heights Near Brooklyn," engraving by John Hill, from watercolor by William G. Wall, 1823. Vol. 3 in *The Iconography of Manhattan Island, 1498–1909*, I. N. Phelps-Stokes (New York: R. H. Dodd, 1915–1928).

Bird's-eye view of New York City from imaginary aerial perspective. Vol. 2 in *The Iconography of Manhattan Island, 1498–1909*, I. N. Phelps-Stokes (New York: R. H. Dodd, 1915–1928).

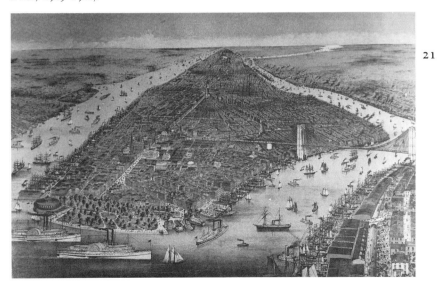

22

Engraving of view from spire of Trinity Church, New York, 1849. Detail from "New York in 1849," drawn by E. Purcell, engraved by S. Weekes, in *The Columbia Historical Portrait of New York*, John Kouwenhoven (New York: Doubleday, 1953), p. 22.

23

"Central panel of the panoramic view of New York City as seen from the Brooklyn Tower of the Brooklyn Bridge prior to the placing of cables," by J. H. Beals, 1876. Courtesy of the New-York Historical Society.

"East River Waterfront, view to the west from Brooklyn Bridge, showing buildings and skyline between Wall Street and Maiden Lane, New York City," 1888. Courtesy of the New-York Historical Society.

(facing) Engraving, view of Wall Street from Trinity Church, New York, 1834. Drawn by Hugh Reinagle and lithographed by Peter Maverick, Jr. Collection of Edward W. C. Arnold. By permission of the Museum of the City of New York.

(*above*) Skyline, New York City, *Harper's Weekly*, August 11, 1894, by G. W. Peters. Drawing entitled "View from North River," one of a pair of panoramas entitled "The Age of Skyscrapers—Tall Buildings in the Business District of New York City." John Kouwenhoven (New York: Doubleday, 1953).

(below) Skyline, New York City, *Harper's Weekly,* March 20, 1897, by Fred Pansing, entitled "The Sky-line of Buildings Below Chambers Street in 1897," it was one of a pair, jointly titled, "New York's Skyscrapers—The Effective Change Wrought by Three Buildings on the City's Appearance within a Few Years."

Church.   Union   Crocker   Cable   Johnston   Standard Building.   Bowling Green   Washington
      Trust.   Building.   Building.   Building.   Building.   Building.

Bander Building.   Manhattan Life.

28

Pre–World War I night skyline, Pittsburgh, Pa., by Lewis Hine. Courtesy of the Russell Sage Foundation.

The Flatiron Building, 1903, by Alfred Stieglitz. The Metropolitan Museum of Art, The Alfred Stieglitz Collection.

Flatiron Building, by Edward Steichen. Reprinted with the permission of Joanna T. Steichen.

"Drizzle on Fortieth Street, New York, 1925." Edward Steichen.

"Sunday Night on Fortieth Street, New York, 1925." Edward Steichen.

Grand Central Terminal, Main Concourse, ca. 1912. Museum of the City of New York.

Grand Central Terminal, cross-sectional perspective. Museum of the City of New York.

Public comfort station, Union Square, New York. Author's collection.

(*facing*) Grand Central Terminal, Main Concourse, north side of Forty-second St. at Vanderbilt Avenue. Museum of the City of New York.

Woolworth Building in *King's Views of New York, 1896–1915*. Reprinted by Arno Press, 1974.

(*facing*) Haughwout Building, 1952. Courtesy of Otis Elevator Company.

38

Haughwout Building, 1859. Courtesy of Otis Elevator Company.

39

40

Broadway and Fifth Avenue. Courtesy of the Brown Brothers.

"Madison Square Garden, view looking south on Madison Avenue from 29th Street, New York City," 1895. Courtesy of the New-York Historical Society.

Metropolitan Life Building, 1909, in *King's Views of New York, 1896–1915*. Reprinted by Arno Press, 1974.

Metropolitan Life Building, 1915, in *King's Views of New York*.

44

A.—NEW YORK'S ARTIFICIAL MOUNTAIN RANGE

B.—THE FUTURE CITY OF TOWERS
SKYLINES OF THE PRESENT AND FUTURE

"Two Views of the New York Skyline," in *The Building of the City* (New York: The New York Regional Plan, 1931).

45

(*above and overleaf*) Taken from the observation deck in Rockefeller Center by Samuel Chamberlain. Courtesy of Rockefeller Center. © The Rockefeller Group.

(*facing*) "Imaginary Metropolis," by Hugh Ferriss, in *Architectural Visions: The Drawings of Hugh Ferriss*, by Jean Ferriss Leich (New York: Whitney Library of Design, 1980).

could swim against the current. Historically, his admired writers were those who made up what he called "the maverick outlaw strain" in American literature. This favored group was composed of writers from Poe and Whitman to Twain, Lardner, and Dreiser, whose accomplishments had been unappreciated and repressed. All of these writers, he felt, bore the wounds of a puritanical society that hated art in any form. What Americans needed most of all was a "civilized aristocracy, secure in its position, animated by an intelligent curiosity, skeptical of all facile generalizations, superior to the sentimentality of the mob, and delighting in the battle of ideas for its own sake."[52] Without such intellectual leadership, Americans constantly fell prey to their own gullibility:

> The *boobus Americanus* is a bird that knows no closed season—and if he won't come down to Texas oil stock, or one-night cancer cures, or building lots in Swampshurst, he will always come down to Inspiration and Optimism, whether political, theological, pedagogical, literary, or economic.[53]

It is interesting to speculate about the sources of the animus and venom that characterized these early excursions into cultural criticism. The war and the inner conflicts that found expression in the events of the war years were the major factors in the bitterness he developed. External circumstances appear to have exacerbated the inner tensions he was experiencing. The position that Mencken had taken on Germany before the outbreak of war in Europe had been more cultural than political. Before the war, Mencken had never concerned himself with German nationality as such, and he had repeatedly distanced himself from German-American Baltimore. The Germany that Mencken came to admire was the modern, enlightened Germany of Nietzsche and Wagner: what he called the "new aristocracy of the laboratory, the study and the shop," not the old tradition-clogged German "aristocracy of the barrack and the court."[54]

As the war in Europe intensified and America dangled closer and closer to involvement, Mencken became more militant. He saw the struggle as one between an enlightened Imperial Germany pitted against the procrustean past personified by the Allied countries. Mencken believed that England had acted out of jealousy of the new Germany in fomenting the war. Fearful of new German efficiency, it had stirred up the French, Russians, and, finally, the Americans. The battle that then raged became, for him, one between the past and the future. England stood for an obsolete and effeminate Anglo-Saxon tradition, the dead hand of gentility that was repressing everything vital in American culture.

The war and the anti-German feelings that accompanied it left Mencken profoundly divided between a passionate nativism and his equally powerful feelings of alienation, between the America he professed to care about and solidarity with Germany and things German. The resulting conflict left him painfully disoriented, stammering out heartfelt American patriotism and vitriolic abuse of England and America by turns. In an essay entitled "On Being an American" that he published in 1922, in the midst of his bitterest attacks on America, he insisted that he was

> unshaken, undespairing, a loyal and devoted Americano, even a chauvinist, paying taxes without complaint, obeying all laws that are physiologically obeyable, accepting all the searching duties and responsibilities of citizenship unprotestingly . . . contributing my mite toward the glory of the national arts and sciences, enriching and embellishing the native language, spurning all lures (and even all invitations) to get out and stay out—here am I, a bachelor of easy means, forty-two years old, unhampered by debts or issue, able to go wherever I please and to stay as long as I please—here am I smugly basking beneath the Stars and Stripes. [55]

Because of this inner conflict, the rebellion took on an intensely personal character, and the tensions he saw in the culture seemed to be mirrored in the struggle within himself.

Americans, Mencken came to feel, were "goose-steppers," stupidly herded into war with Germany by a puritanical and Anglophile Woodrow Wilson. "I am for the hellish Deutsch til Hell freezes over," Mencken wrote to Dreiser in 1914. [56] His *Sun* column, "The Free Lance," until he discontinued it at the end of 1915, carried his pro-German and anti-English diatribes interlarded with protests of American fidelity. "It is my hope and belief that this sick and bogus England will be given a good licking by the Deutsch to the end that truth and health may prevail on the earth," he wrote that year for the September 29 column. The same article passionately disavowed his German national roots and protested his American identity. "I am not German and am not bound to Germany by sentimental ties," he flatly stated.

> I was born in Baltimore of Baltimore-born parents; I have no relatives, near or remote in Germany, nor even any friends (save one Englishman!); very few of my personal associates in this town are native Germans; I read the German language very imperfectly, and do not speak it or write it at all; I never saw Germany until I was 23 years old; I have been there since but twice; I am of English and Irish blood as well as German. [57]

While *Smart Set* eschewed any direct comment on the war, Mencken (with the concurrence of Nathan) on occasion allowed himself impudent macho gestures of his pro-German sentiments, as in a nonsense fragment, probably composed over dinner at Luchow's, that appeared on January 15, 1915: "A rathskeller for my palace, a pipe for my scepter, a waltz tune for my national anthem, a napkin for my flag, a waiter for my subject, a stein for my prime minister, a thousand tomorrows for my harem!"[58] Mencken's defense in 1917 of the submarine captain who had sunk the *Lusitania* further distanced him from American sentiment, even in German-American Baltimore. When it became known at the end of a trip to Germany for the *Sun* that year that Mencken had received favored treatment from the German commander General Ludendorff, he was probably placed under federal surveillance. In any event, he clearly felt cornered and pressured into silence by the Creel Committee (on Public Information) and by the broad terms of the Espionage and Sedition Acts that soon followed. He complained that he was forced to make changes in the text of his *Book of Prefaces* in order for it to pass freely through the mail.[59] "In the United States alone among the great nations of history," he complained in 1918,

> there is a right way to think in everything—not only in theology, or politics, or economics, but in the most trivial matters of everyday life. . . . For an American to question any of the articles of fundamental faith cherished by the majority is for him to run grave risks of social disaster.[60]

Mencken never fully resolved the conflict brought on by the war, which continued for several years to give an unsettling edge to what he wrote. This conflict, it would appear, had roots that went deep into Mencken's nature, stirring up feelings he had not before seriously confronted. The vision of men at war seems to have heightened Mencken's own feelings of being left powerless on the sidelines, as it did other noncombatant writers like F. Scott Fitzgerald. The result for Mencken was an uncomfortable acknowledgment of, and attempt to reckon with, the feminine within himself. This, at least, would be one reading of his puzzling and controversial tract, *In Defense of Women* (1918), which was the work of the war years.

Mencken apparently wrote this curious book, which abuses men and women by turns, as a way of venting raging feelings that the war had both provoked and forced him to muffle. It also formed part, although an inconsistent part, of a running and hostile inquiry into the nature of women and their role in American culture.

Mencken in his critical essays kept returning to his belief that women were somehow responsible for the narrowness and vapidity of American culture. He did not originate such a contention, which he apparently first found in Nietzsche and which was widespread among critical contemporaries like Wright. It had been advanced in one form or another much earlier by Nathaniel Hawthorne and Mark Twain. With Mencken, however, the assault on femininity became close to an obsession, an ugly set of feelings he could not leave alone and returned to repeatedly in these years. He contended on one occasion that the feminine sensibility was one of sentiment and surfaces: "timorous flaccidity," "amiable hollowness," and "pervasive superficiality" were the phrases he used to characterize the state of America's literary culture under feminine dominance. Those critics who were not women, he once sniped, "were sopranos." "The feminine mind, which rules in English fiction, both as producer and consumer, craves inevitably a more confident and comforting view of the world than Conrad has to offer. It seeks not disillusionment but illusion."[61] In Conrad's fictional worlds, Mencken seemed gratified to find, women and romantic love had little place, and, as a result, Conrad was able to free himself from the sentimental pieties insisted on by the restrictive imaginations of women. "His women, in the main, are no more than soiled and tattered cards in a game played by the gods," Mencken reported. "He sees quite accurately, it seems to me, how vastly the role of women has been exaggerated, how little they amount to in the authentic struggle of man."[62]

Mencken at the age of thirty-eight, whatever the population of his "harem," was still a bachelor. Up until this time he appears to have had only one serious, but abortive, courtship to his credit. It seems very odd that he should have sought out this particular avenue of expression. Nonetheless, for over a hundred pages he discoursed confidently and authoritatively on courtship, marriage, family life, childbearing, divorce, prostitution, and the temperamental and aesthetic make-up of the two sexes. His own concept of gender, which he drew in part from Nietzsche, reversed most current stereotypes of men and women.

On the surface, at least, the book contains a favorable portrayal of women. Its title and some of its assertions have misled some Mencken scholars into believing that he had written a proto-feminist tract,[63] as in Mencken's slightly tongue-in-cheek contention that women were

> the supreme realists of the race. They see at a glance what most men could not see with searchlights and telescopes; they are at grips with the essentials of a problem before men have finished debating its externals. . . . Apparently illogical, they are the possessors of a rare and subtle super-logic.[64]

This was a far cry from his contention that women had muzzled reality with illusion. Women came to develop this capacity for realism, Mencken was quick to observe, in the same way that the Jews acquired their intelligence; out of a sense of their vulnerability, out of a need to compensate for their weaknesses.

The significant shift in attitude for Mencken came with his insistence on the bisexual nature of genius. Men who can soar above the quotidian and who are capable of great achievement, he conceded, were necessarily amalgams of male and female traits:

Find me an obviously intelligent man, a man free from sentimentality and illusion, a man hard to deceive, a man of the first class, and I'll show you a man with a wide streak of woman in him. Bonaparte had it; Goethe had it; Schopenhauer had it; Bismarck and Lincoln had it; in Shakespeare, if the Freudians are to be believed, it amounted to downright homosexuality.[65]

Such a concession represented a distinct, if temporary, change of attitude. Gone was the talk of male "sopranos." Running through this discussion of women and marriage there is, nonetheless, a nasty undercurrent of misogyny and grandiosity. Women of great talent and ability, for example—and he cited Catherine the Great, George Sand, and Cosima Wagner as examples—were also gender amalgams. "In women of genius we see the opposite picture. They are distinctly mannish, and shave as well as shine."[66] Mencken found women as a whole ill-shaped and physically unattractive. There is no mistaking the note of sexual horror in observations such as these:

The female body, even at its best, is very defective in form; it has harsh curves and very clumsily distributed masses; compared to it the average milk-jug, or even cuspidor, is a thing of intelligent and gratifying design—in brief, an *objet d'art*.[67]

It is little difficult to know whether to take at face value the taunts at women, at manhood, and at democracy that poured from him during and after the war years. Mencken was an inveterate poseur. What he most admired in Thackeray, he once noted, was "the deep-rooted human impulse to play a part, to pretend, to dissemble, to wear a mask." The masks he assumed, moreover, were not simply those put on for public display. The masking of his private self appears to have been part of his nature, as we have seen. Carl Bode has pointed out that even in his letters to his closest friends, Mencken avoided expressions of deep feeling or hid his feelings behind a comic mask.[68] His correspondence is filled with dramatic role-playing: the more intimate the friendship, the more intense and sustained the drama, as in the comic *Katzenjammer*-like German-Jewish world he evoked in his letters to his close friend and Philadelphia publisher, Philip Goodman.[69]

In order to determine how much of what he said was part of one or another clever public mask he had developed and how much was in some meaningful way personal to him, it may be useful to try to distinguish between his political and his personal crises. Much that he said about democracy was clearly colored by his bitter animosity toward Woodrow Wilson and his increasingly desperate feelings of persecution, but what he wrote was nonetheless cast in his characteristically provocative vocabulary of "goose-steppers, imbeciles, and bounders." For

this cause he was able to draft the familiar cast of Mencken villains—
Comstockers, Rotarians, 100 Percent Americans and the like. In his discussions of women and the feminine, the same jaunty mask was less
adequate or more transparent, and a note of personal bitterness soon
crept in. The war left him painfully conflicted, as we have seen, on the
question of gender. In his eyes the war and its politics were a masculine
business and men had botched it badly. On the other hand, he saw
women in general as domineering and unattractive.

Mencken's personal relations with women in these years do comparatively little to explain or explain away such convictions. In his
posthumous memoir he asserted that he systematically destroyed his intimate correspondence with women. What little evidence remains suggests,
however, that he remained uneasy throughout his life in these relationships. Between 1915 and 1922, he and Marion Bloom, a Washington
woman and would-be contributor to the *Smart Set*, developed a close
friendship, exchanged love letters, and seriously considered marriage.
According to Carl Bode, their relationship may have foundered over,
among other things, Mencken's wish to settle Marion on Hollins Street in
the house with his mother. In 1926, the year after the death of his mother,
there was a rumor that he was engaged to marry film actress Aileen
Pringle, who later married writer James Cain. When Mencken himself
married Sara Haardt in 1930, he asked Aileen Pringle to return his letters
to her, and he burned them. When both women were later divorced after
Sara Haardt's death, Mencken reopened correspondence with them but
did not resume the relationships.

Mencken's marriage to Sara Haardt also raises many questions. Sara
was seriously ill with tuberculosis when they married and remained in
poor health until she died five years later. While the marriage was apparently a happy one and Mencken was considered a devoted husband, there
appears to have been little passion involved, at least on Mencken's side.[70]

Mencken's track record with women, such as it is, speaks more of his
discomfort with them—and his greater ease in the company of men—
than of a deep, embittered misogyny of the kind his writings sometimes
suggest. Less-threatening professional relationships with women, for example, he carried off with his usual comic gusto. Two of his three strong
ties with women, moreover, began as editor-to-contributor relationships.
He was able later in his life to develop warm friendships with the wives of
some of his friends and with intellectual women such as Blanche Knopf.
He was also a loving, indulgent uncle to his niece.

The acidic turn that Mencken gave to his discussion of women originated, at least in part, elsewhere. He tapped a vein of misogyny that was
especially evident among the Broadway writers that he knew. Anyone

familiar with the lives and announced beliefs of New York male journalists in this period—with the views of Damon Runyon, Walter Winchell, "Bugs" Baer, and writers for *Variety*—will recognize in Mencken a more developed version of the Broadway line on women and marriage.

Mencken was above all else a pen for hire, a man who, for a price, would say almost anything. He undertook this campaign against women, one feels, in much the same spirit with which he wrote so much of his other cultural criticism, prompted and guided by his own inner turmoil but with a caricaturist's sure eye for comic exaggeration and the telling detail—and the literary marketplace. At one point he put himself to school studying epigrams on women and marriage written by such masters of misogyny as Oscar Wilde and Ambrose Bierce and then set out to equal them with concoctions of his own.[71] Only in such a way could he have found his way to the cuspidor and the milk bottle as forms more shapely than women's. His ability to say things and to say them in a colorful, provocative way clearly brought him his greatest satisfactions, but it was also what probably precipitated feelings of hollowness and futility. "In brief," he confessed in 1939, "my booth has been set up on a favorable pitch and I have never lacked customers for my ballyhoo."[72] Always behind the screen of his carefully constructed literary persona sat the Wizard himself, empty-handed. By the mid-'twenties, many felt that he had begun repeating himself, that his observations were beginning to lose their provocative edge. Once the Depression had swept the country and FDR and the Common Man had arrived on the scene, his derision of presidential politics and his elitist social philosophy suddenly seemed antediluvian.

Nonetheless, for a time he was able to pour out insults to a surprisingly receptive and appreciative national audience that included many intellectuals. The popular following that he developed is amazing for a literary figure. Traveling by train from New Orleans in the mid-'twenties he was astonished to find crowds gathered to see him at stations along the route. In 1921, the "oleaginous" *New Republic* paid Mencken the highest imaginable praise: "Mencken is the civilized consciousness of modern America, its learning, its intelligence and its taste, realizing the grossness of its manners and mind, and crying out in horror and chagrin."[73] Others, however, were quick to disagree, including *Time* magazine, which printed an article critical of him in its third issue. Other critics chimed in on the general theme that Mencken was something of a cut-up in the literary world with less to offer than his rhetoric promised. Marxist critic V. F. Calverton, who called attention to Mencken's lack of social values, found his cultural criticism empty and bombastic and, because of his staged antics, labeled him "the Vaudeville Critic." The *Freeman*, in

1920, carried an article by Percy Boynton entitled "American Literature and the Tart Set" that poked fun at *Smart Set* authors for uniformly blasting the living and the dead in a critical assault that spared only Mencken himself.[74]

Mencken's influence clearly waned as the 'twenties progressed. Edmund Wilson has argued that Mencken did his most important work as editor of the *Smart Set* (1914–1923) and that his importance diminished by the mid-'twenties when he served as editor of the "more elegant and pretentious" *American Mercury* (1923–1933):

> His own prejudices and mannerisms had hardened, and he tended to try to impose them on other writers in the magazine; he became excessively indulgent to writers like Sinclair Lewis whom he himself had helped to create. Like every other good thing in the period of the boom—like Florida real estate and Lindbergh—the public overdid him.[75]

Certainly, if one excepts his various editions of *The American Language* and the *Supplements* that followed in the 'forties, he wrote little after the mid-'twenties that is memorable today. His fame and his standing as a savant, however, outlasted the period of his greatest originality. The Mencken industries ground on through the 'thirties and into the 'forties. The historian Charles Beard, writing for the *New York Daily Mirror* in 1934, included Mencken in his list of the twenty-five "most interesting persons in America," and described him as a leader "to whom in times of stress we can turn and who is socially conscious."[76]

Beginning in 1934 and continuing through the time of his cerebral thrombosis in 1948, Mencken wrote some sixty-four articles for *The New Yorker.* He wrote travel pieces, reminiscences, and miscellaneous essays of one kind or another. Some of his reminiscences were later incorporated into the three volumes of autobiographical writing that appeared during the 'forties: *Happy Days* (1940), *Newspaper Days* (1941), and *Heathen Days* (1943). Most of this writing has little interest today. Reading through it, it is hard to believe that it was written by the same Mencken who edited *Smart Set* and composed the six volumes of *Prejudices* and the other collections that appeared during the 'twenties.

His later style is that of a Dickensian sentimentalist writing with an eye for human eccentricity and a taste for the out-of-the-way curiosity. By the time he came to this body of writing, the old fire had definitely left him. There was until recently, of course, the mystery still lurking in the auto-biographical writings that had been under lock and key since his death, supposedly to protect the living from posthumous abuse by the old master of invective. These two lengthy typewritten manuscripts, interesting as they are, clearly show, for all their candid assessments of individuals he knew, that Mencken's vituperative powers had lapsed by the 1940s when he compiled these documents. Their most surprising revelation may be in Mencken's insistence that he always felt himself incapable of rage, passion, or malice, and his conviction that he wrote without artifice, saying only what came naturally.[77] It would be hard to believe, in any case, that Mencken at the end of his life could have shown his adversaries the cold steel that he regularly turned on his foes in the 'twenties. The essays written for *The New Yorker*, in fact, refract not Mencken but *The New Yorker* itself. This time it was his friend Harold Ross, the master editor, whose tastes he must have set out to accommodate. Ever the professional, he understood his assignments and completed them like the diligent journalist he was.

Mencken died in 1956 after living for eight years as a semi-invalid following a stroke, unable to read or write. During those long years as he sat silently in his house on Hollins Street, he must have ruminated many times over the events he had retailed in these last assessments of his life, looking for the bright spots. His early life as a reporter would have been one of them. He probably would have accepted as his epitaph the tribute he himself had once paid his mentor James Huneker, one that placed him in the social world he himself found most congenial:

> Whatever the flag [paper or magazine] he served it loyally, and got a lot of fun out of the business. He liked the pressure of newspaper work; he liked the associations that it involved, the gabble of the press-room . . . , the exchanges of news and gossip; above all, he liked the relative ease of the intellectual harness. In a newspaper article he could say whatever happened to pop into his mind, and if it looked thin the next day, then there was, after all, no harm done.[78]

TEN

A Place That Words Built ·
Broadway, Damon Runyon, and
the Slanguage of Lobster Alley

Lobster Alley is the theatrical section of New York as it has grown under the patronage and guidance of the weekly newspaper Variety, *and its inspired editor, Sime Silverman.*[1]
Hiram Motherwell, *The Bookman*, 1930

Every phase of our complex civilization, and every class have contributed something to what is becoming a national slanguage. The bootleggers with their "hooch," "drums," "tail," "frontiers," "fixers"; the underworld with its jargon, almost unintelligible to an outsider; the outdoor show game with its "rag front," "pitch," "ballyhoo," "grift," "rolldowns," and "shills" and hundreds of other words: horse racing with its "front runners," "morning glories," "stoomers," "workouts," "pencil men," "wind suckers," "chumps". . . .

It is not beyond the range of possibility that an entire new language will evolve and that some pioneer will write an entire book in it without recourse to what we now know as pure English. And why not?[2]
Jack Conway, *Variety*, 1926

I took one little section of New York and made half a million dollars writing about it.[3]
Damon Runyon, 1941

Late in 1933, W. J. Funk, the lexicographer, circulated a list of the names of the most prolific makers of American slang. The list was sent to a number of leading newspapers for comment. Almost all the ten names, strikingly, were identifiable figures on the Broadway scene. The list included Sime Silverman, editor of *Variety*; cartoonists Thomas Aloysius (Tad) Dorgan and Reuben (Rube) Goldberg; Eugene Edward (Gene) Buck, songwriter and principal libretticist for Ziegfeld; Damon Runyon, by then famous as a writer of Broadway stories as well as a sportswriter and humorist; Walter Winchell, gossip columnist on McFadden's *Graphic* (and later the *Hearst Mirror*); Indiana's George Ade, humorist and playwright; Ring Lardner; Gelett (Frank) Burgess, coiner of "bromide," "the goops," "blurb," and the quatrain about the purple cow; and H. L. Mencken of the *Baltimore Sun* and the *Smart Set*, published just off Times Square.[4]

A copy sent to Mencken reached him as he was preparing a fourth and enlarged edition of *The American Language*. This list, with Mencken's commentary, was included in the reorganized chapter on American slang. In the chapter, Mencken went on to document the coinages and inventions of the figures on the list and then proceeded to add a few additional figures of his own: Jack Conway of *Variety*; playwright James Gleason, whose 1925 dialect play *Is Zat So?* had been a comic sensation; Milton Gross, whose 1926 comic classic *Nize Baby* had introduced readers to the tenement-dwelling Feitlebaums and his "Yidgin English"; playwright Wilson Mizener; Johnny Stanley and songwriter ("Melancholy Baby") Tommy Lyman.[5]

How Funk and Mencken arrived at their particular choices is not known, but the provenance of the figures they chose was scarcely surprising. Walter Winchell had come up with an almost identical list six years before. Funk and Wagnalls was a Brooklyn house, and Funk himself, the son of the founder and originator of the dictionary, was something of a sport and probably knew the Broadway world first-hand. Mencken was an active if part-time New Yorker. When his work on the *Smart Set* brought him to the city, he stayed at the Algonquin on Forty-fourth Street near the magazine's offices.

By the early 'thirties, word that the Times Square area was a productive site for the coinage of language had traveled far. Eric Partridge, a young New Zealander lecturing at Manchester and London Universities, seems to have been caught up in the vogue for Runyonese that swept England after the publication of the Broadway stories. Soon afterward he turned his attention from the study of Shakespearean English to the contemporary development of slang. The first edition of his *Dictionary of Slang and Unconventional English* was published only a few years later, in 1937. After several periods of American study, he published his *Dictionary of the Underworld, British and American* in 1940. This work, with its lengthy verbatim transcriptions from American prisons, stands as a monument to the belief at the time that there was a special kind of vitality and creativity in the speech of criminals and their sporting associates in the underworld.[6]

World fame had come abruptly, it appears, to an area that a decade earlier was still something of a novelty, even to sophisticated New Yorkers.

In November of 1927, Walter Winchell had published a revealing article of Condé Nast's *Vanity Fair*. *Vanity Fair* prided itself on scooping entertainment news in the city and tracking recreational fashions. The title of Winchell's article, "A Primer of Broadway Slang: An Initiate Reveals Some of the Mysteries of the Much Quoted Theatrical Idiom" tells part of the story. In the article, Winchell proclaimed Broadway "the slang capital of the world," adding that "it is difficult to imagine any other spot on the globe where the citizenry take so readily to slang." He left no doubt, furthermore, that he was inducting his readers into a linguistically coded world. "Most of the argot Broadway invents," he concluded by saying, "is relished and rolled on the lips of 'Main Drag' tongues, but little of it is comprehensive [*sic*] west of the Hudson and north of Harlem."7

It is worth noting that the examples of slang that Winchell cited as localisms in 1927 were mostly in familiar usage a decade later and are commonplace today, some of them scarcely detectable as slang, so rapidly and so expansively did the circle of usage and acceptance spread. He included such words as click, hit, fan, flop, wow 'em, up-stage, bimbo, baloney, push-over, cinch, pay off, gate, turkey, the last word, phoney, racket, bump off, plug, take for a ride, squawk, squeal, a flame, a rat, a heel, burned up, all wet, gyp, crash the gate, wash-out, belly laugh, laugh off, and ball and chain (wife). Winchell also included enough locutions, such as Tad Dorgan's "Yes, we have no bananas," and Texas Guinan's "Hello, Suckers" and "A big butter and egg man," to suggest he was referring to a manner of speaking and not simply some fresh new words.8

In this and similar compilations that appeared over the next decade, one thing is apparent. What was referred to as Broadway slang included a great deal more than "theatrical idiom," to use Winchell's phrase. All the occupational groups of the area made their contributions to it. These contributions included many types of lingo: what was once "trade" cant, a kind of intentional Babel; fan talk; and journalistic coinages, like Winchell's, designed to upstage fellow journalists, as in his description of Broadway as "the hardened artery," and of divorces as "Reno-vations." For Winchell the key to all this inventiveness was provided by the volatile spirit of Sime Silverman's *Variety*, which he joined others in calling "the Bible of the theatrical profession."9

A more satisfactory explanation for the composite character of the language in these lists, as well as for some of its remarkable vitality, probably lies in the human chemistry of Times Square. By the mid-'thirties, the area in the vicinity of Times Square could be divided into roughly three overlapping sectors. In ascending order moving north from Forty-second Street were the newspaper, theater, and sporting and night-life zones. The southernmost sector, extending from Forty-first to Forty-fifth Street and radiating out from the *Times* building at the south end of the square, contained a significant new concentration of newspaper and magazine offices. This concentration represented a significant relocation of newspaper and periodical publication into the midtown area. As late as 1920, for example, key publications, like Hearst's *American*, which printed Runyon, Baer, and Fowler, were located downtown on South Street, and McFadden's *Graphic*, which first carried Winchell's column and Dorgan's cartoons, was located near Park Row not far from Pulitzer's *World*. By contrast, Hearst's *Mirror*, which picked up Winchell and Runyon, along with other Broadway "scribes" such as Lardner, was located far east on Forty-fifth Street, and the *Daily News* on Forty-second Street, three blocks to the South.

In the immediate vicinity of the *Times* and the *Times* Annex around the corner on Forty-third Street was the *Herald-Tribune* on Forty-first Street west of Seventh Avenue. Symbolic of the sector as a kind of beacon of journalistic metropolitanism was the out-of-town newsstand at the northern tip of the *Times* building. The principal magazines specializing in urban sophistication, *Vanity Fair*, the *Smart Set*, and the *New Yorker*, were at one point clustered on Forty-third and Forty-fourth streets east of Sixth Avenue, along with the hostelries and hangouts that "the magazine crowd" preferred, such as the Algonquin and Royalton Hotels. Farthest north were the offices of *Variety*, just west of Broadway on Forty-sixth Street, appropriately situated within the theatrical sector that contained the largest concentration of theaters and para-theatrical institutions.

This sector probably lay between Broadway and Eighth avenues and Forty-fourth and Forty-seventh streets, the area radiating from Shubert Alley. Theatrical life in the more general sense, however, was dispersed throughout a much wider area, stretching from the Metropolitan Opera at Broadway and Thirty-ninth into the Fifties.

This more constricted theater zone also contained an astonishing array of support institutions and facilities of one kind or another. The locus of legitimate theater shifted northward after 1920 as theatrical productions along Forty-second Street dwindled. What gave the mid-Forties further centrality was the presence there of key institutions such as *Variety*. On Seventh Avenue near its junction with Broadway below Forty-seventh Street was the monumental Palace and next door the American Federation of Actors, whose membership consisted mostly of variety entertainers. Central to the theater world were the Astor Hotel, on Broadway just east of Shubert Alley, and the Lambs Club on Forty-fourth Street. The Lamb's Club as a social organization served the vaudeville and music worlds in much the same way as the Friar's Club four blocks north on Forty-eighth Street catered to theatrical promoters and publicity men.

Scattered over these blocks were hangouts that especially catered to different parts of the theatrical world. Sardi's on Forty-fourth Street west of Shubert's Alley; the Blue Ribbon, a German rathskeller on Forty-fourth east of Broadway; Ye Eat Shoppe on Eighth Avenue between Forty-fifth and Forty-sixth streets, were favorite hangouts for groups in the entertainment community. Around the corner from the Palace on West Forty-seventh Street, once known as "Dream Street," the sidewalk in front of *Billboard* magazine was a meeting place for carnival managers and owners. Actor's Equity was just down the street on the east side of Sixth Avenue.

By the 'twenties, Tin Pan Alley, like the newspaper and theater world, had moved north and was dispersed over the area above Forty-fifth Street east and west of Broadway, but its focus and social center after 1931 was probably around the Brill building to the north on the southwest corner of Broadway and Forty-ninth Street.[10]

The Brill Building was located in a sector that during Prohibition had been dominated by nightlife and developed into an important meeting ground for the sporting crowd and the underworld. The ground floor of the Brill Building contained the Turf, an important musical hangout; it also held for a time Jack Dempsey's Café, an important sporting hangout. Irving Berlin's offices were at 1607 Broadway, a block to the south. Dave's Blue Room on Seventh Avenue north of Fifty-first Street was one key place where the music crowd and the sporting world mixed.

It is easy to see why this northernmost sector of the area became prime Runyon country. Its flagship institution after its completion in 1925 was the second Madison Square Garden on Eighth Avenue just west of Broadway, between Forty-ninth and Fiftieth streets. The Garden drew huge crowds to its sporting events, prize fights, rodeos, circuses, and other spectaculars. It also drew its camp followers of ticket scalpers, gamblers, bookies, racing buffs, and minor hoods and knockabouts. It was, because of the rodeos, the locus where the cowboy entered the Broadway scene.

Across the street was one of the locations of "Jacob's Beach," named after fight promoter and impresario Mike Jacobs. Jacob's Beach was the sidewalk hangout for the sporting and racing crowds and their hangers-on. For many years it was located between Forty-ninth and Fiftieth streets on Broadway, a block to the east in front of Lindy's restaurant. Lindy's, named for its owner and manager Leo Lindemann, was Runyon's "Mindy's," and while it remained at this location was a popular late-night (and early-morning) social center.

This northern sector was preeminently the center of nightlife. Most of the famous cabarets and speakeasies were concentrated here, a majority along its upper fringe. Some of the most famous were located in the low

Fifties, well to the east, just beyond Fifth Avenue, but the immediate area was well represented. The Hollywood Club on Broadway above Forty-eighth Street, built by the Grunland Syndicate in 1928, was a huge, new kind of cabaret, which introduced the "cover charge" and was designed to make up in volume what it lost in not selling liquor. For a decade the Hollywood featured big bands, famous acts, and the Ziegfeld girls, who were known to moonlight in its reviews. The Silver Slipper, around the corner to the west on Forty-eighth Street, was probably Broadway's best-known night spot and catered to a mixed crowd from the stage, high society, and the underworld ("gangland"). Earl Carroll's *Vanities*— "Through These Doors Pass the Most Beautiful Girls in the World"—was located two blocks north on the southeast corner of Fiftieth Street.

The lower Fifties were known as speakeasy streets. The various establishments of the colorful Texas Guinan were in this vicinity, along with Runyon's fictional 300 Club, operated by his character Missouri Martin. One of the most famous, Club Napoleon, was located in a townhouse, once the Woolworth mansion, at 33 West Fifty-sixth Street. Leon and Eddie's and the 21 Club were on Fifty-second Street between Sixth and Seventh Avenues. El Morrocco and Sherman Billingsley's Stork Club, where Walter Winchell for many years occupied table number fifty, were farther east.

Other haunts, residential and recreational, were crucial to establishing the character of the area. The Garden Cabaret at Fiftieth and Eighth Avenue, Roth's Grill on Seventh Avenue above Forty-eighth Street, and both Jack Dempsey's restaurants, on Broadway and on Eighth Avenue, were important hangouts for the sporting crowd. Jack Doyle's billiard parlor at Forty-second and Broadway was the headquarters for Runyon's H.B.E. (Hard-Boiled Egg) Club, and a hangout for minor hoods and the press that Runyon, among others, frequented in the 'twenties. For reporters on the crime beat, the Eighteenth Precinct Station far west on Forty-seventh Street and the " Fly-beat" across the street were important places. The Fly-beat ("Ask for Hickie") was a twenty-four-hour office maintained for the press. After Runyon had finished with the scene, one could have said, "Through these doors pass the most famous hoods in the world."

Billy La Hiff's Tavern on Forty-eighth Street west of Seventh Avenue was for a time a key show-business hangout popular with the press. The two floors above the restaurant functioned as a kind of Broadway dormitory for married men like Runyon and Winchell who seldom went home. Winchell lived there after his divorce, and Runyon stayed there "more than somewhat," to steal a favorite phrase. At one point, Runyon, Sherman Billingsley, Jack Dempsey, and Bugs Baer all occupied the rooms simultaneously. For a long time in the 'twenties, Runyon lived in the

Forrest Hotel on Forty-ninth Street between Broadway and Eighth Avenue, next door to the Forrest Theatre and halfway between the Garden and Brill Building, astride the experiential worlds of his fiction.[11]

It is difficult today, looking back, to determine what it was that fused all these elements into the Broadway subject and created such enormous receptivity for almost any version of it. Mere proximity and adjacency do not appear to explain it. Lower Manhattan with its rabbit warren of occupational and ethnic worlds of Wall Street, Chinatown, and the Lower East Side was never linguistically fused in such a way, despite the concentration of newspapers along Park Row and the presence of talented journalists and other writers who might have exploited such an opportunity.

It is tempting to conclude that Broadway, as an idea, was the creation of a particular historical moment as much as it was the product of a place or location. This complex circuitry of special languages and working journalists, in turn, appears to have inspired a unique combination of adoption and invention. Writing of Broadway at the end of the 'thirties, Mencken concluded that "it is from this quarter that most American slang comes, a large part of it invented by gag-writers, newspaper columnists and press agents, and the rest borrowed from the vocabularies of criminals, prostitutes and the lower orders of showfolk. There was a time when it was chiefly propagated by vaudeville performers, but now that vaudeville is in eclipse the torch has been taken over by the harlequins of movie and radio."[12]

To the journalists working the area, the *way* people talked *was* the story. It was their discovery that for a time language was itself something you could take off and run with. "Without slang," Jack Conway once remarked, "I know a lot of guys who would be doing pantomime. On Broadway it was the pay-off. For we all speak and think it. I never knew it could be peddled until I fell into a job at *Variety* and found a home. On this sheet where they use the dictionary for a doorstop, I can rip and tear,—and I have."[13] If the language of the press became a performance medium for the writers, it became a kind of theater for its readers.

This historical moment when slang crystallized as language theater was comparatively brief, a matter of twenty years at the most. The fully fleshed-out Broadway of myth was available only in the barest outline to Fitzgerald in 1925 when he came to compose *The Great Gatsby*, mostly as evoked in the Broadway character of Meyer Wolfsheim. As early as the mid-'thirties, the creative energy that had fired the myth had begun to depart the scene, and the versions of Broadway that were produced by Hollywood and by wordsmiths elsewhere were becoming formulaic and repetitive.

For writers and others who were tracking it, Broadway was always a moving target that required quick responses, as Mencken implies in his reference to the switch from vaudeville to film and radio as the source of slang. One important factor in keeping *Variety*, which had started publication in 1905, at the center of the Broadway scene was Silverman's shrewd sense of the direction show business was moving. Founded when vaudeville and variety entertainment were near their peak, *Variety* moved quickly to cover developments in the film industry and in radio. By the 'thirties, these new media were prominent in the area. Every major Hollywood studio occupied space on Broadway, from the offices of Paramount and Fox on West Forty-fourth Street, to the offices of Universal, RKO, and Goldwyn on Sixth Avenue between Forty-ninth and Fifty-first streets, on either side of Rockefeller Center and behind the new RCA building.

Meanwhile, an important transition had taken place in Times Square, as press replaced theater as the voice of the area; a transfer of energy, one might say, from stage to page. Fundamental to such a shift was the long history of variety entertainment in New York, which stretched back for almost a century and had a vitality that no technological changes seemed capable of dampening. So powerful was its influence that the format of the burgeoning tabloid press soon imbibed its qualities.

Variety entertainment, developed around the enticements of what was known as "naked dancing," was basically a theater of pastiche: swift shifts in substance and tempo to match the expectations of impatient and knowing urban audiences. *Variety* as the bible of variety theater was quick to mimic its moods and pace. By the 'twenties, *Variety*, intended as the medium for communicating within the Broadway world, itself became the message. The distinction between press and theater, in fact, soon became almost meaningless as crossover figures from one area to the other proliferated, until finally the slanguage of the press became the best show in town. Winchell, who began his career in the song-and-dance team of Winchell and Green, was only one of the figures to make the transition into the new era and medium of performance.[14] Reporters like Runyon and Winchell, who were sent uptown as emissaries to cover the entertainment world in midtown, eventually became its stars, dragging the press, so to speak, after them.

A surprising number of journalists, like Runyon, Lardner, and Hecht, themselves wrote plays. No one, not even Winchell, had a greater hand in exploiting this linguistic wealth than Damon Runyon, who came to New York in 1911 as a seasoned journalist from the West. He was born, ironically, in Manhattan, Kansas, the son of a heavy-drinking itinerant newspaperman. After his Broadway years writing for Hearst's *American*, Runyon virtually left New York for a new career writing and producing films in Hollywood.[15] Runyon collaborated with Howard Lindsay in *A Slight Case of Murder* (1931), and Hecht and Charles McArthur together produced the immensely successful *Front Page* (1928). With its enthusiastic reception of a play about the press, one could say that Broadway had completely turned the tables. The press was now the subject, and Broadway theater had become the reporter. The story the press covered in the ensuing years was the sporting life of Broadway: its lingo, its antics, its dirt, and its colorful repertoire of anecdote.

Another factor in the creation of the Broadway subject was traditions in American journalism that had something of the same kind of performing energy as variety entertainment. One of these was the convention of the whimsical, informal essay, highly personal in point of view, that had evolved alongside hard news by mid-century. The first such essays appeared in Western papers. This tradition drew on a tradition of colloquial Western humor going back to newspaper writing by Brett Harte and Mark Twain in the 'sixties. Edgar Watson Howe of the Atchison, Kansas, *Daily Globe*, who began such a whimsical column in the late 'seventies, was an early practitioner whose influence outran the circulation of his paper. Donald Robert Taylor of the *Chicago Tribune*, Finley Peter Dunne of the *Chicago Post*, and Don Marquis of the *New York Evening Sun* were others doing such writing before the 'twenties. Franklin Pierce Adams ("F.P.A.") writing "The Conning Tower" in Pulitzer's *World* and Hecht's essays for the *Chicago Daily News* carried this tradition into the 'twenties. All these essayists created distinctive personas that set their work off from competitors as well as from those doing hard reporting. Some of them, like Dunne, were beginning to experiment with dialect.[16]

There is considerable evidence to suggest that the conventions of theater criticism and sportswriting that were developed during the 'twenties grew out of this tradition of informal, highly personal, sometimes whimsical or humorous commentary. Humorist Robert Benchley, after a brief career as a feature writer for the *World*, went on during the 'twenties to become drama critic for the old *Life*, and, after its founding, *The New Yorker*. Alexander Woollcott served as drama critic for the *New York Times* for almost ten years before 1922. During the 'twenties, Heywood Broun wrote an influential theater column significantly entitled "It Seems to Me," for the *World*. In 1927 Woollcott took it over. It was out of this tradition that figures like Ring Lardner launched such successful careers. Lardner began as a writer for South Bend, Indiana, papers in 1905 and wrote a successful sports column for the *Chicago Tribune* until he moved to New York in 1919. So far had conventions in sportswriting moved from other kinds of reporting, however, that most sportswriters of 1920 were advertised as "humorists" ten years later. The columns that Runyon wrote under the heading of "My Wife Ethel" and under the by-line "A. Mugg" took him into the mainstream of journalistic humor, far from the ring, the stadium, and the racetrack.[17]

This tradition makes the Western origins of Broadway's principal architects a little less puzzling. The extraordinary fecundity and inventiveness of New York journalism during the 'twenties and 'thirties owes much of its vitality to traditions of Western journalism. The flow of talent into New York from San Francisco, Denver, Chicago, and Des Moines was clearly one element. Runyon, who had the ear of Arthur Brisbane and sometimes Hearst himself, brought young journalists he admired from other cities, as he brought Gene Fowler from the Denver paper he himself had left. The *Denver Post* and the *San Francisco Chronicle* in this period were the most abundant sources of journalistic talent; in effect, the "farm teams" for Hearst sports reporting and graphic art. New York papers, with their large circulation and huge advertising revenues, were pots of gold to provincial journalists. Coming to Hearst's *American* or the *Mirror* in those years must have been a little like playing the Palace. The cartoonist Rube Goldberg was earning $150,000 a year from Hearst and national syndication only a few years after he moved to New York from San Francisco.

Coming as they did out of Western journalism, they had already tapped the mainstream of American newspaper humor, most of them, before they arrived in New York. This mainstream of humor in 1920 was defined as much by Will Rogers as by any one figure. Rogers, who galloped into New York as part of a Wild West show that debuted in the Garden in 1905, had become a Ziegfeld star by 1916 just playing his "natchell self." By the 'twenties he had branched off into journalism and was writing a syndicated column, profoundly conservative, in which he poked fun at anything new or unconventional as well as anything old or new that appeared to him fake or stodgy or phoney. He and Runyon together covered the Republican national convention in 1924.

Meanwhile, the kinds of feature writing that were included, especially in Sunday editions of the tabloid press, expanded as such writing became a key factor in expanding circulation. Hearst and other publishers paid the highest salaries to attract such talent, sometimes more than they paid to their editors.

The career of Damon Runyon is more closely associated with the Broadway subject and what was then the New Journalism than that of any other figure, even Winchell; yet his relationship to New York, to the Broadway beat he covered, was unique. Runyon came to personify Broadway, yet he was over thirty and a seasoned journalist when he arrived in New York from Denver and took his first job on Hearst's *American* in 1910.[18]

For journalists like Runyon, Times Square was a crossroad where special languages—dialects, cants, argots—hitherto confined to ethnic or occupational groups, converged in a kind of linguistic funnel to create a new national slang with a pronouncedly New York accent. The sporting world, the underworld, the worlds of vaudeville, theater, and carnival had all developed rich and expressive argots by the beginning of the 'twenties. By the end of the 'thirties, however, Runyon had virtually left New York and was dividing his time between Florida and Hollywood. He thus joined the significant migration westward of Broadway talent. Several Broadway stories, written in the early 1930s for national magazines, were made into successful films. Along with others, therefore, he brought the mythos of Broadway to movie audiences across the country at just the moment when the Broadway world that Runyon knew was on the point of disappearing.

His contributions to the Broadway mythos were distinctive and set him off from all the other figures who haunted the area and wrote about it during the 'twenties and 'thirties. More than anyone else, he was the creator of "slanguage," as *Variety* dubbed it. The linguistic product that emerged during the 'twenties and 'thirties was more than a slang vocabulary. It was less imitation than simulacrum. It more closely resembled a distinctive manner of speech, in effect an amalgam of languages highly expressive of the historical moment: jokes, an inventive punning and toying with words reminiscent of vaudeville, new ways of representing speech in dialect, a distinctive syntax and temporal mode (e.g., Runyon's historical present tense), a repertoire of characters unmatched since the early days of Western humor, a colorful array of "monikers" to designate them, and anecdotal lore and narrative configurations that sealed the locality in myth.

Runyon did not write dialect like Gleason, Milt Gross, and many of his contemporaries. Nothing was further from his style than the gossipy, breathless, staccato columns with their showy neologisms like "Chicagorilla" that brought Winchell fame and national recognition as the personification of Broadway by the end of the 'twenties. In 1931 Winchell appeared on the cover of *Time*, and little wonder, since what he had achieved stylistically was closely akin to the "Timestyle" being manufactured simultaneously a few blocks to the east. Winchell's column was a difficult target for parody since it approached self-parody almost by nature, but Lardner managed to do it by mocking his breezy delivery:

A. Lincoln and Gen. McClellan are on the verge . . .
Jimmy Madison and Dolly Payne are THAT WAY . . .
Aleck Hamilton and Aaron Burr have phfft . . .

Finally, Runyon differed in both style and focus from the writers who created the snappy, slangy, highly elided language of *Variety*. *Variety* was devoted to the world of show business and was probably best known outside its inner circle for its brief, jazzy, comically compressed headlines, such as "Stix Nix Hix Pix" for "movies about farm life play poorly in small towns." Runyon had, moreover, little sustained interest in the theatrical world as such, only in the bright aura with which it surrounded the Broadway scene. It was the Broadway sporting, gaming, and nightlife world that consumed his attention as a writer.

For this reason, Runyon throughout his career remained close to the conventions of the "sporting writer," as the type was then called, unlike Winchell or the writers identified with *Variety* or theatrical writing. Soon after he arrived in New York and began covering sports for the *American*, he fell into the routines as journalist that were to guide the early part of his career. He arose at noon and set off for one of his Broadway haunts, Jack Dunston's restaurant near the old Hippodrome, or later the Garden cabaret, where the sporting crowd gathered and he could listen to baseball or boxing anecdotes and pick up racing tips. After 1913, he was away for several months each year, hanging out with the teams during spring training. In 1914 he traveled to Paris with the Giants and White Sox and covered their tour through Europe, sending home comic accounts of such incidents as the presentation of John McGraw and Charles Comiskey to George V.

For the rest of his career, he divided his energies between what amounted to feature writing, more and more humorous, about sports, and straight reporting. In this sense his career reflected contrary tendencies between factual reporting and opinionating that had been present in American journalism for much of the century.

A writer for *American Speech* in 1927 described this dialectical process of the press with such precision that his comments, though long, seem worth quoting in full. The article, entitled "Color Stuff," begins with a series of complaints about the deterioration and dullness of news reporting, which the author ascribes to a "standardization of the news" imposed by the business office and advertising departments. The writer then pays tribute to "sporting writers" as the sole survivors of that golden age in journalism when color made the news article as intriguing and fascinating as the brightest of short stories.

> But the sports writer—Facts to him are incidental. He molds his stories, often grotesque, usually colorful, and always unfettered by the restrictions which hem in the boys in the city room, out of less tangible substances.
>
> He is a freebooter. He goes into the street for his slang. He invents words when his dictionary fails him. He writes what is in his head, how and as he wishes. The general reporter may not do this even if he could—and generally he couldn't.
>
> Why is this so? For one reason, the sporting writer serves a clientele which is not so much concerned with facts as with good, rollicking tales of the diamond, the mat, the gridiron, and the boxing ring . . .

Of all the sporting writers, he who pictures the stirring battle of the ring is the breeziest. He knows no restraint. Slang, he uses in full measure, and his readers like it and the slangier he is, the higher is he held in their esteem. It is he who invents such spicy phrases as: "honeyed kisses and brotherly love stuff"; "took two more reefs in his wampum belt"; "speared him on the whiskers"; "knocking them bowlegged"; ". . . kid himself into the throne room."

After several paragraphs of further examples, the writer concludes with some general observations.

A fertile imagination coupled with a flair for invention is the sporting writer's greatest asset. Writing stories averaging a column in length six and sometimes seven times a week, and injecting into each of these fresh expressions or phrases, calls for more than ordinary ingenuity. As I have mentioned previously, it is his privilege either to pick up his material in the street or to invent it. Some, possibly many, of the expressions which he has conceived while extolling a fighter have become a living part of the American slang. I do not believe that all the boxing slang which we hear in conversation and later see in the newspapers travelled from the spoken word into print. The contrary is also true.[19]

Runyon during much of his career had clearly internalized some such dialectic of city desk versus sports desk. He wrote straight news accounts of the Chicago trial of his friend Al Capone in 1931 without so much as a hint of their personal relationship. At the same time he was composing humorous, informal feature articles about a range of subjects for almost every Sunday edition of the *Mirror*. He seems, over the course of his newspaper career, to have been fascinated by the drama of court proceedings. He actively sought out notorious trials like that of Bruno Hauptmann in the Lindbergh kidnapping case. As a correspondent in France in 1918, on the other hand, he appears to have seen himself principally as a feature writer concerned with the experience of individual soldiers, and he therefore played to the Sunday editions. Still, he continued to do straight sports reporting, as when he chose to do a serialized biography of his friend Jack Dempsey for King Features in 1919.

When he began writing and publishing his so-called Broadway stories in 1929, therefore, he was clearly embarked on a new phase of his career, one that carried him psychologically away from newspaper work altogether and, for much of his subsequent career, from New York itself. Between 1929 and the end of the 'thirties, Runyon wrote some eighty of these stories. Most of them were completed by 1935 when the third collection of them was published. They appeared in *Colliers, Cosmopolitan, Liberty,* and the *Saturday Evening Post*, all of which commanded large, middle-class readerships. The stories were an instant success and, almost at once, were in great demand. Magazines estimated a Runyon story to be worth 60,000 subscriptions.[20]

Magazine stories are no longer a staple, and it is therefore a little difficult to gauge the qualities that made these stories so instantly appealing. The appeal, moreover, did not wear off with their first publication. Many of these stories were later republished by the Hearst papers and several of them were made into successful Hollywood films. "Madame La Gimp" became *Lady for a Day,* and "Little Pink" became *Big Street,* starring Lucille Ball. Much later, of course, *Guys and Dolls,* based on two stories, played on Broadway as a hit musical.

This instant success would seem incredible if Runyon had been a novice story writer entering the highly competitive field of magazine fiction at the end of the 'twenties where he would have competed with the likes of F. Scott Fitzgerald. Yet in a sense this is what he did. Runyon, it is true, had written a few stories about Western town life before he left Denver in 1911, and some of his feature writing, such as his column "My Wife Ethel," were whimsical fictions, but the Broadway stories still seem to have come out of the blue.

These stories have by now received what seems like an inordinate amount of study from literary scholars, including a book-length critical study by Jean Wagner, entitled *Runyonese.*[21] Another scholar has succeeded in locating 750 slang expressions in a group of stories he examined and has determined that almost half of these expressions derive from the underworld Runyon came to know so well. Still another study has placed Runyon as the last of the Local Colorists. None of these studies, however, seems to me to have addressed the problem that is most interesting today, though they offer some interesting clues.

To read Runyon's Broadway stories today, it strikes me, is to enter a special narrative world, a world that is almost entirely voice. Plot, settings, and the characters with their colorful "monikers" change from story to story. Fewer than half of the Broadway stories, for example, actually take place on Broadway. Some are set at various racetracks across the country, in college stadiums, even in faraway places like the island of St. Pierre off the coast of Labrador. The plots of these stories, one must agree with Runyon, do now, at least, seem formulaic. The rescue of a damsel in distress is a common theme, though all of Runyon's damsels don't make it, as in his story "Little Miss Marker," where the child dies as her hood friends stand weeping at her hospital bedside. Rich, obnoxious society people "get" it in one story after another, just as tough hoods frequently reveal a heart of gold.

If plots were the essence of Runyon's fiction, his success would be unintelligible. There is almost nothing in his fiction, moreover, that would qualify today as "local color." There is very little description of any kind. So much for the appeal that these stories might once have had for those longing for a fictional glimpse of the Broadway scene. There is very little dialogue. While there is slang in abundance, slang is not thrown around in the way that Winchell or *Variety* writers deployed it. It is fused with the narrative voice and, while important, is not an element in itself. Even the famous "monikers" are ultimately a function of voice, for it is the narrator who designates the characters in the stories, just as it is the narrator who in the course of the stories relabels the human goods of the Broadway world. The narrator, of course, is immediately identifiable as a Broadway guy; sometimes named, sometimes not. But it is this Broadway voice, or what we readily come to accept as a Broadway voice, that must have given this fiction its authentic appeal. It is this voice that has survived, as much as anything has, during the fifty years since the last of these stories was written.

"One morning about four bells," "Bloodhounds of Broadway" begins, "I am standing in front of Mindy's restaurant with a guy by the name of Regret." We are at once on familiar terrain surrounded by a repertory company of gangland and sporting world figures that Runyon has concocted out of the impersonal world of hangers-on who frequented the real Broadway, a Micawberish well-meaning crew that, whatever their provenance, are pure invention. In Runyon stories activity is ceaseless but nothing much happens. In this story as in so many others, a sequence of farcical and non-consequential events take place. In this instance the catalyst is an eccentric character from rural Georgia who turns up at Mindy's with a pair of bloodhounds and proceeds to turn the Broadway world upside down, exasperating the police, terrifying the underworld, and eventually tracking down poor Regret, who turns out not to be really guilty of a crime, after all.

So much in a similar vein has been written about Broadway and the underworld since Runyon's time that it is difficult for us to imagine the novelty these stories must have had for their readers and the reassuring charm they must have provided. From *Some Like It Hot*, to *Married to the Mob* and *Billy Bathgate* we have learned to laugh away some of our anxiety about organized crime. Runyon, almost alone, created the format for certain popular representations of Broadway and the Mob. Instead of writing about the complex and impersonal city that had grown up by the 'twenties, Runyon, drawing on the Western towns he had known as a youth, succeeded in de-urbanizing his Broadway and rendering it comically in terms familiar to small-town America. It is little wonder that Frank Capra was drawn to Runyon stories. They provide a version of the pastoral that has escaped notice only because it was so blatantly labelled as "New York." None of the searing emotions, for example, that are evoked by O. Henry stories—the desolating loneliness of his waitresses and shop-girls—are present in Runyon. Out of his stories the endorphins flow freely, subduing the anxieties of Americans who were still uneasy about their big cities, New York most of all.

Taken together, the Broadway stories compose a sequence of timeless fables recounted by a voice that is at once socially accepting and morally firm. This voice appears to know that his Broadway friends cut a comic figure at a Park Avenue party, but their very awkwardness is portrayed as a virtue that places them above the mannered world that is discomfiting them. They are redeemed by their candor and their innocence. They are, in Runyon's description, "citizens" or "peasants."

They belong to what becomes a small, familiar world, what amounts to a village in the center of New York. Rough parallels to Runyon's fictional world can be found in the other fictions of small-town America where narrative voices structure the community, as in Sherwood Anderson's *Winesburg* or Thorton Wilder's *Our Town*. In Runyon's stories, Broadway becomes a small town, very like the towns that figure in Runyon's early Western stories, where everyone knows everyone by name. This aspect of Runyon's stories clearly had effect of giving his readers, who must have felt they were looking for something new, something that was at the same time familiar to them.

Runyon's world, however, is a manic world in some ways closer to that of the Marx brothers or Tad Dorgan's comic strip "Boob McNut" than to that of any literary parallel. In Runyon's fiction, when someone throws a ham, the narrator comments: "Well, this ham hits poor old Bodeeker ker-bowie smack dab on the noggin. The doc does not fall down, but he commences staggering around with his legs bending under him like he is drunk."[23] In general Runyon composes highly visual fiction, but it is a visual fiction that is very dependent on voice. In this world of mayhem, it is the function of the narrative voice to exercise a slightly distant controlling influence. The historical present tense in which he addresses us is a measure of his narrative control. It is, in a sense, the voice of Runyon, the reporter, speaking from location, "I am standing in front of Mindy's. . . ." The success of these stories is also, I suspect, heavily dependent on the even greater popularity of radio drama. It is no coincidence that they appeared at just the moment when radio plays broadcast over national network radio had saturated the airwaves, adding still further authenticity to these New York narrators as on-the-spot reporters. They reached a wide national audience, moreover, that was attuned to drama arriving by voice.

Jean Wagner and most later students of Runyon make a much of certain similarities in career and in storyline between Runyon and one Alfred Henry Smith, an earlier (1858–1914) writer who, like Runyon, was born in Kansas, and also, like Runyon, wrote Western stories of saloons, cattle thieves, and gambles in a succession of stories focusing on a fictional town. Smith then came east, working on newspapers, and then wrote a series of stories about the New York underworld, collected in 1912 under the title *The Apaches of New York*.

The coincidence is striking, but one look at Smith's stories is enough to dispel the idea that Runyon's fiction was in any important sense derived from Smith's. Smith's stories are recounted by a third-person genteel narrator, like those employed by William Sydney Porter (O. Henry) a generation earlier. Porter was another New York writer whose Western origins and preoccupation with petty criminals parallels that of Runyon. It seems less likely that Runyon read these other writers than that all these writers drew from a common tradition of Western storytelling.

This Western tradition may help account for still another and striking feature of Runyon's fiction, a characteristic that it shares with other verbal lore of Broadway. Runyon's world is preeminently a world of men. Women figure in it as obsessions, as hostages, as prizes. They are "dolls" or "molls" or "gams," but never "citizens" or "peasants" or anyone important. In the transformation from the West to Broadway, one is tempted to view them as replacing the cattle in these earlier fictions. They are stolen or hustled. They provoke violence in men, and they seldom talk. In the slanguage of Broadway more generally, they are characteristically the butts of jokes. They are dumbbells or dumb blondes, if they are not the eel's hips or the cat's whiskers. Dumb wives who outsmart their husbands, as in Runyon's column "My Wife Ethel," were a standard feature of variety entertainment from Runyon to the Honeymooners.

The jokes that broke up readers in the 'twenties would make any modern woman "pull in her ears," as in "Bugs" Baer's quip that paying alimony "was like feeding oats to a dead horse." Homoerotic bonding was at the very heart of Runyon's fiction, as in his associations at work. Homoerotic bonding remained, of course, equally a regular feature of the celibate cowboy in "the West of memory." As incorporated into Runyon's fiction, this version of the West as a world of tough, virile men acquired a New York accent with the likes of Marlon Brando playing Runyon's character Skye Masterson in *Guys and Dolls*.

Runyon may, partly for these reasons, turn out to be the most important of the Broadway writers, even though his Broadway stories now seem dated and mechanical. Runyon was, as I have already suggested, an odd kind of New Yorker. Born in Kansas, he launched his career as journalist on small town papers and, later, in Denver and did not come east to New York until 1910 when he was thirty-one years old. Yet during his New York years he seemed to be almost fiercely involved with anything touching on Broadway. Gene Fowler remembered being startled in 1917 when he arrived in New York and heard Runyon, six years after his arrival, talking as though he had invented the place; as in a sense he had. Another friend noted two years later when Runyon was serving in France that he latched onto any snippet of information or any New Yorker with Broadway ties "like a miner jumping a claim."

Yet by the mid-'thirties, as we have seen, Runyon had to all intents and purposes left New York and was dividing his time between his house on Hibiscus Island near Miami (and the house of his friend Capone) and a house in Beverly Hills, where he was by then earning a sizable income as author, scriptwriter, and, finally, producer.

So ambivalent about New York had he become at the end of his life that he hesitated, in making funeral arrangements, whether to have his ashes scattered over Miami or over Broadway. In the end, he opted for Broadway, thereby enhancing the myth, and his friend Eddie Rickenbacker performed the task as he requested. Yet, unlike many of his journalist contemporaries, who had left reporting once they had established themselves as writers, Runyon continued to practice straight news reporting from time to time, reporting proudly and impartially for Hearst on trials and disasters and conducting interviews, including one with Hearst himself in 1941. During the last weeks of his life, as he was dying of throat cancer and literally speechless, he spent the hours, when he wasn't at Winchell's table at the Stork Club, riding around the city in Winchell's car answering police calls.

His life, one could say, encapsulated a central contradiction in the journalism of his time. Reporting was clearly in his blood and a fundamental part of his identity. As the son of an itinerant, quasi-failure of a newspaperman, whose migratory lifestyle and hard-drinking ways Runyon began by imitating, he also prided himself on being a reporter. At the same time, despite his attachment to reporting, his best and most important work, the Broadway stories that he began to write in 1929, were in clear reaction to the restrictiveness of journalism and were published, as he published nothing else, not in newspapers, but in large-circulation national magazines like *Cosmopolitan* and *Liberty*.

In his personal life, too, he seems to have been equally enigmatic and contradictory. Although he surrounded himself with talkative, even garrulous friends with whom he spent the better part of every day, and his stories contain endless accounts of conviviality and partying, he himself was reticent, even taciturn, and, in the eyes of many of his friends, inscrutable. Many of his stories revolve around themes of loyalty and undying affection, yet in his personal relationships he appears to have been aloof, even cold. He shamelessly neglected his first wife and his children by her, with tragic results.[24] Although he imbued his portrayals of nightlife with a manic gaiety and wrote with comic nonchalance about dolls and chorines, speakeasies and bootleggers, he remained personally severe, most of his life a teetotaler.

Finally, although a passion for egalitarian justice and a distrust of wealth and privilege characterize the whole body of his stories, he himself carefully withheld any political criticisms he may have had and avoided any but comic commentary on the events of the day. To the end he remained loyal to, and uncritical of, William Randolph Hearst. His bitterest attack upon the morals of his time appeared, characteristically, on the editorial page of Hearst's *American* in 1921, when he compared the crowds on Broadway to so many hogs grunting and pushing. Commenting on a description of pigs running free on Broadway almost a century earlier in Charles Dickens' *American Notes*, he wrote:

Since Mr. Dickens' time, the pigs of Broadway have changed in form only, having taken on the semblance of humans. You can see them today in street-cars and subway trains, pushing and grunting their way to seats while women stand clinging to straps. You can see them wandering along Broadway, old hogs familiar with every sty in the city, and young porkers just learning the ways of swine, their little eyes eagerly regarding every passing skirt.

Of an evening they gather in cabarets, wallowing in illicit liquor and shouting their conversational garbage made up of oaths and filthy stories and scandal. A pig is a pig even when it wears evening clothes. . . .[25]

Over and over he repeated his credo to other reporters, who criticized his determination to remain emotionally and politically aloof: "Never bite the hand that feeds you," and "Go for the money!"[26] Yet friends who felt they understood him hesitated to call him either a cynic or a hack. He always struck them as in the grip of some slightly elusive and mysterious passion.

He seems to have been by nature a listener, always withholding a bit of himself from what he did and said. In some sense, of course, these contradictions may be less personal to Runyon than an embodiment of some more general ideal he had internalized and nourished of the newspaper writer. In the end, his life and career, in other words, may have been defined less by the personal and the enigmatic than by the model he had chosen. What he left behind may, in other words, prove to be more a measure of the newspaper culture he worked in than of personal idiosyncracy.

His success and the wide popularity of his stories about gangsters may in fact have been the result of the degree to which his work embodies a tension between respectability and prurience that was central to his time. In portraying petty criminals and hoods as sympathetically and engagingly as he did, he was catering to what Winchell once described as society's "underworld complex," a middle-class love affair with the underworld that began during Prohibition. In striking out at the ruthlessness of wealth and privilege as he did, he may simply have been inverting the class spectrum, leaving its pieties intact.

To reach such a conclusion about Runyon is to raise certain larger questions about the meaning of the Broadway mythos and about what we have been calling commercial culture. One is tempted to ask some fifty years later what the consequences of this seemingly liberating moment in our history have been. It is a sobering fact, first of all, to recall that this moment occurred during economic good times and faded during the system failure of the Great Depression. Certainly the vitality and energy that went into transforming everyday speech and the language of the press have left a permanent stamp on our culture, but we may have lost the passion for city life and the excitement about other subcultures that informed this linguistic transformation.

The most important question concerns our use of the concept of commercial culture. Much that I have written about it in this chapter assumes that the era of commercial culture represents an historical moment before the intervention of mass culture when cultural production still reflected in some way the interactions of the city as a community. I have implied, if not stated, that cultural exchange and monetary exchange were for a time closely and generatively interrelated in the urban setting of New York City. One product of this interrelationship was the stimulation given to linguistic invention across the whole spectrum of urban occupational life: songwriters, gag-writers, publicity men, sportswriters, playwrights, copywriters, poets, and socialists were all during these years engaged in some kind of intensified linguistic invention. In this sense, the 'twenties and 'thirties were a fecund moment in the history of American cultures. The coming of mass culture appears to have brought this creativity to an end. If this is so, it is ironic that the very circuitry of press, radio, and film that delivered Broadway slang and all the other freshly minted lingoes to the nation at the same moment deprived us of the vital communal impulses that made Broadway itself possible. One wonders in retrospect whether the ashes of Broadway should be dropped on Times Square or on Hollywood.

22. Ibid., p. 664.

23. Ibid.

24. Montgomery Schuyler, "The Towers of Manhattan," *Architectural Record* 33, no. 2 (February 1913), p. 108 (emphasis added).

25. For more on display and store windows, see William Leach, "Strategists of Display and the Production of Desire,"

26. Redding, "Woolworth's Story," p. 664.

27. Joseph Nathan Kane, *Famous First Facts* (New York: H. W. Wilson, 1981), p. 667. Gary Jennings describes the grand celebration in 1899 for Dewey and claims that ticker tape was thrown on his parade in Gary Jennings, *Parades! Celebrations and Circuses on the March* (Philadelphia: J. B. Lippincott Co., 1966), p. 81.

Chapter Four

1. Cooper, Eckstut Associates, *Forty-Second Street Development Project: Design Guidelines* (New York, 1981).

2. Arthur O. Lovejoy, *The Great Chain of Being* (Cambridge, 1936), chap. 1; idem, *Essays in the History of Ideas* (Baltimore, 1948), chap. 1.

3. Sullivan quoted in Siegfried Giedion, *Space, Time and Architecture: The Growth of a New Tradition*, 5th ed. (Cambridge, 1965), p. 854.

4. Giedion, *Space, Time*, p. 780.

5. Montgomery Schuyler noticed the increased presence—both because of numbers and because of their growing self-confidence and aggressiveness—of Beaux-Arts–oriented architects in New York in the 1890s. Montgomery Schuyler, *American Architecture*, 2 vols., ed. William H. Jordy and Ralph Coe (Cambridge, 1961), I:575–78.

This is not the place to identify all Beaux-Arts influences in New York, but it may be useful to say a bit about the leading architects, mostly born in the 1850s, who came of age professionally in New York in the 1890s. These architects were either trained directly at the École des Beaux-Arts or they studied in New York offices of École graduates. The first American trained at the École was Richard Morris Hunt (b. 1827), and his New York office provided training on the École model for many men who later became leaders in the profession in New York, most notably George B. Post (b. 1837) and William Ware (b. 1832), the latter having decisively shaped the training programs of the architecture schools at MIT and, later in the 1880s and 1890s, Columbia University. Charles McKim (b. 1847), who was trained at the École, in turn trained one of New York's most important architects, Cass Gilbert (b. 1859), who had very little other study beyond his experience in the McKim, Mead, and White firm. McKim's later partner Stanford White (b. 1853) studied in the New York office of Beaux-Arts–trained Henry Hobson Richardson (b. 1838). John Carrère (b. 1858) and Thomas Hastings (b. 1860), architects of the New York Public Library, were both trained at the École, as was Ernest Flagg (b. 1857). Whitney Warren (b. 1864), who was primarily responsible for the architectural design work of Grand Central Terminal, studied at the École des Beaux-Arts, returning to New York City in 1896, after an extended residence in Paris. Finally, Henry Hardenberg (b. 1847), architect of the Plaza Hotel and the Dakota, studied in New York with Beaux-Arts–trained Detlef Lienau.

6. On the École des Beaux-Arts and urban planning, see the forthcoming work by Gwendolyn Wright, *At Home and Abroad: Colonialism and French Urban Planning, 1870–1930*, Chap. 1.

7. While we were working on this paper—and developing this notion of the progressivist side of the Beaux-Arts tradition—Domenico Cecchini shared a brief and helpful paper developing the notion of conservative and progressive sides of classicism ("The Meanings of Classicism and the Image of the City," 1981).

8. Louis Sullivan, *The Autobiography of an Idea* (1924; reprint New York, 1956), pp. 324–25.

9. Giedion, *Space, Time*, pp. 393–95.

10. Schuyler, *American Architecture* II, pp. 559–60; *Architectural Record* (July, 1916), pp. 3–4. It should be noted that Schuyler in the essay cited above also saw (and quite rightly) certain dangers in misreading the urbanistic lesson of the Fair, pointing out that it was unreal, that it was not fitted into the dense fabric of the city.

11. On Charles McKim's special influence at the Fair and at Washington, see John Reps, *Planning Monumental Washington* (Princeton, 1967), p. 93 (on the Fair), and *passim* for Washington.

12. "New York Daguerrotyped," *Putnam's Magazine* I (1853): 13.

13. Schuyler, *American Architecture* II, pp. 424–28.

14. Ibid., pp. 595–96. Schuyler is cited frequently in part for convenience' sake, but also because he is a contemporary observer of the evolution of modern architecture generally appreciated by modernists.

15. Dorothy Norman, *Alfred Stieglitz: An American Seer* (New York, 1973), p. 45.

16. Le Corbusier, *When Cathedrals Were White* (New York, 1947), pp. 59–60.

17. Louis Sullivan, *Kindergarten Charts and Other Essays*, ed. Isabella Athey (New York, 1947), p. 206.

18. Hugh Ferriss, *The Metropolis of Tomorrow* (New York, 1929), p. 109.

19. Harvey Wiley Corbett, "New Heights in American Architecture," *Yale Review* 17 (July 1928), pp. 692–93.

20. Lewis Mumford, *From the Ground Up* (New York, 1956), pp. 20–60.

21. They may be seen in New York Regional Plan, *Building the City* (New York, 1931), pp. 69–70.

Chapter Five

1. David Hammack, *Power and Society: Greater New York at the Turn of the Century* (New York: Russell Sage Foundation, 1982).

2. Richard W. Fox and J. Jackson Lears, eds., *The Culture of Consumption: Critical Essays in American History, 1880–1890* (New York: Pantheon Books, 1983); Stuart Ewen, *Captains of Consciousness: Advertising and the Social Roots of Consumer Culture* (New York: McGraw-Hill, 1976). The theoretical root of much of this writing lies in Gramsci and Adorno; see especially T. W. Adorno, *Zeitschrift für Sozialforschung*, vol. II (1949): 14–48.

3. Peter Burke, "The World of Carnival," *Popular Culture in Early Modern Europe* (London: M. T. Smith, 1978), pp. 178–205; Richard D. Altick, *The Shows of London* (Cambridge: Harvard University Press, 1978), pp. 35–36.

4. Peter Burke, *Venice and Amsterdam: A Study of Seventeenth Century Élites* (London: Allen & Unwin, 1974).

5. Diane Lindstrom, "Economic Structure, Demographic Change, and Income Inequality in Antebellum New York," in *Power, Culture, and Place: Essays on New York City*, ed. John H. Mollenkopf (New York: Russell Sage Foundation, 1988), pp. 3–23.

6. See Mark Sharman Farber, "The Conquering Hero Comes: Urban Celebrations of Public Figures in America, 1879–1910" (Ph.D. diss., New York University, 1978), pp. 142–95.

7. Thomas Bender, "The Cultures of Intellectual Life; the City and the Professions," in *New Directions in American Intellectual History*, ed. John Higham and Paul Conkin (Baltimore: Johns Hopkins University Press, 1979), pp. 181–95.

8. Daniel Czitrom, *Media and the American Mind: From Morse to McLuhan* (Chapel Hill: University of North Carolina Press, 1982); John E. Kasson, *Amusing the Millions* (New York: Hill and Wang, 1978); Roy Rosenweig, "The Conflict over the Saloon: Working Class Drinking and the Legal Order in Worcester, Massachusetts, 1870–1900," paper presented at the annual meeting of the American Historical Association, December 1979.

9. Oliver Zunc, "Inside the Skyscraper," *Making Corporate America, 1870–1920* (Chicago and London: University of Chicago Press, 1990), pp. 103–24. Marquis James, *The Metropolitan Life Insurance Company* (1935). One of the most revealing sources for examining the new office culture is the Metropolitan Company photographs in the Byron Collection of the Museum of the City of New York.

10. William R. Leach, "Transformations in a Culture of Consumption: Women and Department Stores, 1890–1935," *Journal of American History* 71, no. 2 (September 1984), pp. 319–42.

11. Zunc, op. cit. See Miriam Cohen, "From Workshop to Office: Italian-American Women in New York," *Class, Sex, and the Woman Worker*, ed. Milton Candor (Westport, Conn.: Greenwood Press, 1977); Deborah S. Gardner, "'A Paradise of Fashion': A. T. Stewart's Department Store, 1862–1875," in *A Needle, a Bobbin, a Strike: Women Needle Workers in America* (Philadelphia: Temple University Press, 1984); Margery Davis, *Woman's Place Is at the Typewriter* (Philadelphia: Temple University Press, 1982); and Elyce Rotella, *From Home to Office* (Ann Arbor: University of Michigan Press, 1981).

12. Leach, "Culture of Consumption"; Émile Zola, *An bonheur des dames* (Paris, 1908).

13. Lewis A. Erenberg, *Steppin' Out: New York Nightlife and the Transformation of American Culture, 1890–1930* (Westport, Conn.: Greenwood Press, 1981).

14. Jervis Anderson, *This Was Harlem: A Cultural Portrayal* (New York: Farrar, Straus and Giroux, 1982). The best first-hand account of this phenomenon is that of Carl van Vechten in various articles written for *Vanity Fair* and other periodicals during the 1920s and in correspondence in the Van Vechten Papers in the New York Public Library.

15. Robert C. Tool, *On with the Show: The First Century of Show Business* (New York: Oxford University Press, 1976), 295–326; and Cynthia Ward, "Vanity Fair and Modern Style" (Ph.D. diss., State University of New York at Stony Brook, 1983).

16. Steven L. Kaplan, ed., *Understanding Popular Culture: Europe from the Middle Ages to the Nineteenth Century* (New York: Berlin, 1984), has especially interesting essays by Roger Chartier and Carlo Ginzburg; Roger Chartier, *Popular Culture in Early Modern Europe* (London: Oxford University Press, 1978); Carlo Ginzburg, *The Cheese and the Worm: The Cosmos of a Sixteenth-Century Miller* (Baltimore: Johns Hopkins University Press, 1980); Raymond Williams, *The Long Revolution* (New York: Random House, 1972): Peter Bailey, *Leisure and Class in Victorian England* (London: Routledge & Kegan Paul, 1978); and Richard Hoggart, *The Uses of Literacy* (London: Peregrine Books, 1975). Important work by Americans has also been done in the area of studies in popular and folk culture in early modern Europe—most notably, by Natalie Z. David, Robert Darnton, and Richard Altick.

17. Hutchins Hapgood, *The Spirit of the Ghetto: Studies of the Jewish Quarter of New York* (New York: Schocken Books, 1965), xii.

18. See note 21, this chapter.

19. Lindstrom, "Economic Structure, Demographic Change, and Income Inequality in Antebellum New York," in *Power, Culture, and Place: Essays on New York City,* ed. by John Hull Mollenkopf (New York: Russell Sage Foundation, 1988).

20. Grace M. Mayer, *Once Upon a City: New York from 1890 to 1910 as Photographed by Byron* (New York: Macmillan, 1958), contains numerous citations from the daily press recording the progress of new buildings; Daine Lindstrom, "Economic Structure, Demographic Change, and Income Inequality in Antebellum New York," *Power, Culture and Place: Essays on New York City,* ed. by John Hull Mollenkopf (New York: Russell Sage Foundation, 1988), pp. 25–53.

21. Christine Stansell, "Women, Children, and the Uses of the Streets: Class and Gender Conflict in New York City, 1850–1860," *Feminist Studies* 8 (Summer 1982): 309–35.

22. Daniel T. Rodgers, *The Work Ethic in Industrial America, 1850–1920* (Chicago: University of Chicago Press, 1978); Joseph F. Kett, *Rites of Passage: Adolescence in America, 1790 to the Present* (New York: Basic Books, 1977), does not discuss this publishing phenomenon. The best treatment to date is still Frank

L. Mott, *A History of American Magazines* (Cambridge, Mass.: Harvard University Press, 1938), vol. 3, chaps. 6–8, pp. 174–80.

23. Mott, *American Magazines*, 3.

24. Rodgers, *op. cit.*; Mott, *American Magazines*, v. 4, p. 174.

25. Allan Stanley Horlick, *Country Boys and Merchants Princes: The Social Control of Young Men in New York* (Lewisburg, Penn.: Bucknell University Press, 1975). See William R. Taylor, *Cavalier and Yankee: The Old South and the American National Character* (Cambridge, Mass.: Harvard University Press, 1979).

26. Horatio Alger, Jr., *Ragged Dick and Mark the Match Boy* (New York: Collier Books, 1962).

27. Three examples of these genres of writing are: James D. McCabe, Jr., *Lights and Shadows of New York Life; or, Sights and Sensations of the Great City* (New York, 1872); Junius Henri Browne, *The Great Metropolis: A Mirror of New York. A Complete History of Metropolitan Life and Society, with Sketches of Prominent Places, Persons, and Things in the City, as They Actually Exist* (Hartford, Conn., 1869); and Inspector Thomas Byrnes, *Darkness and Daylight, or Lights and Shadows of New York Life* (New York, 1982).

28. See, for example, in W. Parker Chase, *New York: Wonder City* (New York: New York Bound, 1983), "Working Girls," p. 35, and "Chorus Girls," p. 41.

29. See note 27 for complete citation of the McCabe work.

30. McCabe, *Lights and Shadows*, p. 524.

31. Ibid., p. 741.

32. Frank Luther Mott, *American Journalism, A History: 1690–1960* (New York: Macmillan, 1962), p. 440.

33. Ibid., pp. 402–4, 481, 546–47.

34. Quoted in ibid., p. 429.

35. Quoted in ibid., p. 440.

36. Ibid., pp. 525–26.

37. Richard Felton Outcault, *My Resolutions, Buster Brown* (Chicago, 1910).

38. Peter Bailey, "Alley Sloper's Half Holiday: Comic Art in the 1880s," *History Workshop* 16 (Autumn 1983): 5.

39. Quoted in Richard O'Connor, *O. Henry: The Legendary Life of William S. Porter* (New York: Doubleday, 1970), p. 67.

40. William Sidney Porter, "The Unfinished Story," in *The Complete Works of O. Henry* (New York: Doubleday, 1970), p. 71.

41. Porter, "Brickdust Row," in *Complete Works*.

42. Ibid.

43. See Philip Furia, *Poets of Tin Pan Alley: A History of America's Great Lyricists* (New York: Oxford University Press, 1990). For this part of the chapter, I am indebted to Carol Seldman, whose 1983 research paper, "The American Popular Song and the Creation of a Common American Culture," explored some of these ideas about popular songs.

44. See John R. Williams, *This Was Your Hit Parade* (Rockland, Maine: Courier Gazette, 1973), pp. 88–89. Cited by Carol Barchas, "The American Popular Song."

45. Furia, *op. cit.*; quoted in Michael Freedland, *Irving Berlin* (New York: Stein and Day, 1974), p. 53.

46. Quoted in Richard Rodgers, *Musical Stages* (New York: Random House, 1975), p. 88. Cited by Barchas, "The American Popular Song."

47. Mark Slobin, *Tenement Song: The Popular Music of the Jewish Immigrant* (Urbana: University of Illinois Press, 1982), Chap. 1.

Chapter Six

1. "Times Square: Secularization and Sacralization," *Inventing Times Square: Commerce and Culture at the Crossroads of the World*, edited with an introduction by William R. Taylor (New York: Russell Sage Foundation, 1991). Hereafter referred to as *Times Square*.

2. See note 1. This essay is adapted from the introduction to that volume, and most of the references are to essays included in it.

3. Eric Lampard, introductory essay to "Structural Changes," *Times Square*.

4. William Leach, "Brokers and the New Corporate Industrial Order," *Times Square*.

5. Neil Harris, "Urban Tourism and the Commercial City," *Times Square*.

6. Richard W. Fox, "The Discipline of Amusement," *Times Square*.

7. David C. Hammock, "Developing for Commercial Culture," *Times Square*.

8. Betsy Blackmar, "Uptown Real Estate and the Creation of Times Square," *Times Square*.

9. Philip Furia, "Troubadour of Tin Pan Alley," *Times Square*.

10. See Chapter 10.

11. Margaret Knapp, introductory essay to "Entertainment and Commerce," *Times Square*.

12. Robert W. Snyder, "Vaudeville and the Transformation of Popular Culture"; Peter A. Davis, "The Syndicate/Shubert War," in *Times Square*.

13. Knapp, *op. cit.*

14. Lewis Erenberg, *Steppin' Out: New York Nightlife and the Transformation of American Culture, 1890–1930* (Westport, Conn.: Greenwood Press, 1981); Erenberg, "Impresarios of Broadway Nightlife," *Times Square*.

15. Brooks McNamara, "The District at the End of the 1930s," *Times Square*.

16. William Wood Register, "New York's Giant Toy," *Times Square*.

17. William Leach, introduction to "Aesthetics of the Commercial World," *Times Square*.

18. Gregory Gilmartin, "Joseph Urban," *Times Square*.

19. Ibid.

20. Timothy J. Gilfoyle, "The Policing of Sexuality from 'Tenderloin' to Times Square," *Times Square*.

21. Peter Buckley, "Tracing the Boundaries of Respectability," *Times Square*.

22. Laurence Senelick, "Private Parts in Public Places," *Times Square*.

23. George Chauncey, "Strategems of Survival in Times Square," *Times Square.*

24. Ibid.

25. Ada Louise Huxtable, "Re-Inventing Times Square," *Times Square.*

Chapter Seven

1. Alfred Kuttner, Lippmann's Harvard classmate and translator of Sigmund Freud's *Interpretation of Dreams.*

2. Walter Lippman, manuscript diary, July 4 and 5, 1914. Lippmann Collection, Yale University.

3. Ronald Steel, *Walter Lippmann and the American Century* (Boston, 1980), p. xiv. Steel's biography, comprehensive and authoritative on most matters, has been of immense help in this study although Steel, like most students of Lippmann, underestimates the cultural basis of Lippmann's political odyssey from socialism to anti-New Deal Democrat.

4. On December 20, 1924, Lippmann devoted an editorial in the *World* to Houdini's efforts to expose sham mind-readers. Correspondence and meetings between Lippmann and Houdini continued until Houdini's death in 1926. For the visit to Houdini's house and the experiment conducted there, see Steel, *Walter Lippmann*, pp. 205–6.

5. "Blazing Publicity," *Vanity Fair* (September 1927).

6. *Drift and Mastery* (Prentice-Hall, 1961), p. 118.

7. Van Wyck Brooks, *'Highbrow' and 'Lowbrow', America's Coming of Age* (New York, 1915). Brooks and Lippmann had met in London in 1914 and found they had much in common.

8. Cynthia L. Ward, "*Vanity Fair* and Modern Style" (Ph.D. diss., State University of New York, 1983).

9. Ibid., p. 68.

10. Lippmann, "Candidates Who Have Lived Before," *Vanity Fair* (September 1920).

11. *Vanity Fair* (January 1921).

12. *Vanity Fair* (April 1922).

13. "The problems that vex democracy," Lippmann had concluded, "seem unmanageable by democratic methods." *The Phantom Public* (New York, 1925).

14. Ibid., p. 65.

15. "Al Smith: A Man of Destiny," *Vanity Fair* (December 1925).

16. Lippmann to Frankfurter, June 14, 1926, Lippmann Papers, Yale.

17. Lippmann to Crowninshield, June 29, 1928, Lippmann Papers.

18. *New York World*, December 26, 1924.

19. *Vanity Fair* (March 1928).

20. Lippmann to Adolph Ochs, December 26, 1924, Lippmann Papers.

21. Malcolm Cowley, *Exile's Return* (New York, 1931), is the classic statement

of this discovery. For a more general and modern historical account, see Daniel Aaron, *Writers on the Left* (New York, 1964).

22. Lippmann to Harcourt, May 4, 1927, Lippmann Papers.

23. "Blazing Publicity," *Vanity Fair* (September 1927).

24. "Two Revolutions of the American Press," *Yale Review* XX (March 1931): 3, 433–41.

25. Cited by Steel, *Walter Lippmann*, pp. 276–77.

26. Ibid., pp. 174.

27. Ward, *Vanity Fair*.

Chapter Eight

1. Djuna Barnes, "Greenwich Village As It Is," *Pearson's Magazine* (October 1916), p. 2.

2. Ibid., p. 3.

3. Ibid.

4. Malcolm Cowley, *Exile's Return* (New York, 1951), p. 48.

5. Ibid.

6. John Reed, "The Day in Bohemia, or Life Among the Artists, Being a *jeu d'esprit* containing Much that is Original and Diverting. In which the reader will find the Cognomens and Qualities of many Persons destined one day to adorn the Annals of Nations, in Letters, Music, Painting, the Plastic Arts, and even Business; Together with Their Foibles, Weaknesses, and shortcomings, and some Account of the Life led by Geniuses in Manhattan's Quartier Latin by John Reed Esq. Printed for the Author." New York, 1913.

7. The title is itself a clear take-off on eighteenth-century titles. Note also the suggestion that these particular Bohemians in "Manhattan's Quartier Latin" will someday be celebrated in the various arts, "even business." On the comparable development in France in this period, see Jerrold Seigel, *Bohemian Paris* (New York, 1986).

8. "The Day in Bohemia," *Collected Poems*, p. 51 ff.

9. Reed, cited in Mabel Dodge Luhan, *Intimate Memories*, v. 3, *Movers and Shakers*, p. 173.

10. Ibid., p. 174.

11. Ibid.

12. Ibid., pp. 174–75.

13. June Sochen, *The New Woman: Feminism in Greenwich Village, 1910–1920* (New York, 1972).

14. Judith Schwarz, *Radical Feminists of Heterodoxy: Greenwich Village, 1912–1940* (Norwich, Vt., 1986).

15. Ibid.

16. See, for example, Walter Winchell, "A Primer of Broadway Slang," *Variety* (Nov. 1927).

17. Philip Fisher, "Appearing and Disappearing in Public: Social Space in

Late–Nineteenth-Century Literature and Culture," in Sacvan Bercovitch, ed., *Reconstructing American Literary History* (Cambridge, Mass.: Harvard Univ. Press, 1986), p. 164.

18. Ibid., pp. 155–85.

19. Cited by Lois P. Rudnick, Mabel Dodge Luhan, *New Woman, New Worlds* (Albuquerque, New Mexico, 1984), p. 62.

20. Hutchins Hapgood, "A Promoter of Spirit," *New York Globe*, June 12, 1913.

21. Ibid.

22. Cited by Hapgood, *op. cit.*

23. Cited by Rudnick, *New Woman*, p. 86.

24. Cited by Rudnick, *op. cit.*, p. 74.

25. These plays include *Trifles* (1916), *The Outside* (1917), *Inheritors* (1921), *In the Verge* (1921), *Alison's House* (1930).

Chapter Nine

1. H. L. Mencken, *Prejudices: Fourth Series* (New York: Alfred A. Knopf), pp. 139–40.

2. "The Ruin of an Artist," *The New Yorker*, May 27, 1939, p. 26.

3. Lippmann, *Men of Destiny* (New York: Macmillan, 1927), p. 70. Cited by Douglas C. Stenerson, *H. L. Mencken: Iconoclast from Baltimore* (Chicago: University of Chicago, 1971), p. 13.

4. Letter from Dreiser to Isaac Goldberg dated August 24, 1925, in Goldberg, *The Man Mencken* (New York, 1925), p. 19. Cited in Stenerson, *H. L. Mencken*, pp. 124–25.

5. On Mencken's hypochondria, see George Jean Nathan, *The Intimate Notebooks of George Jean Nathan* (New York: Alfred A. Knopf, 1932), p. 95: "I have alluded to his maladies. In the twenty-odd years that I have known him, I have received thousands upon thousands of letters and telegrams from him, and in not a single one has he failed affectingly to mention some hypothetic physical agony that was making life intolerable for him."

6. Ellen Moers, *Two Dreisers* (New York, 1969), p. 179.

7. Dreiser to Goldberg, *op. cit.*

8. Ibid.

9. Cited by M. K. Singleton, *H. L. Mencken and the American Mercury Adventure* (Durham, N.C.: Duke University Press, 1962), p. 19fn.

10. Mencken, *Prejudices, Fifth Series* (New York: Alfred A. Knopf, 1927), p. 240.

11. Ibid., p. 242.

12. Ibid., p. 240.

13. Ibid., *Sixth Series* (1927), p. 211–15.

14. Stenerson, "Child of Baltimore, The German-American Heritage," in *H. L. Mencken*, pp. 47–59.

15. Ibid.

16. Ibid.

17. Mencken, *Prejudices, Fifth Series*, p. 240.

18. Cited by Stenerson, *H. L. Mencken*, p. 234. In the manuscript memoir just released, Mencken acknowledges his feelings for his mother in recalling the circumstances of her death in 1925. "My father's death in 1899 was really a strike of luck for me, for it liberated me from the tobacco business and enabled me to attempt journalism without his probable doubts and disappointments to hamper me, but the loss of my mother was pure disaster, for she had always stood by me loyally, despite the uneasiness that some of my ventures must have aroused in her, and I owed to her, and to her alone, the fact that I had a comfortable home throughout my youth and early manhood. Her death filled me with a sense of futility and desolation. It was weeks before I was fit for any work beyond routine." Mencken Papers, New York Public Library, "Thirty-Five Years of Newspaper Work," p. 469.

19. On Mencken's sense of release, see note 18 above.

20. Mencken, *The New Yorker* (May 27, 1939), pp. 23–26.

21. Mencken, *Newspaper Days* (New York: Alfred Knopf, 1947); Gerald W. Johnson, H. L. Mencken, et al. *The Sunpapers of Baltimore* (New York: Alfred A. Knopf, 1937).

22. Johnson et al., *Sunpapers of Baltimore*, p. 321n.

23. The belief, prevalent by the mid-'twenties, that news had to be "objective" was different from the earlier belief, prevalent in the 'nineties with figures like Richard Harding Davis, that reporters should get their facts straight. The belief in objectivity that emerged was in part a reflection of the young reporter's brushes with science and scientific ideas—taking the *self* out of reporting was distinct from getting it right. The danger was not simply bias but the tangle of subjectivism that characterized the human psyche as its dimensions were untangled by psychoanalysis and the new scientific studies of human behavior. Also, objectivity, according to Schudson, was connected with the Progressive idea of science as embodied in scientific social investigation. Michael Schudson, *Discovering the News: A Social History of American Newspapers*, p. 152.

24. H. L. Mencken, *Newspaper Days (1899–1906)*, pp. 14, 23. Cited by Michael Schudson, *Discovering the News: A Social History of American Newspapers*, p. 80.

25. Shelley Fisher Fishkin, *From Fact to Fiction: Journalism and Imaginative Writing in America* (Baltimore: Johns Hopkins, 1985).

26. Alfred Knopf, "For Henry with Love," *Atlantic Monthly* (May 1959), pp. 50–54; Geoffrey Hellman, *The New Yorker* (December 4, 1948), pp. 40–51.

27. The background material on magazines in this period has been drawn from Frank Luther Mott, *A History of American Magazines*, 5 vols. (Cambridge, Mass.: Harvard University Press, 1968).

28. Edna Woolman Chase, *Vogue* (1943), cited by Mott, *History*, vol. 1, pp. 756–62.

29. Mott, *op. cit.*; see also Cynthia L. Ward, "Vanity Fair and the Modern Style, 1914–1936," (Ph.D. diss., S.U.N.Y., Stony Brook, 1983).

30. Mencken Papers, New York Public Library, "My Life as Author and Editor," p. 203.

31. According to Mencken, the circulation of the *Smart Set* reached 50,000 a month by 1913, almost all of it in newsstand sales; by 1917 circulation had fallen to about 35,000. Mencken Papers, NYPL, "My Life," p. 177.

32. Mencken to Louis Untermeyer, July 20, 1916. Cited by Stenerson, *H. L. Mencken*, p. 9.

33. Mencken Papers, NYPL, "My Life," p. 179.

34. The *Smart Set* had offices at a succession of locations before it settled on Forty-fifth Street between Fifth and Sixth avenues at the beginning of the 'twenties. It remained at its original location at 331 Fourth Avenue, where it shared quarters with *Field and Stream*, until 1915, when it moved to 456 Fourth Avenue. A third move took place in 1916 when the office was moved to Eighth Avenue and Thirty-fourth Street. It seems to have followed the movement of entertainment industries, the theater and Tin Pan Alley, uptown.

35. Quoted by Stenerson, *H. L. Mencken*, pp. 208–9.

36. Mencken, *Prejudices, Series 2* (New York: Alfred A. Knopf, 1920), p. 36.

37. Mencken, "A Massacre in a Mausoleum," *Smart Set*, v. 48 (February 1916), p. 157. Cited by Stenerson, *H. L. Mencken*, p. 195.

38. Ibid., p. 19.

39. Ibid., p. 29.

40. *Los Angeles Times*, December 10, 1910, cited in Mencken Papers, NYPL, "My Life," pp. 161–62.

41. Mencken, *A Book of Prefaces* (New York: Alfred A. Knopf, 1918), p. 15.

42. Ibid., p. 12.

43. Ibid., p. 89.

44. Mencken, *Prejudices: First Series*, p. 36.

45. Marius Bewley, *The Complex Fate* (London: Chatto and Windus, 1952), p. 210.

46. Mencken, *Prejudices III*, pp. 9–11.

47. Cited by Stenerson, *H. L. Mencken*, p. 5.

48. Stenerson comments on the inconsistency in the positions taken by Mencken as a critic: "Just as we think we have grasped the quintessential Mencken, another and contradictory phase of his thought emerges"; p. 226.

49. I have been able to find only a single reference to Sacco and Vanzetti in the posthumous memoir: Mencken Papers, "Thirty-five Years," p. 504: "Two of the celebrated cases of the time [1927], the Sacco-Vanzetti case and the Snyder-Gray Case, got my attention, the first on August 15 and the second on November 28."

50. "On Being an American," *Prejudices: Third Series*, p. 93.

51. Ibid., pp. 35–36.

52. Ibid., p. 65.

53. Ibid., p. 15.

54. Stenerson, *H. L. Mencken*, pp. 168–69.

55. Mencken, "On Being an American," *Prejudices: Third Series*, p. 93.

56. Mencken to Dreiser, loc. cit.

57. *Baltimore Evening Sun*, September 29, 1915.

58. Stenerson, *H. L. Mencken*, p. 175.

59. Mencken, *In Defense of Women*, p. xx.

60. Ibid., p. xix.

61. Mencken, *A Book of Prefaces* (New York: Alfred A. Knopf, 1918), pp. 32–33.

62. Ibid., p. 35.

63. See, for example, Charles A. Fecher, *Mencken: A Study of His Thought* (New York: Alfred A. Knopf), p. 124.

64. Mencken, *In Defense of Women*, p. 18.

65. Ibid., pp. 6–7.

66. Ibid., p. 7.

67. Ibid., p. 30.

68. Carl Bode, *The New Mencken Letters* (New York: Dial Press, 1977), p. 5; *The New Yorker*, (May 27, 1939), p. 26.

69. See, for example, the letter to Goodman, dated October 19, 1922, in Bode, *The New Mencken Letters* (New York: Dial Press, 1977), pp. 161–62.

70. Bode, *op. cit.*, p. 5.

71. Mencken quotes Bierce's epigrams in *Prejudices: Sixth Series*, pp. 264–65; for his own epigrams, see "The Jazz Webster," *A Book of Burlesques* (New York: Alfred A. Knopf, 1920), pp. 205–6. Cited by Stenerson, *H. L. Mencken*, p. 132fn.

72. *The New Yorker* (May 27, 1939), p. 26.

73. Cited by Marius Bewley, "Mencken and the American Language," *The Complex Fate*, p. 194.

74. Edmund Wilson, *The New Republic*, 1921. *Time*, March 10, 1923; V. F. Calverton, "The Vaudeville Critic, H. L. Mencken," *A Sociological Criticism of Literature* (New York, 1925), pp. 165–79; Percy Boynton, "American Literature and the Tart Set," *The Freeman*, (April 7, 1920), p. 88.

75. Wilson, *Shock of Recognition*, pp. 1,155–1,159.

76. *New York Daily Mirror*, August 26, 1934.

77. *Mencken papers*, NYPL, "My Life," p. 3.

78. Mencken, *Prejudices, Third Series*, p. 78.

Chapter Ten

1. "The Language of Lobster Alley," *The Bookman* LXXII (March 1930), pp. 396–99.

2. "Why I Write Slang," *Variety* (December 29, 1926).

3. Cited by John O. Rees, "The Last Local Colorist," *Kansas Magazine* (1968), pp. 73–81.

4. H. L. Mencken, *The American Language: An Inquiry into the Development of English in the United States*, 4th ed. (New York, 1936).

5. Ibid.

6. Eric Partridge, *In His Own Words* (London, 1980); *A Dictionary of Slang*

and Unconventional English, Including Language of the Underworld (London, 1938).

7. Walter Winchell, "A Primer of Broadway Slang," *Variety,* (Nov., 1927), p. 67.

8. Ibid.

9. Ibid.

10. Stanley Walker, *The Nightclub Era* (New York, 1933); Jack Lait and Lee Mortimer, *New York Confidential* (Chicago, 1948).

11. The best account of the layout of the Broadway locale is to be found in Jack Lait and Lee Mortimer, *op. cit.,* pp. 1–35.

12. H. L. Mencken, *The American Language,* 4th ed. (1936), p. 646.

13. Conway, "Why I Write Slang," *Variety* (December 29, 1926), pp. 5, 7.

14. Herman Klurfeld, *Winchell, His Life and Times* (New York, 1976).

15. Edwin P. Hoyt, *A Gentleman of Broadway* (Boston, 1964), chap. 15.

16. J. Willard Ridings, "Use of Slang in Newspaper Sports Writing," *Journalism Quarterly* 7 (December 1934): 348–60.

17. Ibid.

18. Standard biographical sources on Runyon's life are: Tom Clark, *The World of Damon Runyon* (New York, 1974); Edwin P. Hoyt, *A Gentleman of Broadway* (Boston, 1964); Jean Wagner, *Runyonese: The Mind and Craft of Damon Runyon* (Paris, 1965). No fully satisfactory biographical study of Runyon was available to me. Jimmy Breslin, *Damon Runyon: A Life* (New York, 1991) appeared too late to be of use to me in this study.

19. "Color Stuff," *American Speech* 3 (October 1927), pp. 28–36.

20. Hoyt, *Gentleman of Broadway.*

21. Jean Wagner, *Runyonese: The Mind and Craft of Damon Runyon* (Paris, 1965).

22. *The Bloodhounds of Broadway and Other Stories by Damon Runyon,* ed. by Tom Clark (New York, 1981), p. 124.

23. Ibid., "Damon Runyon, a Very Honorable Guy," p. 23.

24. Hoyt, *op. cit.*

25. Cited in Jack Lait and Lee Mortimer, op. cit., pp. 248–49.

26. Ibid., p. 125.

Index

Abbott, Berenice, 66; "Exchange Place," 66
Actor's Equity, 167
Adams, Franklin Pierce, 171
Adams, William T., 76
Addams, Jane, 13–14
Ade, George, 163–64
Adult guidebooks, 76
Advertising, 17, 19–20, 45, 46, 49, 81, 82, 95, 96
Advice literature, 76
Aerial perspectives, 23–24, 25, 49
Aesthetics: and architecture, 18–19, 51–67; and a commercial culture, 75–76, 102–4; and culture, 51–67; and horizontal space, 52–67; and movement, 61; and photography, 17–18, 29–30, 31, 32; and skyscrapers, 65; and vertical space, 52–67
Agnew, John, 93
Alger, Horatio, 74, 76–78
Algonquin Hotel, 136, 149, 164, 166
Algonquin Round Table, 109
Allen, Woody, 49
American Federation of Actors, 166
The American Language [Mencken], 99, 160, 164
"American Literature and the Tart Set" [Boynton], 159–60
American Mercury [magazine], 160
American Museum, 38
American Notes [Dickens], 181
American Speech [magazine], 174–75
America's Coming-of-Age [Brooks], 147
Amusement parks, 70, 102
Anderson, Margaret, 126
Anderson, Sherwood, 112, 178
Andrews Sisters, 9
The Apaches of New York [Alfred Henry Smith], 179
Apartment houses, 49, 74
Apollo Theater, 89
Arbus, Diane, 21

Architecture: and abstraction, 18–19; and abstract design, 15–16; and aesthetics, 18–19, 51–67; and the Columbian Exposition [1893], 36, 53–55, 56; and culture, 51–67; and domination of the environment, 21; and engineering, 17; and horizontal space, 52–67; and movement, 56; and painting, 19; and public space, 36, 47; Putnam's Magazine series of drawings about New York, 58; reputation of New York's architecture, 52–53; and skylines, 51–52, 55; and social reform, 51; and technology, 54; and the training of architects, 53; and vertical space, 51–67
Armory Show [1913], 8, 121, 130
Art Deco, 19
Associated Press, 114–15
Astor family, 41, 106
Astor Hotel, 60, 106, 116, 117–18, 166
AT&T Building, 49

Baer, "Bugs," 158–59, 166, 168, 179
Baltimore, Md. See Mencken, H. L.
Barnes, Djuna, 119–20, 123
Barnum, P. T., 38, 61
Bath/washhouses, 43, 44
Battery, 26, 48–49, 56–57
Battery Park, 72
Battery Park City, 51
Bauhaus group, 18, 19, 104
Baum, L. Frank, 102–3
Beard, Charles, 160
Beaux-Arts design, 36, 52, 53, 55
"Bei Mir Bist Du Schoen" [song], 89
Belasco, David, 114
The Bell Jar [Plath novel], 21
Benchley, Robert, 112, 117, 142, 143, 171
Bender, Thomas, 72
Bergson, Henri, 127–28
Berkeley, Busby, 18
Berlin, Irving, 89, 98–99, 110, 167

Bewley, Marius, 151
Bicycle clubs, 30
Bierce, Ambrose, 159.
The Big Parade [film], 114
Billboard [magazine], 167
Billingsley, Sherman, 168
Biltmore Hotel, 41–42
Bishop, John Peale, 112, 142, 143
Black community, 74, 89, 90
"Blazing Publicity" [Lippmann], 115–16
"Bloodhounds of Broadway" [Runyon], 177
Bloom, Marion, 158
Bly, Nellie [a.k.a. Elizabeth Cochran], 81
Bode, Carl, 157, 158
Bohemian [magazine], 141
Bohemias, 126
"Boob McNut" [Dorgan], 178
A Book of Prefaces [Mencken], 146, 148, 149, 155
Bowery, 71, 96–97, 104
Boyce, Neith, 121, 128
Boynton, Percy, 159–60
Brecht, Bertolt, 19
Brevoort Hotel, 120, 122, 123
"The Bridge" [Harte Crane poem], 20
"The Brief Debut of Tildy" [O. Henry], 87
Brill Building, 98, 167, 168–69
Brisbane, Arthur, 172
Broadway: and a commercial culture, 35, 71, 72, 74, 75, 85–86, 182; and democracy, 112–13; Dickens' views of, 181; as an entertainment center, 93–94, 96–97, 100, 170; and film, 169, 170, 173, 182; and gender issues, 158–59; and Greenwich Village, 124, 128, 129; as an idea/myth, 169, 182; illumination of, 48, 103, 129; and journalism, 94, 107, 169; and language/slang, 99, 128, 164, 165–66, 169, 172–73; Lippmann's views of, 110–18; Mencken's views of, 169–70; and moral issues, 114; and movement, 61; Nathan's reputation on, 142; as part of Times Square, 97, 98; and radio, 94, 182; and Runyon, 163, 167, 168–69, 172, 174, 175–79, 180; in short stories, 85–86; as a small town, 178; as a style, 93–94; and Winchell, 172, 173
Brooklyn Bridge, 25, 26–27, 48
Brooklyn Heights, 25
Brooks, Van Wyck, 111, 147
Broun, Heywood, 113, 171
Brown, Buster, 84
Buck, Gene [Eugene Edward], 163
The Building of the City [New York Regional Plan], 65
Burgess, Frank [Gelett], 163–64
Burlesque, 72, 101, 106
Burnham, Daniel H., 30–31, 36, 53–55, 56, 59–60, 62, 66–67

Cabarets, 73–74, 167–68
Cafe des Beaux-Arts, 136
Cain, James M., 140, 158
Calverton, V. F., 159
Camera clubs, 30
Camera Work [quarterly journal], 4, 8, 19, 30–31, 32
Cameras, 11, 13–14, 15, 17, 29–30
Campanile tradition, 63–65. *See also specific buildings*
Capone, Al, 175, 180
Capra, Frank, 177
Carnegie Hall, 98
Carroll, Earl, 101, 168
Cather, Willa, 120
Celebrities, 128–30
Central Park, 38–39, 45
Century [magazine], 76, 111
Cezanne, Paul, 20
Chambers Street, 59
Chaplin, Charles, 15, 19, 21, 32, 91, 110
Chartier, Roger, 80
Chase, W. Parker, 78
Chauncey, George, 106
Chicago, Ill., 1–2, 53, 54, 55, 56, 66, 126. *See also* Columbian Exposition [1893]
Chicago Renaissance, 126
Children: abuse of, 105; in comics, 83–84; photographs of, 11, 12, 13, 15; and recreation, 102
Chrysler Building, 65
Cité industrielle [plan by Garnier], 56
Citicorp Building, 49, 50, 67
Cities: and Bohemias, 126; centers of, 106–7; European, 4, 24, 43; origins of modern, 1; panoramic views of, 3
City Hall Park, 71, 72, 75, 96–97
Civic space, 52, 59, 60, 67, 107
Classicism, 54, 55. *See also* Neoclassicism
Club Napoleon, 168
Coburn, Alvin, 7–8, 30
Cochran, Elizabeth [a.k.a. Nellie Bly], 81
College literary magazines, 144
Colleges/universities, 127–28, 132
"Color Stuff" [*American Speech* article], 174–75
Columbia University, 60
Columbian Exposition [1893], 36, 53–55, 56, 102, 129
Comfort stations, 42–45, 73
Comics, 76, 83–84, 178
Commercial art, 103, 104
Commercial culture: and aesthetics, 75–76, 102–4; benefits of a, 90; and Broadway/Times Square area, 35, 129, 182; as a culture of pastiche, 74–90; evolution of a, 69–91; forms of a, 90; and gender issues, 73–74, 77, 128; and Greenwich Village, 123–24, 125–26,

117, 166, 172, 176, 180, 181. *See also*
  New York Journal
Heathen Days [Mencken], 160
Hebrard, Ernst, 53
Hecht, Ben, 125, 140, 170, 171
Hell's Kitchen, 74
Hemingway, Ernest, 21, 120, 140
Henry, O. *See* Porter, William Sidney
Herald Square, 75, 96–97
Heterodoxy [feminist group], 127, 128
Hill, John, 25
Hine, Lewis, 3, 7–8, 9–16, 17, 29; "Black
  Man Dying of Tuberculosis," 13; "Bowery
  Derelict," 15–16; "Breaker Boys," 10, 13;
  "Empire State Building," 17; "Family in
  New York Tenement," 11–13;
  "Forty-Year-Old Woman," 11; "Madonna
  of Ellis Island," 10, 15; "Man at
  Dynamo," 14; Danny Mercurio, 15;
  "Negro Orphan," 13; "Newsboys," 13, 15;
  "Steamfitter," 15
Hippodrome Theater, 101–2
Historical preservation, 50
Hoffmannsthal, Hugo von, 19
"Hogan's Alley" [comic], 83, 84
Hollywood. *See* Film; Film industry
Hollywood Club [cabaret], 168
Homoerotic bonding, 179
Homosexuality, 105–6, 127–28, 157
Hood, Raymond, 65, 66–67
Horizontal space: and aesthetics, 52–67; and
  architecture, 52–67; bias toward, 58, 63;
  and civic space, 52, 59, 67; and
  modernism, 56–57; and monuments, 60,
  67; and movement, 61; and underground
  transportation, 61, 65. *See also specific
  buildings*
Hotels, 72, 73, 100–101. *See also specific
  hotels*
Houdini, Harry, 110
Howe, Edgar Watson, 171
Humor, 144, 171, 172, 177
Huneker, James, 134, 161
Hunt, Richard Morris, 58, 60, 61, 63, 75

Ibsen, Henrik, 138, 141
Illumination, 48, 103, 107, 129
Immigrants, 39, 90, 147
In Defense of Women [Mencken], 155–57
Intellectuals: mediocrity of, 123–24;
  Mencken's attacks on, 146–48, 150, 152,
  159
Inventing Times Square [William R. Taylor],
  94
Invisible Man [Ellison], 21
Italian Renaissance, 63
Italianate architecture, 58, 61, 75
Ivins, William, 29

J. Walter Thompson [advertising firm], 32
Jack Dempsey's Cafe, 167

"Jacob's Beach" [hangout], 167
Jacobs, Mike, 167
James, Henry, 29, 57
James, William, 127–28, 150
Jazz, 74, 90
Jews, 10, 89–90, 147, 156
Journalism: as the basis for other types of
  writing, 140–41; and Broadway/Times
  Square area, 94, 99, 107, 168, 169, 170;
  and a commercial culture, 70–71; and the
  control by writing, 115; and essays, 171;
  and feature writing, 172, 174; and gender
  issues, 158–59; and Greenwich Village,
  126–27; investigative, 9; and
  language/slang, 99, 170, 174–75, 182;
  and liberalism, 116; magazine, 142–43,
  144; New, 172; and objectivity, 139–40,
  147; and politics, 82; and Progressivism,
  146–47; and style, 140; and the theater,
  170–71; Western influences on New York,
  171–72. *See also* Newspapers; *specific
  people*
Joyce, James, 145
Judge [magazine], 142
Judson Hotel, 123
Juvenile literature, 76–78, 102

"Katzenjammer Kids" [comic], 84
Keaton, Buster, 91
Keith, B. F., 100
Kellogg, Paul, 9, 14
Kelly, Florence, 13–14
Kelly, Gene, 21
Kern Jerome, 89
Keynes, John Maynard, 115
"Killers" [Hemingway], 21
King, Moses, 64
Knickerbocker Bank, 60
Knopf, Alfred, 141
Knopf, Blanche, 158
Kouwenhoven, John, 27

La Hiff, Billy, 168
La Hiff's Tavern, 168
Ladies of the Night [play], 114
Lady for a Day [film], 176
Lafayette Hotel, 122, 123
Lambs Club, 166
Lamont, Thomas, 116, 118
Landscape painting, 2, 17, 20, 28–29
Language/slang: and Broadway/Times
  Square area, 99, 128, 164, 165–66, 169,
  172–73; and a commercial culture, 182;
  and film, 19, 99, 169–70, 182; of fluids,
  38; Funk's survey about, 163–64; and
  gender issues, 179; and Greenwich
  Village, 128, 131; and journalism, 99,
  170, 174–75, 182; and Lardner, 99,
  163–64; Lippmann's views of, 113; and
  Mencken, 99, 163–64, 169–70; and

Merchandising: sidewalk, 45–48
Merchant's Exchange, 25
"The Metropolis of Tomorrow" [Ferriss], 65–66
Metropolitan Life Insurance Building and Tower, 46–47, 48, 63–64, 72, 73
Metropolitan Museum of Art, 60
Metropolitan Opera House, 98, 166
Midnight Cowboy [film], 106
Midnight Frolic [Ziegfeld], 100
Millet, Jean Francois, 2, 17
Minsky family, 101
Minstrels, 70
Mizener, Wilson, 164
Modern Times [film], 15, 21
Modernism, 8, 36, 54, 55, 56–57, 97, 103, 104, 135, 149
Monist Society, 126
Monroe, Harriet, 129
Monuments: buildings as personal, 46; and horizontal/vertical space, 60, 67
Moore, Marianne, 120
Moral issues: and Broadway/Times Square area, 97, 104–6, 114; and a commercial culture, 75–76, 84, 85, 87–88, 96, 97, 104–6, 114; and gender issues, 105; Mencken's views of, 150; and Runyon, 180; and the theater, 104–6; and visual experiences, 96
Motherwell, Hiram, 163
Movement/kinetics, 19, 32, 56, 61
Movie houses, 70, 72
Mumford, Lewis, 67
Municipal Building, 47, 59, 61
Munsey's [magazine], 111
Museums, 70, 72
Music Box Theater, 99
Music industry, 93–94, 98, 128. *See also* Tin Pan Alley
Musicals, 18, 21, 24, 91, 98, 100, 104
Mutual Life Building, 27
"My Heart Belongs to Daddy" [song], 89–90
"My Wife Ethel" [Runyon column], 171, 176, 179

Napoleon LeBrun & Sons, 63
Nast, Condé, 32, 74, 110, 111, 143
Nathan, George Jean, 114, 136, 141–42, 143, 144, 145, 150, 152, 154
National Child Labor Committee, 9
The National Police Gazette [magazine], 76, 143
Neighborhoods, 20, 71–72, 79
Neoclassicism, 52, 53, 54, 55–56, 59, 60, 66–67
New Amsterdam Theater, 101
New Journalism, 172
New Republic [magazine], 109, 117, 147, 159
"The new urbanity," 142, 144

New Year's Eve, 94
New York American [newspaper], 99, 166, 170, 172, 174
New York Central, 59–60
New York City: architectural reputation of, 52, 56–57; as the embodiment of modern urban life, 1–2; European cities contrasted with, 4; imitations of, 36; and the mainstream of American culture, 93; as the marketing center, 95, 96; as a vertical city, 23
New York Daily News, 166
"New York from Heights near Brooklyn" [Hill], 25
New York Herald, 97, 142
New York Herald-Tribune, 117, 166
New-York Historical Society, 78
New York Journal, 27, 81, 84
New York Mirror, 166, 172, 175
New York Post Office, 59
New York Public Library, 60, 67
New York Regional Plan, 65, 66–67
New York society, 142–43
New York State Urban Development Corporation, 51–52
New York, the Wonder City [Chase], 78
New York Times Building, 49, 94, 97–98, 107–8, 165–66
New York Times [newspaper], 171
New York Tribune Building, 49, 58, 61, 63, 75
New York Tribune [newspaper], 116
New York World, 81–83, 87, 109, 110, 111, 113, 116, 118, 166, 171
New Yorker [magazine], 85, 142, 160, 161, 166, 171
Newspaper Days [Mencken], 160
Newspaper industry, 165, 166, 169
Newspaper Row, 75
Newspapers: advertising in, 81, 82; comics in, 83–84; and a commercial culture, 70, 75, 81–88, 90; format of, 81–82; and Greenwich Village, 125; photographs in, 30; short stories in, 76, 83, 84–88; and social classes, 82, 83–88; and the standardizaton of the news, 174
Night clubs, 100
Nightlife, 73–74, 75, 96–97, 98, 104, 105, 136, 165, 167–68, 174
Norton, Charles Dyer, 66
Number One Fifth Avenue, 66

Ochs, Adolph, 114, 115, 116, 117
Office buildings, 72, 73, 74
Olmsted, Frederick Law, 36, 38–39, 55
"On Being an American" [Mencken], 154
O'Neill, Eugene, 125, 132, 145
Opera houses, 72
Optic, Oliver, 76, 78
Our Town [Wilder], 178
Outcault, Richard Felton, 83

Pulitzer, Joseph, 81, 82, 166. *See also New York World*
Putnam's Magazine, 58

Queensboro Bridge, 33

Radiator Building, 65
Radio: and Broadway/Times Square area, 94, 182; and a commercial culture, 70–71, 75, 90; and language/slang, 99, 169–70, 178, 182; magazines about, 170; and popular music, 90
Ragged Dick [Alger], 74, 76–78, 80, 84
Ragtime, 90
Rauh, Ida, 127
RCA Tower, 74
Reed, John, 109, 121–24, 125, 126, 127, 129, 130, 131
Regional Plan Association, 65
Religion, 78, 96, 102, 103
Renaissance, 54, 65
Restaurants, 72, 100–101
Restrooms, 42–45, 73
Rickenbacker, Eddie, 180
Riis, Jacob, 4, 9
RKO Studios, 170
Robinson, Walter C., 142–43
Rockefeller Center, 59, 67, 74
Rodeos, 167
Rodgers, Richard, 89
Rodman, Henrietta, 121
Roger's Chop House [restaurant], 145
Rogers, Will, 172
Roof gardens, 73–74
Roosevelt, Theodore, 48–49
Rose, Billy, 100, 101
Ross, Harold, 144, 161
Roth's Grill, 168
Royalton Hotel, 166
Runyon, Damon: and the Broadway stories, 175–79, 180; and Broadway/Times Square area, 163, 167, 168–69, 172, 174, 175–79, 180, 181; by-lines of, 171; and a commercial culture, 98, 126–27; death of, 180; and Dickens' views of Broadway, 181; family background of, 179, 180; and feature writing, 174, 175; focus of, 173–74; funeral of, 180; and gender issues, 128, 158–59, 179; as a Hearst journalist, 180; and Hollywood/Florida, 170, 173, 176, 180; and humor, 171, 177; and language/slang, 98, 163–64, 170, 172, 173, 175, 176–77, 179; and magazine journalism, 166, 175–79, 180; as a mentor, 172; and moral issues, 180; and the "My Wife Ethel" column, 171, 176, 179; personal life of, 180, 181; as a playwright, 170; and politics, 172, 181; professional background of, 124, 125; self-image of, 140; and social classes, 175,

178, 181; and the sporting world, 177; style of, 173–74; and the theater, 174; and the underworld, 175, 176, 177, 180, 181; Western influences on, 172, 177, 179; and Winchell, 180
Runyonese [Wagner], 176
Russell Sage Foundation, 9, 29, 66

Sacco and Vanzetti case, 113, 152
Saloons, 44, 72, 89
Saltus, Edgar, 150
Sandburg, Carl, 145
Sardi's [restaurant], 167
Saturday Evening Post [magazine], 99, 146
Saucy Stories [magazine], 141
Schiele, Egon, 15
Schlesinger, John, 106
Schudson, Michael, 139
Schuyler, Montgomery, 28–29, 33, 47, 55, 58–59, 60
Science: and photography, 15–16
Scripps-Howard Publications, 117, 118
Self-amplification, 128–30
Self-photographs, 11–13
Senelick, Laurence, 105
Sexual issues: and Broadway/Times Square area, 104–6; and Greenwich Village, 130; Mencken's attacks on, 135, 147
Sheeler, Charles, 15, 19
Sherman, Stuart, 150
Sherwood, Robert, 112
Short stories, 76, 83, 84–88
"A Short View of Gamalielese" [Mencken], 151
Shubert Alley, 166
Shubert family, 100
"Sidewalk generation," 47–48
Sidewalks: and merchandising, 45–48
Silver Slipper [night club], 168
Silverman, Sime, 163, 165, 170
Singer Sewing Machine Company Building, 46, 64
Singin' in the Rain [film], 21
Sister Carrie [Dreiser], 42, 129
Sixth Avenue, 35, 97
"The Sky-line of New York, 1881–1897" [Schuyler], 28–29
Skylines: and aesthetics, 28–29; and architecture, 51–52, 55; as chaotic, 28; and corporate power, 33; and culture, 51–52; as distinct, towering peaks, 65; evolution of, 23–33; and films, 24, 49; first use of word, 27; as the identifying signature of a city, 23; as mountain ranges, 65; and painting, 28–29; and photography, 24, 27–28, 29–30, 31–32; and skyscrapers/vertical space, 23, 25, 31–32, 49, 65; as symbols, 33
Skyscrapers: as advertising, 46; and aesthetics, 65; and Broadway/Times